Lutheran Salvationists?

Lutheran Salvationists?

The Development Towards Registration
as an Independent Faith Community
in The Salvation Army in Norway
with Focus on the Period 1975–2005

Gudrun Maria Lydholm

Foreword by John Larsson
Preface by Roger Green

WIPF & STOCK · Eugene, Oregon

LUTHERAN SALVATIONISTS?
The Development Towards Registration as an Independent Faith Community in The Salvation Army in Norway with Focus on the Period 1975-2005

Copyright © 2017 Gudrun Maria Lydholm. All rights reserved. Except for brief quotations in critical publications or reviews, no part of this book may be reproduced in any manner without prior written permission from the publisher. Write: Permissions, Wipf and Stock Publishers, 199 W. 8th Ave., Suite 3, Eugene, OR 97401.

Wipf & Stock
An Imprint of Wipf and Stock Publishers
199 W. 8th Ave., Suite 3
Eugene, OR 97401

www.wipfandstock.com

PAPERBACK ISBN: 978-1-4982-9787-5
HARDCOVER ISBN: 978-1-4982-9789-9
EBOOK ISBN: 978-1-4982-9788-2

Manufactured in the U.S.A.   FEBRUARY 24, 2017

*With gratitude for the heritage and interpretation
of faith, hope, and love my officer parents,
Senior Majors Gestur and Katrine Arskog,
passed on to me*

Contents

Foreword by John Larsson | ix
Preface by Roger Green | xi
Abbreviations | xiv
Introduction | xv

Chapter 1	Identifying the Issues	1
Chapter 2	The Start and Development of The Salvation Army	12
Chapter 3	The Foundation of Significant Factors for the Process Towards Registration in Norway	29
Chapter 4	Changes and Challenges from the Wider Norwegian Society and Frelsesarmeen's Response to These	50
Chapter 5	The Work of Frelsesarmeen's Commission 1975–78	70
Chapter 6	Developments in the Interim Period 1978–1993	95
Chapter 7	Frelsesarmeen's Church Commission 1993–96	125
Chapter 8	Frelsesarmeen's Registration as a Faith Community in 2005	162
Chapter 9	The Theory of Civil Religion in Relation to Salvationists' View of the Norwegian church	191
Chapter 10	Which Ecclesiology?	207
Chapter 11	Conclusion	234
Appendix I	Doctrines of The Salvation Army	243
Appendix II	Soldier's Covenant	245
Appendix III	Officer's Covenant	248
Appendix IV	Commissioning and Ordination	249

Bibliography | 251
Index | 261

Foreword

"The Army's achievements are built on the great fundamental principle of adaptation," wrote Catherine Booth, the Mother of The Salvation Army, in 1880.

The fascinating story that Gudrun Lydholm tells in these pages is how The Salvation Army, on arrival in Norway, took hold of the principle of adaptation and aligned itself with the national church scene in a unique and almost eyebrow-raising way, and then applied the principle again more than a hundred years later to adapt to changed circumstances.

In very broad strokes, the challenge the Army's pioneers in Norway faced was that virtually everyone was a member of the state church by having been baptized into it as an infant. And so interwoven was the Lutheran Church in the civic and religious life of the nation that to ask anyone to give up their membership of the state church when they became Salvationists seemed out of the question. So with inspired application of the principle of adaptation, the pioneers decreed that Norwegian Salvationists could be members of both the Lutheran Church and The Salvation Army. Like people with dual nationality, they could have two passports.

The Lutheran passport was not only for decoration. Most Salvationists had their children baptised in the church and many took communion. But the system of dual allegiance worked well in practice and the Army's striking progress in Norway could be chalked up as yet another achievement built on the principle of adaptation.

However, with the passage of years bringing changed thinking in the church and Army, changed national legislation, and changed attitudes in society, the rightness of the two passports solution was increasingly called into question. Was it time to apply yet again the principle of adaptation?

The discussions grew heated in the period 1975–2005. Some felt that the Army could be even more effective if it had a clear and separate identity. Salvationists needed only one passport. But others questioned whether a Salvationist passport would be all-sufficient. Issues that had lain dormant for years sprang back to life. The ramifications seemed endless. There were strong divergences of opinion within the Army.

The debate reached its conclusion in 2005 when The Salvation Army in Norway registered as an independent faith community. The principle of adaptation had triumphed yet again.

In tracing the course of the debate, its background, and the nature of the conclusion that the Army arrived at, Gudrun Lydholm draws on a wide range of Norwegian cultural and ecclesiastical writings together with international Salvation Army material. She has also had access to all the documents in the Army's Norwegian archives relating to the issue.

The book is groundbreaking in that the remarkable story it tells has never been told before. With its clear marshalling of complex material and its considered judgments, the book makes a unique contribution to both Salvation Army and Norwegian church history. We stand indebted to Gudrun Lydholm.

John Larsson
General (Retired)
Beckenham, London
October 2016

Preface

HISTORY CAN BE VIEWED from two fields of vision. When seen from above the large picture emerges. But history can also be viewed from below, from local events and from the lives of people whose names may be unknown except to interested historians. The history of The Salvation Army has often been told from above, from the perspective of the greater movement since its founding in 1865. But it is equally important to tell the stories of the work of The Salvation Army on the ground, in the local and sometimes obscure settings. And with this narrative we learn of the work of great men and women whose stories have not been told in the broader denominational narrative, and we learn also of significant events that shaped local history and eventually had an impact upon the broader denomination.

This book is a fine example of local history coming to life—the events, the people, the ideas that created the narrative of unique circumstances that informed the development of The Salvation Army in Norway. The Salvation Army, founded as The Christian Mission in 1865 and evolving into The Salvation Army in 1878, inherited both the doctrines and the mission of the Methodism that was the background of its founders, William and Catherine Booth. The Army observed the sacraments of baptism and the Lord's Supper until 1883 when the practice of both sacraments was dropped. However, as this book reminds us, such was not the case in Norway. Salvationists in Norway were also members of the Lutheran Church, baptized by that faith communion. And Salvationists in Norway continued to participate in the Lord's Supper.

Trained in theology and with a broad knowledge of history, Commissioner Gudrun Lydholm brings her scholarly acumen to the service of the question of the uniqueness of the Norwegian experience in the history and development of The Salvation Army. There are many vital issues raised in this study, but three are especially critical. First, this work is a valuable study of the relationship of history from above and history from below. How, specifically, does the local history of the Army in Norway relate to the larger picture of the history of a worldwide movement, and to the history of the Church in Norway? Researching material in several archives was crucial to examining that question. In many respects this was a unique situation. Salvationist readers, aware only of the Methodist background of the Army, will be surprised to learn that Salvationists in any country belonged to another denomination but retained their identity as Salvationists. They might ask how this was possible. But there were several local idiosyncrasies that emerged as the Army was founded in different cultures, and this study is one of the most important studies of such local history.

Second, broader questions emerge that relate The Salvation Army to the Norwegian Church. What is the relationship of the Church to the broader culture, and especially a broader religious culture that has a distinct civil religion? What some might consider the specific issue addressed in this work as adaptation and therefore as a means to the central mission of the Army, others might think of it as accommodation to the broader culture that supported a State Church and therefore acted as a hindrance to the mission of the Army. This book carefully examines the sometimes complicated work that led finally to the Army's registration in Norway as a faith community, and the ramifications of such a move.

Third, this study raises the question of the nature of the Church, and well articulates the Army's self-understanding as a mission and a movement. However, the local issue of the relationship of The Salvation Army to the Norwegian Church naturally, and eventually, raised questions of ecclesiology. This was a matter of both theology and identity with which the international Salvation Army struggled at the same time as the questions related to the Army and the Norwegian Church were raised. The inquiry of the Army's identity with the Church was difficult for some outside of the Army because of the Army's position of non-practice of the sacraments that finally evolved after 1883. The very nature of the institutional Church was, for many Christians, tied to the observance of baptism and the Lord's Supper. However, the international Army worked hard to articulate an ecclesiology that demonstrated a clear sacramental theology while at the same time remaining non-practicing.

While the theology and history of this study is complicated, Dr. Lydholm does a remarkable job in working out the ramifications of the central questions raised by this topic. Readers who follow the carefully constructed argument in this text will understand why this is such an important work on several levels. It is a book that is extremely helpful to an understanding of The Salvation Army in the light of critical historical, cultural, and theological developments.

Roger Green, PhD
Professor of Biblical and Theological Studies
Terrelle B. Crum Chair of Humanities
Gordon College, Wenham, Massachusetts

Abbreviations

CO	Commanding Officer (Leader of a corps)
CoS	Chief of Staff (Second in command—worldwide)
CS	Chief Secretary (Second in command in a territory)
BEM	*Baptism Eucharist and Ministry,* The Lima Document, WCC
DC	Divisional Commander
DHQ	Divisional Headquarters
IHQ	International Headquarters of The Salvation Army
IS	International Secretary
LWF	The Lutheran World Federation
O&R	Orders and Regulations
TC	Territorial Commander
THQ	Territorial Headquarters
WCC	World Council of Churches

Introduction

THIS BOOK BEGAN AS a doctoral dissertation at Oslo University where I was privileged to be a doctoral student for four years, exploring The Salvation Army in Norway through academic study in a scholarly setting with inspiring dialogues and supervision. I am very grateful for this opportunity, which the Theological Faculty offered me.

A special relationship to Norway began as my husband and I were appointed by The Salvation Army to the Norway, Iceland and Færoes Territory as Territorial Leaders in the summer of 2005. We stayed for five and a half years. During these years I gathered knowledge and insight from the administration of the Army as well as from extensive travels and visits to all corps and institutions around the country. The opportunity of listening to Norwegian officers, soldiers, and employees in discussions, dialogues, and work evaluations, as well as sharing fellowship in worship and ordinary social settings enriched me and raised my curiosity. I wanted to know the background of different attitudes and opinions which had puzzled me. I wanted to know the history that was hidden behind official history books. My curiosity concerned the way The Salvation Army in Norway had accommodated itself to Norwegian culture and especially in its relationship to the Lutheran State Church. With the help of the archivist, Lt. Colonel John Bjartveit, I found documents of processes that became central in my work. Turning to the confidential archives which are kept in the Leadership office at The Salvation Army's Headquarters in Oslo I began to gather correspondence between Territorial Commanders and officers, soldiers, church leaders, and governmental departments as well as reports and correspondence with The Salvation Army's International Headquarters in London. These unpublished and confidential letters, reports and minutes from different councils constitute the foundation of the primary sources for my research. Added to these are correspondence concerning Norway from the Europe Department at the International Headquarters, material from The Salvation Army Heritage Center in London as well as from my personal archives. I have had the privilege of being given access to all these sources and acknowledge the support from the leadership of the Norway territory, the archivists and the Europe Department during my four years of research after we left Norway as territorial leaders. I also acknowledge all the encouragement, insight, and advice from friends and colleagues in different countries in the writing of this book. Two friends and fellow Salvationists have given me special support: Major Christine Parkin for reading through my original dissertation as well as this revised book and giving helpful comments and advice concerning the English language; and Dr. Helen Cameron for encouragement, advice, and mentorship during the whole process.

Last, but not least I give warm words of thanks to my husband, Carl, who has travelled with me to the archives in Oslo and London, joined in search of material, copied a substantial number of papers, helped with the tagging of the manuscript of this book, and discussed thoughts and ideas as they appeared. I am grateful for his continual support.

I hope readers find that the focus on the relationship between a minority religious movement and a Lutheran state church, including the question of civil religion, has application beyond Norway and the Nordic countries and beyond The Salvation Army. I also hope that this example of enculturation and adaptation can apply to other situations of mission into different cultures and subcultures.

Gudrun Maria Lydholm
Copenhagen
October 2016

Chapter 1

Identifying the Issues

THE NORDIC COUNTRIES OF Europe have been Lutheran countries since the Reformation in the sixteenth century. Because of the strong adherence to the King and subsequently to the state, these churches became established and dominant state churches. As national identity developed, membership of the State Church became part of it. One of the consequences was that in order to be regarded as properly Danish, Norwegian, Swedish, or Finnish, membership of the Lutheran State Churches was considered to be of great importance. This book concentrates on the situation in Norway mainly in the last quarter of the 20th century, as it was experienced by a minority religious group, The Salvation Army (Frelsesarmeen). It gives an insight into how this group accommodated itself both doctrinally as well as practically to the situation of a dominant state church.

A Dissenter Law came into being in 1845 in Norway giving religious freedom. The law made it possible for dissenters to form dissenter communities, propagate their faith, educate their children in their own religion, and also citizens could be without religion or membership of a religious community. Even so only a very small percentage of the population resigned their membership of the State Church. When in 1969 a new Non-Conformist Act was passed through parliament, it removed the dissenters designation and gave more equality to faith communities outside the State Church, as for instance offering financial support from the state to these communities. However, it was still a dissenter law as the State Church was not included, but regulated by its own laws. In spite of this new law the percentage of people who resigned their membership of the State Church was still very limited. The vast majority stayed within the State Church and for many this meant retaining a nominal membership—their children would be baptized and confirmed, weddings would be in the church as well as funerals. Salvationists acted as ordinary Norwegians and kept a nominal membership of the church because Frelsesarmeen never pursued registration as a faith community or as dissenters during its history from 1888 until 2005. This made it distinct from other free churches. Most probably the main reason for this was that the consequence would have been resignation from the State Church because it was not possible to retain membership of the church as a member of a registered faith community. Apparently neither Frelsesarmeen nor ordinary Salvationists wanted to resign.

The dominating position of the State Church shaped the religious life in the country not only by having the vast majority of citizens as members, nominal or not, but also by its close adherence to Stortinget (the parliament) on behalf of the king. Section 2 of the Constitution of 1814 of Norway stated: "All citizens of the country will have freedom of religion. The Evangelical-Lutheran religion will remain the official religion of the state. The citizens who adhere to this religion are under the obligation to educate their children in the same religion." And Section 16 added: "The king will arrange all public worship, all meetings and gatherings concerning religion and make sure that the official teachers of religion follow the laws." This constitution was not changed until 21 May 2012. Conflicts concerning matters of faith were not internal matters within the church, but became public matters where Stortinget's Church Department became involved and made final judgments. For example, a conflict in 1953 concerning belief in eternal perdition, which was the focus of a radio sermon by Professor and leader of the Home Mission Movement, O. Hallesby, escalated in the public square. The message of the sermon was challenged by one of the bishops, Kristian Schjelderup, whereby his position as a bishop was questioned because his opinion was considered outside the faith of the Church. The process involved judgments from a professor in Constitutional Law as well as from the Theological Faculty, and the verdict was that the bishop had not violated the faith of church concerning this matter and could stay as a bishop and guardian of the faith. Professor Hallesby and other conservative Christians did not agree with the verdict. Situations like this one had an impact on religious life not only for State Church members, but also for the dissenters, as they had to define themselves in relation to the official faith of the state. The State Church was the one setting the agenda for religious teaching and religious truths. The small dissenter communities were challenged by the agenda set by the church as all had to relate to the church in some way or another, because of its dominance. Their own agendas remained to a large degree within these smaller communities. An important issue on their agenda was the fight for religious freedom. It was not enough to be given freedom to gather and organize the dissenter communities through the goodwill of the State Church, but they wanted to obtain religious equality as well. The dissenters had hoped that the Non-Conformist Act of 1969 would have been a law concerning all religions including the State Church, but instead it turned out as another dissenter law. Towards the middle of the century the designation "the Norwegian Church" became usual instead of "the State Church." The name itself implied that there was only one church in Norway and signaled the dominance of the church in religious life in the country. The Non-Conformist Act of 1969, or a more correct translation from Norwegian, "Law concerning faith communities and other matters of 13 June 1969," did not use the word church for the dissenter congregations, but had the designation—faith community—as a common description for religions outside the Norwegian Church. This use of language narrowed the concept of church down to total identification with the Norwegian Lutheran Church. For ordinary people the word "church" would always mean the Norwegian Church.

Frelsesarmeen never called itself a church, rather a movement, an Army, an organization with the aim of proclaiming salvation and holiness, forming corps communities where Salvationists would be taught and trained as disciples of Christ, and involving itself and its members in serving people in need and giving voice to the voiceless. In avoiding calling itself church it followed not only Norwegian custom, but also Salvation Army tradition, as during The Salvation Army's history there had been a resistance against not only using the word church, but also using the concept of church when describing the Army. The following words from William Booth had lasting influence: "It was not my intention to create another sect . . . we are not a church. We are an Army, an army of salvation."[1] Church was identified with a formal, inflexible institution representing sacerdotalism and sacramentalism, the opposite of what the Army wanted to be. It wanted an image of informality and the flexibility to be easily mobilized and convey the gospel in a simple and direct way. Even though Bramwell Booth in 1925 made the following claim that the Army remained reluctant to describe itself as a church:

> "Of this, the Great Church of the Living God, we claim, and have ever claimed, that we of The Salvation Army are an integral part and element—a living fruit-bearing branch in the True Vine."[2]

Bramwell Booth stated that the Army was an integral part and element of the Church of the Living God and connected to the church, while

---

1. Nicol, *General Booth and the Salvation Army*, 85.
2. Booth, *Echoes and Memories*, 79.

avoiding calling the Army a church. The international Mission Statement which came into use in the early 1970s struck a similar note as it stated that: "The Salvation Army, an international movement, is an evangelical part of the universal Christian Church. . . . " It is a part of the universal church, rather than stating that this part is a church.

This inspiration coming from the international Army fit well into Norwegian Salvationists' concept of church. Frelsesarmeen was something different from the church, a movement, or an organization. The church was the place for rituals and rites of passage common for nearly all Norwegian citizens. It stood in Norwegian society as a symbol of a thousand-year long tradition of Christianity their forefathers had adhered to. The overall rite was the baptism of infants. Here the child got its name and was entered into the church's protocol where all the names of the family many generations back would be. It was the official registration as a citizen as well. The certificate of baptism was an important document which would follow the child for the rest of their life, for example when it entered school. It was the socially accepted thing to have such a document, and it could provoke ridicule or questioning at school if the child had not been baptized and lacked such a document, as it was outside the ordinary custom. For ordinary Norwegians, including Salvationists, the Norwegian Church would identify what a church was. The close affiliation to the state was considered a natural part of being a real church which people were connected to through ceremonies and rites at important stages in life. The use of the word dissenters for those outside the church for more than 120 years signaled how strong the tradition of membership was. It was the norm to be members, those outside the church were dissenting from this norm and tradition. When introducing the concept of faith community in the Non-Conformist Act of 1969, the language described the nature of the communities included in the law. It no longer underlined abnormality, but gave the groups an identity grounded in faith. It could be the Christian faith, the Mosaic faith, or any other faith expressed in different religions. This situation, where the concept of faith was underlined in the name of these communities, made them stand apart from the church. The church in the minds of ordinary people did not necessarily focus on faith, at least not a personal faith. What was important was membership or belonging and then making use of the rituals the church offered. Because of this situation, it has been relevant to evaluate the question of the State Church as an expression of civil religion within the context of theories of civil religion. In particular, I have evaluated Salvationists' affiliation to the church to see if they implicitly considered the Norwegian Church as an expression of civil religion in the country and if this adherence was a way of accommodating to Norwegian society. The title of the book, Lutheran Salvationists, ends with a question mark. The reason is that the praxis of Salvationists would indicate that they were Lutherans, as they kept their membership of the Lutheran church and they participated in the sacraments of the church as well as the ceremonies. This would identify them as Lutherans, but looking into the question of civil religion might alter this. According to their praxis they were Lutherans, but according to their faith they were Salvationists.

The Salvation Army has expanded during its 150-year history from a local mission in the east end of London to a global Christian community. It works presently in 127 countries. All through its history the Army has shown the hallmarks of accommodation and pragmatism in order to be rooted into the local culture of the different countries where it had a presence, in spite of being ultimately international in its administration, structure, and theology. This book focuses on Frelsesarmeen as an illustration of such an enculturation. It scrutinizes how the Army accommodated itself into Norwegian society. It interprets the successful enculturation as a result of compromises and choices made at an early stage—compromises which remained unquestioned until the main period of research which is 1975–2005. In the years close to this time the consensus about the enculturation broke down as the Army's emerging identity as an independent faith community, rather than as a religious organization, began to be detected. Changes in society had challenged the Army's usual way of working and led to questions of identity and self-understanding among Salvationists. The period was marked by a search for its unique Salvationist identity and the strengthening of such an identity as well as internal evaluations, research, debate, and an update on its mission in order to communicate better with contemporary society for serving the present age.[3] This was both an impetus and outcome of the work of two commissions, which looked into the question of the Army's registration as a faith community. After thirty years discussing this question Frelsesarmeen[4] finally registered as a faith community in 2005. Frelsesarmeen remained integrated within the international Army while developing a distinct identity and ecclesiology.

---

3. There is a well known band piece called "The Present Age" by Lesley Condon. It signals the importance of this focus. Charles Wesley's song "A Charge to Keep I Have" puts this into words. The second verse is: "To serve the present age/ my calling to fulfil/ o may it all my powers engage/ to do my Master's will!" *The Songbook of The Salvation Army*, No. 472.

4. Throughout the book I will be using the Norwegian name for The Salvation Army, Frelsesarmeen, when it concerns Norway, while I will be using The Salvation Army for the international Army.

One crucial issue in the Army's accommodation into Norwegian society was the relationship between Salvationists and the State Church. The question of regaining membership of the Norwegian church for Salvationists who had initially left the church came to the forefront at the end of the time of nation building and formation of the state between 1900–1910. Most probably this happened as, at a time of intense national pride, Salvationists wished to be considered proper Norwegians. They had entered into nominal membership as infants by baptism, a tradition they continued concerning their own children. Salvationists also participated in the Eucharist at special occasions in connection with family celebrations, but not regularly. By retaining or regaining membership they avoided being classed as dissenters. The double membership which was the outcome continued for the vast majority of Salvationists until the registration as a faith community in 2005 and even beyond. Two commissions, one from 1973–78 and the other from 1993–96, worked on the question of registration as a faith community. The main reason for establishing these Frelsesarmeen commissions was the reports from different commissions within the State Church as well as the Public Commission of 1971 for Research on Questions concerning State and Church. The reports from within the church concerned identity as a Lutheran church and the report from the public commission recommended separation between state and church. The identity question was important in connection to Salvationists' search for their own church identity as well as their nominal membership of the State Church. The prospect of separation between state and church made it urgent to establish the Army's first commission concerning registration, because it was considered crucial to register the Army as a faith community if this happened. Seemingly it had been unproblematic for Frelsesarmeen's leaders that Salvationists had double membership, as long as the Norwegian Church was a state church while a separation between state and church would alter the situation. The opinion that Frelsesarmeen would have to register as a faith community in the event of a separation between state and church continued for the next thirty years. This argument is another reason why the question of considering the State Church as an expression of civil religion has been relevant. This mixture of state and church blurred the concept of what it meant to be church and opened up for the possibility of seeing the church as an expression of civil religion, which Norwegians adhered to through their membership of the church.

The outcome of the mode and choices for accommodation into the Norwegian society meant that Frelsesarmeen really established itself as a true Norwegian Christian organization and was accepted as such. In November 2003 Norwegian Information Advisers gave Omdømmeprisen (Reputation Prize) to Frelsesarmeen. The reason given was, "Its strong brand which everybody associates with something important and very positive, being creative in its communication and making use of new and exciting means in order to communicate its message. Over a long time it has built up its fantastic reputation in a low-voiced, consistent and clear manner in spite of attitudes that the majority of the population do not agree with."[5] Here was a brand that had managed to communicate its message clearly and build up a reputation that was known by everybody as positive in spite of the majority not agreeing with its attitudes. It described Frelsesarmeen's situation in Norway after 115 years of presence in the country. It was quite an achievement to retain a positive reputation in spite of attitudes that were neither politically correct nor modern. Another example of it being considered a Norwegian household name was a letter from a reader of the Norwegian *War Cry (Krigsropet)* from June 1993[6] pointing out that Frelsesarmeen was considered to belong to everybody. It illustrated that a smaller denomination had accommodated itself successfully within Norwegian society in spite of its governance being ultimately international rather than national.

The main question this book is based upon is: Why did Frelsesarmeen register as a faith community in 2005? Implicit in this question were further questions. Why seek registration after 117 years of successful integration into Norwegian society and why had this not been a concern before? In order to find an answer, specific areas such as identity, theology, sociology, legislation, and The Salvation Army's internationalism have been looked into and evaluated to discover where there have been changes that influenced Frelsesarmeen in these areas. A historical narrative that describes how Frelsesarmeen developed during these years leading to the decision of registration as a faith community has been the method chosen of finding answers to the questions.

This study of the development of Frelsesarmeen and its interaction with Norwegian society is an illustration of the fast changing religious landscape and the impact of pluralism developing from a pluralism of minority Christian denominations to a pluralism of other religions. Even though pluralism has often been marked by retreat from the public square, this has not been the case for the Norwegian Church nor for Frelsesarmeen. The dominance of the church made it stay in the public square. Frelsesarmeen has continually tried to deprivatize religion and made a conscious effort to be vocal and visible in the public square in matters of public concern. It also

---

5. http.//www.na24.no/propaganda/arkiv/article2012700.ece.

6. Letter to the leadership of Frelsesarmeen, 9 June 1993, from a lady in the Norwegian Mission Society.

illustrates how the concept of civil religion is not outdated, but still being revisited and reformulated.

This book has 11 chapters. Chapter 2 gives a short historical view of the formation of The Salvation Army as a background for Frelsesarmeen in Norway and its development as a faith community. The sociological and religious factors that were the soil The Salvation Army grew out of in the United Kingdom, from where it crossed the borders of Scandinavia and into Norway are mentioned. There is a focus on the founders, William and Catherine Booth, and the kind of people they attracted to this new working class religious movement. It took the shape of an Army, even an Army that included women leaders, seemingly a discrepancy as the military metaphor was generally considered masculine, and not feminine, at least at the time of the Army's beginning. But this clash of images attracted the crowds that came to see and experience this new religious phenomenon. As pragmatism marked the founder's decisions in the beginning and continued to characterize the Army's accommodation to changing societies and cultures this is included as well. The Salvation Army's development as a faith community in its own right is illustrated by a focus on the sources of the most important elements of the Army's faith and practice. The question of the sacraments is dealt with, because this issue was crucial for the development of Frelsesarmeen, for Salvationists' practice of dual membership—the State Church and Frelsesarmeen; a practice known also in the other Scandinavian countries. This is important for understanding the Army's identity—movement or church—both internationally as well as nationally in Norway. It had a long lasting influence not only on the pioneering work of Frelsesarmeen in Norway, but also on its identity and development over the period that is central for this book. Finally, William Booth used the argument of not professing to be a church as one of the reasons for taking the decision of non-observance. In a way he distanced the Army from the institutional church by making this claim with the consequence that the non-observance position of The Salvation Army has made it stand apart from other churches. The Army's social outreach cannot be ignored either, as diaconia is an indispensable notae ecclesiae for The Salvation Army. This historic research is valuable in order to understand the choices made within Frelsesarmeen and their significance.

Chapter 3 develops the expansion into Norway, the theological opposition from the State Church, Frelsesarmeen's pragmatism towards issues such as registration and follows the development among officers from resigning their membership of the State Church at an early stage to regaining the membership between the years 1900 and 1910, when Norway became independent from its union with Sweden. The overall focus concerns the policy of translating the doctrine books into Norwegian in 1901 and 1930.

The translations deviated from the official international doctrine books which emphasized the Army's non-observant position on the sacraments. It had far reaching consequences and supported the choice of retaining membership of the State Church and participation in the sacraments in the church. Salvationists had a Lutheran praxis, but retained a Salvationist faith.

Chapter 4 looks at the social changes, secularization, and pluralism as a background for the changes within Frelsesarmeen from the 1950s to 1975. The whole question of identity is crucial for changes and challenges. The influence from the commissions within the Norwegian Church is also included.

Chapter 5 concerns the work of Frelsesarmeen's Commission 1975-78. It highlights the main reasons for initiating such a commission, the possible separation between state and church and the question of Salvationists' identity. It describes the influences and development of the work of the commission, such as a meeting with Professor Block-Hoell from the Theological Faculty and his very strong opinion concerning the Army's non-observance of the sacraments, which he called false doctrine and false practice. His influence became profound as his paper was printed in the final report in 1978 and referred to in the report of 1996. The findings from a questionnaire concerning Salvationists' relationship to the Norwegian Church stand central in the chapter, as does a dissertation concerning the Army's identity as a congregation in Finland by Tor Wahlström, and the comparison between the Norwegian and the Finnish situation.

Chapter 6 pays particular attention to the interim period 1978-1993, with all the recommendations from the commission being followed up and an evaluation of Frelsesarmeen's response to challenges from changes in society during these years, such as democratization, women's liberation, youth culture, and music. The growing influence of ecumenism during the period, especially the Lima document from the World Council of Churches and the international Army's response to the document is looked into in light of the reception and translation in Norway.

Chapter 7 focuses on Frelsesarmeen's Church Commission 1993-96. It opens with the influence of the collapse of the Soviet Union and the following changes in Eastern Europe from the perspective of The Salvation Army, especially Frelsesarmeen, as it was in charge of the reopening of the Army's work in Russia. This work influenced Norwegian Salvationists and their perception of being a church and being registered as such. Another influence was the digitalization of people's daily lives such as PCs and the internet, which strengthened the influence coming from abroad from The Salvation Army on Frelsesarmeen. The body of the chapter is the work of the commission, the responses to the work from officers and soldiers and what this reveals. It is clear that there was no enthusiasm to register as a faith community because of reluctance to resign membership of the Norwegian Church as long as state and church had not separated. Through these responses the implicit attitude to the Norwegian Church as an expression of civil religion comes to the forefront. Another issue which is revealed concerns the sacraments as half of the corps answering questions about registration referred to the place of the sacraments in a registered Frelsesarmeen faith community. It was not included in the questions, but nevertheless was dealt with in the different corps. For some it was inconceivable to be registered as a faith community without the sacraments, because sacraments belonged to the being of the church, even though the sacraments in themselves were not that important, for others the sacraments as such were central and needed to be there. The third group wanted more clear teaching concerning the Army's non-observance of the sacraments. The model of a possible registration is outlined as well as the commission's recommendation for such a registration.

Chapter 8 opens with the influence of information technology and how this renewed Frelsesarmeen's communication strategy. It removed the dust and a modern Frelsesarmeen appeared in the mind of the public. This change also altered the attitudes within Frelsesarmeen as it corresponded to the image given to the public. The influence concerning theology coming from the International Army grew stronger through the 1999 doctrine book *Salvation Story* and *Salvation Story Study Guide* as well as the report from the Spiritual Life Commission, *Move forward in Freedom*. They were translated into Norwegian within a year. *Krigsropet* followed this development and published part of the report from the commission. Both *Salvation Story* and *Move forward in Freedom* moved away from the traditional apologetic view concerning the non-observance of the sacraments. Instead they interpreted the sacraments as embedded in Salvation Army practice. *Salvation Story* included an outline of Salvationists ecclesiology. The body of the chapter focuses on the actual registration in 2005 and the consequences of this. The registration of Frelsesarmeen became a dual registration—an organization where all the notae ecclesiae of the Salvation Army were included, but the members, such as soldiers and adherents, did not need to resign their membership of the Norwegian Church. The other part of the registration was a congregation where those wanting to register legally as members of a faith community could be registered. It demanded resignation of the Norwegian Church. Anybody could be a member of this Frelsesarmeen congregation. With such a registration the way of nominal membership was opened. The chapter also looks at the impact of registration on different people as well as the consequences of the open membership of the congregation in the new book of ceremonies that was published at the same time as the registration was finalized. Central ceremonies were changed in order to accommodate this new situation.

Chapter 9 concerns the theory of civil religion in relation to Salvationists' view of the Norwegian Church. It opens with a short view of the development of civil religion from Rousseau to Robert Bella ending with Gerald Parsons looking at the definitions of civil religion. The Nordic scene is presented through LWF's consultation in Finland in 1984. "The Church and Civil Religion in the Nordic countries of Europe." and the definition of civil religion from this consultation. The Finnish researcher, Susan Sundback and her work on civil religion and the State Churches in the Nordic countries, as well as the Norwegian researcher Inger Furseth and her work concerning Norway, are evaluated. In the discussion the attitudes to the Norwegian Church from the two Frelsesarmeen leaders, Solhaug and Dalstrøm, are compared to definitions on civil religion to see if Salvationists implicitly considered the Norwegian Church as an expression of civil religion. The chapter closes with civil religion in connection to pluralism, and pluralism and the renewed effort to deprivatize religion in the public square.

Chapter 10 concerns what kind of ecclesiology is revealed through the work of Frelsesarmeen's two commissions. The documents from these took up the term "spiritualistic Christianity" as a description of the Army and linked it to the concept of the invisible church. This was their understanding based on Block-Hoell's lecture. These concepts are dealt with and the Lutheran thinking concerning invisible/visible church is evaluated in light of Salvationist's ecclesiology. The Salvation Army's publications such as the Army's response to the Lima document, *Community in Mission*, as well as *Salvation Story*, and *Move Forward in Freedom* are dealt with in order to spell out the ecclesiology revealed in these documents. The chapter closes with an evaluation of possible ecclesiological tensions within Frelsesarmeen as well as between Frelsesarmeen and the international Army.

Chapter 11 offers conclusions to the study.

There are four appendices: The Doctrines of the Salvation Army, The Soldier's Covenant, The Officer's Covenant, and the Ceremony of Ordination. All Norwegian or Nordic quotations from documents, letters, books, and legislation are translated into English by the author.

Chapter 2

The Start and Development of The Salvation Army

THE SETTING FOR THE Salvation Army was twofold. First of all, the social and economic changes that transformed England during the nineteenth century are crucial for its formation. The industrial revolution with its urban industrialization made the rural population migrate to the cities in great numbers. London exemplified this. Even though in 1800 it was a great city of one million people it had grown to over four million by 1900.[1] Most working class people were managing life from day to day with little prospect of future improvement. Even here there was a distinction between the poor and the helplessly poor. Workers below the artisan level were considered to be poor. The helplessly poor were the lowest in the social hierarchy, described by William Booth[2] as "the submerged tenth." He estimated their number at about three million, or roughly one-tenth of the population. Leisure was related to the streets, the public houses, and the music halls. That was where the Army was born and where it developed its characteristics. It picked up urban working class culture to create "a uniquely urban working class religious movement."[3] It was sensational in its expressions, but it communicated the gospel to the people of the East End of London.

The other setting for The Salvation Army was the religious situation. The Emancipation Act of 1829 made the church and state separate entities, although the Church of England remained the official church. Many dissenting Christian bodies regarded the nominal Christian environment as soil for evangelistic endeavor. The idea of mission was not only seen in

---

1. McLeod, *Religion and the People of Western Europe 1789–1970*, 75.
2. Booth, *In Darkest England and the Way Out*, 17.
3. Walker, *Pulling the Devil's Kingdom Down*, 243.

terms of overseas mission, but in terms of mission at home. Religion was greatly influenced by the evangelical movement. The Salvation Army was an offspring of Evangelical religion[4] in the understanding of Evangelical as expressed by D.W. Bebbington.

> He gives "four qualities that have been the special marks of Evangelical religion: *conversionism,* the belief that lives need to be changed; *activism,* the expression of the gospel in effort; *Biblicism,* a particular regard for the Bible; and what may be called *crucicentrism,* a stress on the sacrifice of Christ on the cross. Together they form a quadrilateral of priorities that is the basis of Evangelicalism."[5]

This quadrilateral describes very well the essence of Salvation Army belief and practice. Added to that is the stress on the Holy Spirit's inward work in regeneration and outward work in sanctification, the Holy Spirit's guidance and inspiration in all matters of life and especially in interpreting the scriptures. The Army was not a typical expression of religion in its time, but it certainly adhered to these fundamentals of the Evangelicals in the Wesleyan version.

The military metaphor that proved successful picked up on the spirit of the time, not so much the religious, as the secular spirit. Thomas Carlyle expressed this well:

> "Man is created to fight, he is perhaps best of all definable as a born soldier; his life 'a battle and a march' under the right General."[6]

The British Empire was huge. The military had a significant status as the empire was dependent on military presence in all the colonies. The image of an Army certainly communicated to the man on the street and it was exactly these ordinary, working class people the Army tried to reach out to.

The Salvation Army's founders were William and Catherine Booth. William Booth was born in Nottingham, 10 April 1829, and baptized into the Anglican Church, but was introduced to the local Wesleyan chapel where he was converted. Catherine Booth was born the same year as William in 1829 and reared as a Methodist. William Booth was ordained as a

---

4. According to Bebbington the term Evangelical with capital letter is applied to any aspect of the movement beginning in the 1730s. There was much continuity with earlier Protestant traditions, but Evangelicalism was a new phenomenon of the eighteenth century.

5. Bebbington, *Evangelicalism in Modern Britain,* 3.

6. Carlyle, *Past and Present* (1843) as quoted by Rightmire, *Sacraments and The Salvation Army,* 25.

minister in the Methodist New Connection. After ordination in 1858, while the couple was in Gateshead near Newcastle-upon-Tyne, Catherine Booth first published her position on female ministry in a pamphlet (December 1859) and later commenced her own preaching career.[7] Catherine Booth had not yet entered public ministry herself when she wrote it, so she was defending the principle of female ministry and not her own right to preach. The pamphlet argued that this right to preach/teach was because of God's intention and will for humanity as expressed in the Bible, not in spite of it.

The right for women to preach was stated in the first Doctrine Book of The Salvation Army from 1881[8] and in the following editions of this style of catechism. This shows that it was not a practical matter, but a matter of faith, a faith that was being argued for. As this pamphlet on female ministry came out long before there were any beginnings of The Salvation Army, the equality between men and women became a settled question between Catherine and William Booth. Therefore, women were involved in preaching and leading stations from its very start. A Salvation Army without this doctrine is difficult to imagine in view of the substantial number of women officers in the history of Frelsesarmeen in Norway as well as all over the world.

William Booth resigned from the Methodist New Connection in July 1861 two years after his ordination. It is important to note that the resignation had to do with disagreement on itinerant ministry or settled work at a circuit and not on doctrines or ecclesiology. It could reflect his pragmatism. He wanted to conduct evangelistic revivals and took the opportunities that came his way concerning denomination. He started with the Reformers within Methodism, interrupted by three months with the Congregationalists until he, in March 1854, began his training for ministry with the Methodist New Connection. The following four years after the resignation the couple engaged themselves in independent itinerant ministry, first as a couple, but later each of them conducted their own itinerant ministries in different parts of the country. The first meeting William Booth conducted in the East End of London, 2 July 1865, in a tent in an unused Quaker burial ground is considered the birthday of The Salvation Army. The group William Booth started working together with came from various missions, all of them committed to ministry in East London. They belonged to different

---

7. Walker, *Pulling the Devil's Kingdom down*, 26–31 has an extensive analysis of the pamphlet: *Female Teaching: or, the Rev. A.A. Rees versus Mrs. Palmer, Being a reply to a Pamphlet by the Above Gentleman on the Sunderland Revival.* Green, *Catherine Booth*, 308 in note 22 gives an account of the history of printing and publication of the pamphlet.

8. Booth, *The Doctrines and Disciplines of The Salvation Army*.

agencies such as The Christian Community, originally a Huguenot community, or The East London Special Services Committee.[9]

Through her preaching and ministry at this time Catherine came into touch with classes of people who were well off, as most of her engagements were in the West End. Her income was important for the family during the coming years where William's was more uncertain than it had been previously.[10] She also helped finance the beginnings of the mission in East London by raising money from her West End audiences as she informed them about the growing ministry in the East End.

The large majority of workers in the mission and early Army came from a Methodist background as can be seen in Horridge's study:

> "Of those officers with previous religious experience, two-thirds were Methodists of Wesleyan or Primitive ideology. A small but growing number of Anglican women were joining and in late 1878/79 there was a marked influx of women."[11]

By 1880 the numbers of men and women joining were approximately equal.

Walker's research into the class background of Salvationists—even with all the cautions she states for the uneven character of her material—gives a picture of the people the Army attracted:

> "Over three-quarters of the women were employed in unskilled or semiskilled work. Another 17 percent were employed in skilled occupations . . . nearly half the men were artisans or skilled laborers, and another 14 percent were small employers, retailers, wholesalers, or clerical workers. Only 24 percent were semiskilled workers and 13 percent were general or unskilled laborers."[12]

These figures do not conform to the image of the people The Salvation Army gathered as totally destitute people, an image that has lingered on both inside the Army as well as outside. One reason for this was that the Army gathered a lot of people, but not all became members. Another issue was the widespread abuse of alcohol that ruined people's lives whatever skills they might have had and made the whole family destitute.

During the consolidation of the work and transformation into an army the outline of a denomination appeared through the development of

9. Green, *William Booth*, 107.
10. Ervine, *God's Soldier*, vol. I, 270–71.
11. Horridge, *The Salvation Army*, 225.
12. Walker, *Pulling the Devil's Kingdom Down*, 71–72.

doctrines, mission focus, and structures based on a military metaphor. The conversionism and the activism that Bebbington stated as two of the four characteristics of Evangelicalism were very clearly in focus in the programs of the first mission stations. The other two characteristics, Biblicism and crucicentrism, could be seen in the doctrines of the mission. The transition from a mission to an army was gradual. The military idioms had been developing for some time. In August 1878 a "War Congress" was announced in *The Christian Mission Magazine* and also that The Mission would be called The Salvation Army.

William Booth became the General. *The Deed of Constitution of 7 August* 1878 had three main points: a) the eleven doctrines, b) that one person, the General, had the oversight and control over the Army, c) that the General had the power to appoint his successor.[13] The right to appoint the successor became part of the later constitutional crisis of The Salvation Army in 1929, where it was replaced with an election of a General by the High Council.[14]

The name of *The Christian Mission Magazine* was changed to *The Salvationist* in 1879. This was the monthly paper. The weekly paper *The War Cry* was published the first time Saturday, 27 December 1879, to the price of a half penny. The first article in the paper began in this way: "Why a weekly War Cry? Because The Salvation Army means more war!" *The War Cry* was the paper that would characterize the Army in whatever country it began its work. It was aimed at the public and sold on the streets and in public houses, as for example in the opening of the work in Denmark *Krigsråbet* (*The War Cry*) was published the day before the opening. In Norway the first issue was four months later than the opening on 17 May 1888. The Swedish paper was used in the beginning. The paper became a means of raising funds as well. The aspect of raising funds by publishing and selling *The War Cry* became a lasting feature of The Salvation Army both in Britain and internationally. To go into the pubs with the papers has been usual from the very beginning to recent years. The Salvation Army's start in Russia in 1913 was as a publisher of the Army paper and the officers were registered as paper sellers.

---

13. This last point was modified by a supplemental Deed Poll signed by William Booth 26 July 1904. It allowed for a High Council to be established with the duty to appoint a new General in case a successor had not been appointed or there were reasons for such a succession to fail.

14. 1929 crisis: Bramwell Booth's health deteriorated. The constitution of 1904 came into use and a High Council was formed to remove Bramwell from office. This High Council also elected a new General. The newest book on this issue is Larsson, *1929 A Crisis that Shaped The Salvation Army's Future*.

The mission statement of The Salvation Army was expressed in an article entitled "Our New Name":

> "We are a salvation people—this is our speciality—getting saved and keeping saved, and then getting somebody else saved, and then getting saved ourselves more and more until full salvation on earth makes the heaven within, which is finally perfected by the full salvation without, on the other side of the river."[15]

Here both the *conversionism* and the *crucicentrism*, as two of the characteristics, Bebbington links to Evangelicalism were markedly present. The doctrine of holiness, called full salvation, was in focus as well. The Army flag was created and it was centered on crucicentrism and holiness. The three colors, red, yellow, and blue represented salvation through the blood of Christ, the baptism of the Holy Spirit, and purity of heart, holiness. The motto inscribed on the flag—Blood and Fire—signified the blood of Christ and the fire of the Holy Spirit.

The leadership of the Army developed into a strong, effective, and autocratic leadership that seemed to serve the purpose. At least the statistics affirmed this. The Salvation Army experienced a tremendous growth, as can be seen in the following figures. In 1878 the number of corps was 57, the year after in 1879 it had risen to 104 and after five years in 1883 to 519.[16]

Rightmire describes the ecclesiology of the Army very well as a functional ecclesiology, conceiving the church as act rather than substance[17] and dominated by its soteriological task. This pragmatic mission orientated ecclesiology has been evident as the Salvation Army established and developed its work in whatever country.

Pragmatism

Pragmatism as well as the principle of accommodation were hallmarks of William Booth and became integrated into the Army's DNA when it developed and crossed the borders to other countries. During William Booth's time pragmatism developed as a philosophical tradition originating in USA around 1870. The three fathers of pragmatism were contemporaries of William Booth. They were all Americans, William James (1842–1910), Charles Sander Peirce (1839–1914) and John Dewey (1859–1959). They saw

---

15. Booth, "Our New Name," 1.
16. Horridge, *The Salvation Army*, 38.
17. Rightmire, *Sacraments and The Salvation Army*, 79.

themselves as providing return to common sense and the facts of experience as a corrective to earlier thinkers. William James defined pragmatism as:

> "The attitude of looking away from first things, principles, 'categories', supposes necessities, and looking towards last things, fruits, consequences, facts." And "Rationalism sticks to logic and the empyrean. Empiricism sticks to the external senses. Pragmatism is willing to take anything, to follow either logic or the senses."[18]

William Booth was willing to make use of anything that worked, always looking towards the ultimate goal of his mission. His ideas had to be tested by the practical consequences, by reality as he conceived it. He dealt with a specific situation of mission among working class people and people on the fringe of society and not ideas and theories as such, but he developed his ideas or theories on the basis of these specific situations.

The American influence marked by pragmatism and adaptability came more explicitly from revivalists such as James Caughey and Charles Finney, who both had revival campaigns in England. Their writing also influenced the Booth couple, such as Finney's analysis of revival techniques in *Revivals of Religion*. He addressed the demands of the American frontier for religion. Booth applied these measures for the frontier of East London. William Booth always posed the crucial question: "Does it work?" It had to give results and be useful in the situation of mission in which he worked. Rightmire refers to William Booth as developing "a theology of action rather than reflection. Pragmatism and simplicity were the hallmarks of Booth's strategy. His pragmatism, however never lost sight of its spiritual goal."[19] The pragmatism of William Booth not only concerned practical matters, but was also present when it concerned theology and ecclesiology. Rightmire[20] claims that Booth's pragmatic theology was the basis of the Army's ecclesiological self-concept as well as its sacramental position, which I do agree with. Because pragmatism influenced not only methods, but theology and ecclesiology, it became embedded within the Army in whatever country it started its work. William Booth's pragmatism had already become visible in connection with his uncertainty of which denomination within Methodism to choose. The aim was to come into ministry, preferable itinerant ministry as an evangelist, and he connected to different denominations that opened the possibility for him. He left when his aim could no longer be

---

18. James, *Pragmatism*. Reference in Rightmire, *Sacraments and The Salvation Army*, 71.

19. Rightmire, *Sacraments and The Salvation Army*, 71.

20. Ibid., 69–79.

fulfilled and therefore pursued his goal independently. The success of the Army's methods confirmed the principle of accommodation in its mission for Booth and his co-workers. This also influenced Catherine Booth as she began to support the adaption of all lawful means to reach people with the gospel. She began to consider that traditional church forms were no longer relevant to the needs of people. She took 1 Corinthians 9.22 as her proof text in the principle of adaptation: "To the weak I became weak, to win the weak. I have become all things to all men so that by all possible means I might save some" (NIV).

A year before the Christian Mission became The Salvation Army, William Booth explained his methods in this way:

> "Beginning as I did, so to speak, with a sheet of clean paper, wedded to no plan, and willing to take a leaf out of anybody's book that seemed to be worth adopting, and, above all, to obey the direction of God the Holy Spirit, I have gone from step to step. . . . We tried various methods, and those that did not answer we unhesitatingly threw overboard and adopted something else."[21]

As can be seen he felt free to adapt whatever means that worked and felt the freedom to ignore tradition and to start afresh when it concerned his mission and the structures of it. He also was open to adapt methods from different sources or traditions. Catherine considered new ways of spreading God's kingdom on earth as necessary and self-evident as long as not all ideas in the Divine mind had been explored. God gave new light and insight to different people as he called people to find new paths that might differ from what had been. They believed that God wanted a true revival of Christianity.

In the following section the pragmatism was present in the question of the sacraments. The history of Frelsesarmeen in Norway and the choices made by individual Salvationists as well as the organization illustrated this principle of accommodation and of pragmatism.

Salvation Army Faith and Practice

The beginning of the 1880s was a crucial time for the Army as the formation of a denomination became visible in spite of the reluctance to deal with this theologically. For example the first doctrine book was published in 1881 (the eleven doctrines evolved from seven in 1866 to eleven by 1874), the

---

21. Sandall, *The History of The Salvation Army* Vol. I, 208.

Soldier's Covenant, The Articles of War[22] was formed in 1882, the Wedding Ceremony, the Articles of Marriage, was also ready in 1882. The Soldier's Guide was published in 1883 with three daily Bible readings for the year. Orders and Regulations for the Salvation Army came in 1878.[23] The training of officers began for men in 1879 and for women in 1880. The trained officers were commissioned and given a rank. All these were signs of a denomination.

During 1882 a committee was formed from the Anglican Church to investigate a possible union between the Army and the church.[24] The work lasted a year. The negotiations between the committee and the Army did not end in a dispute, just recognizing a difference that was too great to bridge. These negotiations made the Army decide to keep its distinctiveness and its ministry separate from any other established church. That decision in itself could be seen as a step toward denominationalism. The question of the sacraments that had been in focus during the negotiations with the Anglicans was forcing itself on the agenda.

The 1870 the Constitution of the Christian Mission explained the mode and meaning of the sacraments of Baptism "Baptism (mode left to members. Discussion of the subject strictly forbidden. Not to be imposed upon any having conscientious scruples against it. No baptism by immersion at any station—if desired, to be administered elsewhere)"[25] and, "The Lord's Supper (once a month unless two-thirds of the members of a society desire it oftener. Confined to holders of members' tickets or notes of admission. Unfermented wine only to be used)."[26] It is interesting that the mode of baptizing was left free for personal choice, but discussion on the matter was forbidden. By closing any discussion on the matter the Booths must have realized the potential for making this issue both central and dividing. For them baptism should be neither. The baptism administered was infant baptism. This is clear from Bramwell Booth, who claimed to have "sprinkled" thirty infants in one service.[27] According to Rightmire the understanding

---

22. See appendix II.

23. The Heritage Centre in London has two dates 1878 or 1881. The bombing of IHQ during World War II destroyed the original archives so there are some uncertainty concerning dates and material. From 1885 to 1899 a number of Orders and Regulations for Divisional Officers, Field Officers, Staff Officers, Soldiers, Social Officers, Territorial Commissioners, and Chief Secretaries etc. appeared.

24. See Green, *The Life and Ministry of William Booth*, 140–145. Walker, *Pulling the Devil's Kingdom Down*, 134. Booth, *Echoes and Memories*, 68–69.

25. Sandall Vol I., appendix L, 277.

26. Ibid.

27. Booth, *Echoes and Memories*, 191.

of baptism in the nineteenth century among Evangelicals was "as a sign, pledge, or promise of a future regeneration. Rather than conveying grace, baptism pointed to regeneration conditioned by repentance and faith."[28] The dedication ceremony that replaced baptism within The Salvation Army was in harmony with the evangelical understanding of baptism as a dedication.

There are not many primary sources available to substantiate the Army's view concerning the sacraments in the first years of the Army's existence, but a couple of William Booth's songs illustrates the concepts and the vocabulary. William Booth's song, "O, boundless Salvation"[29] has developed into a sort of national anthem of The Salvation Army used internationally in most languages, including all the Nordic. It could be interpreted as a baptismal hymn (without the baptism) or a sacramental hymn as it is the blood of Christ—"who opened his bosom to pour out his sea"—that forms the sea. There is no drinking of the sea, but an immersion into the "life-giving flood." The images of the sacraments, especially baptism are present.

> O Boundless salvation! Deep ocean of love, / o fullness of mercy, Christ brought from above, / the whole world redeeming, so rich and so free, / now flowing for all men, come roll over me.

The following verses have an ending describing the effect of the waters:

> 2) "thou great crimson sea/ thy waters can cleanse me, come, roll over me! 3) Beneath thy blest billows deliverance I see, / O, come mighty ocean, and roll over me! 4) If once thy pure waters would roll over me. 5) Once more I have reached this soul-cleansing sea, / I will not go back till it rolls over me". 6) The tide is now flowing, I'm touching the wave, / I hear the loud call of the mighty to save;/ my faith's growing bolder, delivered I'll be;/ I plunge 'neath the waters, they roll over me. 7) And now, hallelujah! The rest of my days/ shall gladly be spent in promoting his praise / who opened his bosom to pour out his sea / of boundless salvation for you and for me."

By using sacramental images, the song transmits the centrality of Salvationist faith. It does not explain the meaning or status of the sacraments, but it does clothe the all-important blood of Christ as the vehicle of salvation in sacramental language. The *Book of Common Prayer*[30] described

---

28. Rightmire, *Sacraments and The Salvation Army*, 39.

29. *The War Cry*, December 23, 1893. It was written in connection with a "Boundless Salvation" campaign culminating in two day meetings in Exeter Hall, London in the autumn.

30. Davies, *A New Dictionary of Liturgy & Worship*, 101–103.

the sacraments as "an outward sign of inward grace," an expression that continued in the Methodist church and later in the Salvation Army. William Booth concentrated on the inward grace and kept the outward signs to the language. The holiness theme, called full salvation, is also present in the song. Holiness teaching was closely linked to the founders' stance on the sacraments—the constant presence of God through the Holy Spirit in personal lives.

Catherine's understanding of the true sacraments was connected to this constant presence of Christ:

> "The abiding Christ could not have intended to teach that through the earthly medium of bread and wine his people were to remember him on whom their thoughts were to be constantly concentrated, or commune with him in any special sense above that in which they were to commune with him always and everywhere. The water which Jesus gives, and to which he alone attaches any importance, is that which is "in us a well of water springing up into everlasting life"; and the wine which he values and promises to drink with us in his Father's kingdom, is that wine of the kingdom which is righteousness, and peace, and joy in the Holy Ghost."[31]

Holiness experience, the purity of heart that expressed itself in sacramental living, was at the center of her belief. Her fear was that any reliance on outward material forms could become a substitution for the real experience of Christ. She wrote the following:

> "Furthermore, another mock salvation is presented in the shape of *ceremonies and sacraments*. These were only intended as outward signs of an inward spiritual reality, whereas men are taught that by going through them or partaking of them, they are to be saved. Amongst these may be classed Baptism, the last Supper, and the ceremonials of ancient and modern Churches.
>
> Oh, the thousands of souls who are resting their hopes of salvation on the fact that they have been baptized, not only such as believe in the palpable delusion of baptismal regeneration, but amongst ordinary church and chapel-going people. As I look at our Army congregations in the Rinks, Theaters, and other similar places, and note the signs of sin, debauchery, and crime on many of their faces, I say to myself, I suppose all these people have been baptized; but I do not think there are many thieves, or harlots, or drunkards, or openly immoral people who

---

31. Booth, *Popular Christianity*, 45–46.

claim baptismal regeneration. Thank God! It is only genteel sinners who can bring themselves to believe in such palpable sham, and yet, if baptism possesses any efficacy, it should be as effective in the one class of sinners as in the other.

What an inveterate tendency there is in the human heart to trust in outwards forms, instead of seeking the inward grace! And where this is the case, what a hindrance, rather than help, have these forms proved to the growth, nay, to the very existence, of that spiritual life which constitutes the real and only force of Christian experience."[32]

These attitudes to the dangers of reliance on the sacraments were predominant in Catherine's thinking. She feared such reliance upon outward signs instead of reliance upon the work of the Holy Spirit in changed hearts and lives. For her the full presence of Christ was realized in sanctification being lived out in sacramental living. Her description of the army congregations I consider to be used mainly polemically, but also as a partial description of an Army congregation. It would hardly be the full description[33], if the characteristics of the people the Army attracted which Walker and Horridge described were true.

The Bible was considered an important means of grace, but even so William Booth saw the greatest value of the Bible when it was translated into the lives of Salvationists:

> "I want to see a new translation of the Bible into the hearts and conduct of living men and women. I want an improved translation—or transference it might be called—of the commandments and promises and teachings and influences of this Book to minds and feelings and word and activities of the men and women who hold onto it and swear by it and declared it to be an inspired Book and the only authorized rule of life . . . it is no use making correct translation of words if we cannot get the WORDS TRANSLATED INTO LIFE."[34]

This "new translated Bible" revealed the focus on sacramental living, a focus that has continued to present days.

---

32. Ibid., 42–43.

33. A large painting in the Temple corps in Copenhagen from the first years of Frelsens Hær's existence in the country illustrates exactly such faces she is describing. The painter is unknown, but the painting is from 1901 and called "Meeting in Valhalla" (Valhalla was the first name of the Temple corps based on the name the building had when it was bought. The name is from the Nordic mythology).

34. Barnes, *The Founder Speaks Again*, 198.

The sacramental life can be illustrated by another song, *Thou Christ of Burning, Cleansing Flame*[35] by William Booth. It shows this focus on the gift of holiness, on the power to live holy lives:

> ... to burn up every trace of sin, / to bring the light and glory in, / the revolution now begin, / Send the fire! (v.2)

> ... for strength to ever do the right, / for grace to conquer in the fight, / for power to walk the world in white, / Send the fire! (v.3)

> To make our weak hearts strong and brave, / Send the fire! / to live a dying world to save, / Send the fire! / O see us on thy altar lay / Our lives, our all, this very day, / To crown the offering now we pray, / Send the fire! (v.4)

In "Boundless Salvation" the water's cleansing power was central. Here it is the fire that burns up "every trace of sin." The outcome is the same, but the image totally different with no association to the sacraments. The figure of the fire underlines the Army's belief in the baptism of the Holy Spirit as the essential baptism, the spiritual experience or the inward experience. The song also plainly describes what a holy life means—"*strength* to ever do the right, *grace* to conquer in the fight, *power* to walk the world in white." These three gifts were marks of the essential baptism.

The decision on non-observance of the sacraments within the Army was finally published in William Booth's New Year's article January 17, 1883 in *the War Cry*:

> "Now if the Sacraments are not conditions of Salvation; if there is a general division of opinion as to the proper mode of administering them, and if the introduction of them would create division of opinion and heartburning, and if we are not professing to be a church, nor aiming at being one, but simply a force for aggressive Salvation purposes, is it not wise for us to postpone any settlement of the question, to leave it over to some future day, when we shall have more light, and see more clearly our way before us?
>
> Meanwhile, we do not prohibit our own people in any shape or form from taking the sacraments. We say, 'If this is a matter of your conscience, by all means break bread.'"

---

35. 1986 *The Songbook of The Salvation Army* no. 203. It was first printed in *the War Cry* April 14, 1894 and has been in the S.A. Songbook since 1899.

The statement was not the usual statement for the autocrat William Booth. The decision was for the time being, the final decision was postponed for some future day. Normally decisions would be definitive and not left for future days. He made it optional for Salvationists to take the sacraments. As mentioned, the focus for William and Catherine was on the sacramental life that should be lived in the constant presence of Christ and that included to follow Christ's example. Jesus responded to vulnerable people, therefore diaconia belonged to Christian discipleship and became a central issue in Salvationist theology.

Social and Personal Redemption

Diaconia is what the Army is known for everywhere in the world where it has a presence. It has been part of the Army's work during all the time it has been in Norway as this aspect was being developed and formalized during the years of expansion into Scandinavia. It is a nota ecclesiae for The Salvation Army.

Activism as one of Bebbington's four characteristics of Evangelicalism was evident from the early beginnings of The Christian Mission/The Salvation Army. The practical outcome of it was very much in line with what other Evangelicals did during the early years. This situation altered through the 1880s, so the focus on the poor was not only an outcome of evangelical activism, but changed to a much greater involvement in social activism and social work. Diaconia became imbedded into the Salvation Army's DNA—into its theology as well as its ecclesiology. It happened gradually. Salvationists working in the slum areas responded to social challenges by trying to relieve the immediate and growing need caused by the economic depression of 1884–87. The social evils surrounding Salvationists and their response to it, together with William Booth's own experience during his involvement in East London during a life time, changed the theology as well. It must have happened gradually, but the first expression of this change is found in an article by William Booth "Salvation for Both Worlds," pointing out that salvation was social as well as personal:

> "But with this discovery, there also came another, which has been growing and growing in clearness and intensity from that hour to this; which was that I had two gospels of deliverance to preach—one for each world, or rather, one gospel which applied alike to both. I saw that when the Bible said, "He that believeth shall be saved," it meant not only saved from the miseries of the future world, but from the miseries of this also. That it came

with the promise of salvation here and now; from hell and sin and vice and crime and idleness and extravagance, and consequently very largely from poverty and disease, and the majority of kindred foes."[36]

Booth developed his vision that was implied in the article in his most influential book and consequent social scheme *In Darkest England and the Way Out*.[37] The book described his Darkest England Scheme, a crusade to assist the "submerged tenth"[38] of England's population. By this he was providing a model for social salvation. The first part of the book dealt with an analysis of the problems, this was called "The Darkness." The second part, labeled "Deliverance" proposed solutions to the problems. He used the London Cab Horse "as a very real illustration of poor broken-down humanity; he usually falls down because of overwork and underfeeding. If you put him on his feet without altering his conditions, it would only be to give him another dose of agony; but first of all you'll have to pick him up again."[39] He continued his argument such:

> "The second is that every Cab Horse in London has three things; a shelter for the night, food for its stomach, and work allotted to it by which it can earn its corn. These are the two points of the Cab Horse's Charter. When he is down he is helped up, and while he lives he has food, shelter and work."[40]

This illustration of the Cab Horse caught the imagination of people to support the Darkest England Scheme and the fundraising that followed.[41] In the book Booth tried to explain the relationship between personal and social salvation, a natural order of redemption as he understood it. The social redemption was preparatory, necessarily, to the work of spiritual redemption:

36. *All the World* January 1889, 2.

37. The editor W.T. Stead helped William Booth to edit the massive material of statistics and case stories into a book of 285 pages plus an appendix of 31 pages.

38. It was Booth's descriptive term of the poorest of the poor. It was the heading of chapter two, 17. The submerged tenth was illustrated by a four color poster attached inside the cover of the book showing people drowning in the sea. All the waves were named such as unemployment, starvation, homelessness, drunkenness etc. and a figure stating 3000.000 in the sea. At the sides were statistics. Above the sea the Army's programs for solutions to the problems were illustrated by the City Colony, the Farm Colony and the Colony across the Sea.

39. Booth, *In Darkest England and the Way Out*, 19.

40. Ibid., 20.

41. In order to account for the scheme a weekly paper *The Darkest England Gazette* started in July 1893. After a year the name changed to *The Social Gazette*. The paper continued until 1916.

"If these people are to believe in Jesus Christ, become the Servants of God, and escape the miseries of the wrath to come, they must be helped out of their present social miseries."[42]

He wanted to maintain a balance between personal and social salvation.[43] From the beginning of the book he tried to keep such a balance. The message of social and personal salvation could be described as one being the means to reach the goal, but even so they could not be separated as they belonged together. The influence of the book upon Salvationists was profound. As far as I can judge it became part of the Salvation Army's DNA in whatever country it opened its work.

On the first page of *Darkest England and the Way Out* is written: "To the memory of the companion, counsellor, and comrade of nearly 40 years. The sharer of my every ambition for the welfare of mankind, my loving, faithful, and devoted wife this book is dedicated."

Catherine Booth died, 4 October 1890, and *Darkest England* was published 20 October. She had followed the whole process while fighting the cancer that ended her life. She got the message of her condition in February 1888. Her last public address was on 21 June 1888 in the City Temple in London. In the tribute to her in *Manchester Guardian* it was stated: "She has probably done more in her own person to establish the right of women to preach the Gospel than anyone else who has ever lived."[44] She had also been deeply involved in social issues especially concerning women.

Conclusion

The most important issue was to see The Salvation Army's development as an independent denomination with the theological focus on holiness expressed in a sacramental life, and to scrutinize the reasons behind the non-observance of the sacraments. Diaconia as a nota ecclesiae of The Salvation Army has been well known, but still a focus on the origins of it is essential for any discussion on ecclesiology. Diaconia can be seen as constitutive of The Salvation Army as a church. While the word preached pure and the sacraments administered rightly are constitutive for the Lutheran Church, The Salvation Army considers, "saving souls, growing saints and serving suffering humanity" as related to mission to be constitutive for its identity as a church. The Salvation Army had developed as an independent

---

42. Ibid., 257.
43. Green, *War on Two Fronts*, 85–95.
44. Green, *Catherine Booth*, 290.

denomination with doctrines, practices, and structures in place, when it crossed the borders of Norway to commence its work there.

The last time William Booth appeared in public was, 9 May 1912, in the Royal Albert Hall. He died 20 August 1912. A few years prior to his death William Booth had written: "My arms are around the world and my heart set upon its salvation."[45] The Salvation Army had expanded to most parts of the world during his lifetime. The Year Book 1913 gave an account of all the countries: United States, Canada, South Africa, Japan, West Indies, Sweden, India and Ceylon, Australia, New Zealand, Germany, South America (Argentina, Uruguay, Chile, Peru, and Paraguay), Switzerland and Italy, Denmark with Iceland, Holland, Dutch Indies, Korea, Norway, France and Belgium, Finland. The Army's Naval and Military League in St. Helena, Malta, Gibraltar, and Burma was also mentioned.

William Booth's claim that his arms were around the world is justified by this statistic. The Salvation Army's expansion also concerned Norway.

---

45. Ibid., 232.

Chapter 3

The Foundation of Significant Factors for the Process Towards Registration in Norway

THE ROOTS, CULTURALLY FROM the working class and religiously from Evangelicalism, the characteristics of The Salvation Army with the military metaphor, female ministry as well as the influence of pragmatism, did not change in the Army's transition into Norway. The two first issues, working class and evangelicalism, the Army shared with other free churches that had settled in Norway in the years previous to Frelsesarmeen, but even so the Army did not pursue registration as dissenters like the other free churches had done. It did not see itself as a church, on the contrary it claimed not to be a church, but an Army of salvation. The focus was not on building a dissenter church, but on getting people saved and making soldiers. The most effective mode for that purpose would be pursued wherever the Army opened its work. The pragmatism became a mark of The Salvation Army. Pragmatism was passed over to Frelsesarmeen as a DNA and has been visible throughout its history. Pragmatism was evident in 2005 at the actual registration as a faith community in Norway. For William Booth the question would always be: "Does it work?" If things worked there would be no reason for making things more difficult than necessary, as for instance a registration as dissenters would be. The importance of female ministry was illustrated in the pioneering of Frelsesarmeen in Norway as the first leader was a woman and a great number of women have been leading corps, institutions and held THQ appointments throughout the years

The pioneer of the Salvation Army in Sweden, Hanna Ouchterlony also opened the work in Norway. She listened to Bramwell Booth[1] in her hometown of Värnamo which became a turning point for her. She was forty

---

1. Petri, *Hanna Cordelia Ouchterlony*, 36.

years of age and the owner of a bookstore. Through the next four years from 1878 to 1882 she corresponded with Bramwell.² The correspondence became a teaching tool with a clear focus on holiness of life as he became her mentor and teacher of Army belief and praxis. Looking into the start of the Salvation Army in different countries it is difficult to find any parallels to the beginning in Sweden, even though all beginnings were different from each other. Even so the beginning on Scandinavian soil was unique in the way of maturing the soil through spiritual and doctrinal teaching via these letters over four years. Apart from the letters she received the *War Cry* every week and was recommended different books to read. Some books were sent to her as well. In the Scandinavian setting, with its strong Lutheran state churches, this focus on doctrinal teaching was important. In a Lutheran setting orthodoxy was essential. The Army came from a tradition where orthopraxis was as important and it became essential to Salvationism. It was necessary for the Scandinavian scene to combine the somewhat stronger doctrinal teaching with orthopraxis to have a more solid foundation.

Walker's and Horridge's research substantiates the claim of the Army as a working class religion. That was how it started and it stayed that way as it spread beyond the borders of England. It was a ready-made religious movement that settled in Norway. It did not have its roots within Norwegian culture, but it adapted to a certain extent to the culture especially the working class culture. Inger Furseth's work was natural to search in order to find something about Frelsesarmeen in combination with the Labor Movement in Norway as the two started at the same time. This was not the case. The argument for not comparing the labor movement to a religious movement was:

> "No significant religious movement emerged during the years 1870s-1905. It could be argued that the Home Mission movement was a parallel movement to the labor movement, since this movement was constituted as a nationwide movement during this period. However, the Home Mission movement began in 1850s and therefore, its movement formation process took place decades before the labor movement appeared. It could also be argued that Pentecostalism was a parallel movement to the labor movement, but it did not appear until 1906. Therefore the labor movement will not be compared with a parallel religious

---

2. The letters from Bramwell to her, forty-four altogether, can be seen on www.Bootheum.se. Her letters to Bramwell cannot be found. The bombing and destruction of IHQ during World War II might be to blame. Laura Petri mentions three letters from Hanna Ouchterlony that had been preserved, but that was in 1924.

movement, but comparisons will be made with previous movements in this study."³

That was quite a statement and certainly out of touch with historic evidence. Frelsesarmeen started in January 1888 and the labor movement in the 1880s, the Norwegian Labor Party was founded in August 1887, only five months separated the two. That was very close in time. From the criteria above this would be close enough for parallel studies. Frelsesarmeen could convincingly have met some of the criteria for the movements in question: "widespread support, longevity, and public influence."⁴ Frelsesarmeen could not have failed in meeting these criteria to be accepted as "significant," but it was never part of the study.

Industrialization, urbanization, and an increase in the population also characterized the period of the Army's beginnings in Norway as it had done in England and Sweden, as well as other western countries. The population increased from 1.7 million in 1865 to 2.4 million in 1910 with nearly 40 percent of the population living around the capital, in the towns along the Oslo Fjord, and in the area north toward Lake Mjøsa.⁵ The migration from the country to the cities had great importance for the beginning and rooting of the Army. The Salvation Army was an urban religion and to a certain extent dependent upon urban life and leisure for its mission strategy. Kristiania, where the Army first started, grew from 75,000 citizens in 1875 to 230,000 in 1900. A great number of rural workers migrated to the cities to compete with the urban workers and craftsmen for work and housing. The number of rural workers migrating to the cities was nearly as high as those who immigrated to the United States.⁶

The Army appealed to the same segment of the population as the labor movement and some of the same issues were on the agenda for both movements. The equality between women and men was an important issue for the labor movement and could be seen in the demand for general suffrage, but also in its struggles for equal rights and equal obligations for all in relation to gender and class. In the Army the agenda was different, because women's participation at all levels had been the case since the beginning of the Army, but to make women aware of their potential and gifts was certainly an issue. Another issue of mutual interest was to give dignity and self-confidence to working class people and to improve their situation. The ideas

---

3. Furseth, *A Comparative Study of Social and Religious Movements in Norway 1780s–1905*, 49–50.
4. Ibid., 38.
5. Ibid., 314–15.
6. Ibid., 317. See also Ohman Nielsen et al., *Norvegr* vol. III, 35–39.

of what would make the difference for people were certainly different. The Army believed in salvation for all, that salvation changed people, and that changed people would improve their own situation and the society's. The real revolution was believed to be a change in people's hearts, not so much a change in society as the first step. Both movements made use of the press, of their own papers, pamphlets, and books and perhaps most importantly of public meetings. Both movements had their own banners and songs. Furseth mentions the religious language used in socialist songs, a resemblance to the language of religious revivals.[7] The use of music in choirs and bands for use in different gatherings was similar. All these similarities could simply be called working class culture. The temperance question was an issue also in the labor movement. In 1903 the Labor Party had temperance as a point in its program. In the Army temperance was a condition for membership.

It would be one thing to find a resemblance between the two movements, another if there were some co-operation, for instance, involvement in the trade unions or an overlapping in membership. There seems not to be a lot to find, but this quote from a worker from Sapsborg indicates some co-operation:

> "The religious ones were in forefront of the trade unions. Many people with religious backgrounds were elected representatives in the trade unions and political organizations. Especially people who belonged to The Salvation Army, to which I belong and which is my church, and members of the Methodist church were in the forefront of these movements." (Workers' Memoirs 12:4–5)[8]

Nils Ivar Agøy[9] refers to Sapsborg as well as the place where the religious especially those connected to The Salvation Army and the Methodist Church were representatives both in unions as well as in the Labor party around 1910.

In culture the influence of Georg Brandes had reached Norway from Denmark,[10] a culture that rejected a religious worldview. The segment of the population to which the Army appealed was not greatly influenced by this "modern breakthrough." The main influence concerning religious skepticism would come from the labor movement, especially from the leadership

---

7. Ibid., 331–32.
8. Ibid., 349.
9. Agøy, *Kirken og arbeiderbevægelsen*, 93.
10. His daily paper *Politiken* reported extensively from the Army's beginnings in Denmark and gave in that way invaluable press coverage. Jensen, *Suppe, sæbe, frelse i 125 år*, 13.

and the press of the movement and the anti-religion inherent within socialism. The opposition from within the State Church towards cultural radicalism was the same that viewed the labor movement as a threat to religion.

Opposition from within the State Church was also strong towards Frelsesarmeen. It was considered a threat toward purity of religion or true Lutheran Christianity. It came from ministers and bishops alike in the form of articles published in newspapers and Church periodicals as well as in lectures and books. The most important and widespread book was translated from German and called *The Salvation Army* (original title: *Die Heilzarmee*) by the German professor of religious history, Theodor Kolde from the University of Erlangen.[11] The foreword in the Norwegian edition of 1888 was written by Gisle Johnson, professor at the Faculty of Theology and leader of the Norwegian Home Mission movement. According to his foreword the aim was to provide a more comprehensive "enlightenment" about the Army than the press gave. The intention was to warn against the growth of Christian religious movements, which he looked upon as "unhealthy." The opposition from the church concerned mainly the Army's working methods, especially the methods of recruitment, and its doctrine that was considered "false doctrine" from a Lutheran perspective. The meetings were in focus because the critics saw them as crucial success factors. Kolde highlighted the recruiting effect of the meetings, especially the preaching in the language and tone of the people, but also the testimonies of the new converts. Kolde referred to testimonies published in *The War Cry*. Open air meetings were considered an essential part of the Army's popularity. The military organization was another major objection to the Army's methods. Kolde acknowledged William Booth's talent for organization and called the Army's organization "a hierarchical monarchy." Several of the critics drew parallels to the Jesuit Order, a parallel that has been drawn several times in other countries as well. It can be seen in Tor Wahlström's dissertation,[12] which asserted that the orders of the Jesuits were regarded by some as similar to Orders and Regulations for officers. The opponents judged that the conversions and rebirths witnessed to in Frelsesarmeen were much too easy. It was not that quick to free oneself from sin and be sure of eternal salvation. Kolde focused on what he considered the main problem—the doctrine of salvation, especially the emphasis on the subjective dimension, the subjective emotion people felt at the mercy seat when they surrendered themselves to God. Sanctification understood as full salvation was considered with

---

11. Elstad, "Næsten Alting er ualmindeligt og ubeskrivelig excentrisk," 243–61.

12. Wahlström, *Frälsningsarmeen i Finland som Trossamfund*, 90–97. Sandall, *The History of The Salvation Army*, Vol.II, 31–32.

skepticism, that a second step or second experience was taught as necessary. Most critics interpreted the Army's holiness teaching as conveying a belief in being utterly without sin,[13] including Kolde. Non-sacramental practice and the teaching concerning the sacraments were naturally an aspect of severe criticism from Lutheran clergy. The Army's position was considered as contempt or even a ridicule of the sacraments. Catherine's lectures in *Popular Christianity* could very well be perceived in that way. The link between holiness teaching and non-sacramental practice was not understood as the whole matter of the Army's view of sanctification was rejected as false teaching. On top of the actual teaching came the problem that women taught, preached and were pioneers. It was considered unbiblical and against the order of creation. In the area of equality for women the Army was considered a part of the contemporary culture of infidelity.[14] This short review shows some of the religious hostility in which the Army started its work in Norway. It was different or even alien not only from the established church, but also from what was expected of a religious movement from the secular press or the man on the street. This strange movement had an appeal both for ridicule and for fascination and entertainment.

The Salvation Army came into Norway late in the wake of the Dissenter Law of 1845 and soon after its beginning the extended Dissenter Law of 1891[15] became the legal situation. The Dissenter Law of 1845 gave

---

13. This understanding or misunderstanding was not only reserved for the critics. It was part of the holiness crisis in Norway around 1892. The fine line between the belief in freedom from sin or from the sinful nature and the belief in the possible freedom from the power of sin was difficult. The last had to do with the Army's belief in the freedom of the will, that man had a choice between surrendering to the power of sin or to fight the power of sin by the Holy Spirit. It had to do with freedom from deliberate sinning. The concept of *simul justus and peccator* was part of Army teaching, but the stress was on *justus* more than *peccator*. Doctrine 9: "We believe that continuance in a state of salvation depends upon continued obedient faith in Christ" shows that the experience of salvation or full salvation had to be guarded, it was possible to lose it.

14. Elstad, "Næsten Alting er ualmindeligt og ubeskrivelig excentrisk," 255–56.

15. "Lov angående kristne Dissentere og andre, der ikke er medlemmer af Statskirken" (Law concerning Christian dissenters and others who are not members of the State church). The law of 1845 included restrictions such as ban on private meetings, meaning that all meetings had to be open to the public. This restriction was continued in the law of 1891. New for the 1891 law was that it opened up the possibility of a written resignation from membership in the State Church, instead of the demand of meeting up at the pastor's offices and personally giving in a resignation according to the 1845 law. The age for giving in a resignation had been 19 years in 1845, but was lowered to 15 (already in a revision in 1888). The 1845 law demanded the superintendent of the dissenter community to take the oath to the State, this clause was removed in the 1891 law. New for the 1891 law was that pastors of the dissenter communities could perform legal weddings. According to the 1845 law they had to have a civic wedding. The 1891

religious freedom to form dissenter churches, to be members of these or to stay outside any churches or religious societies. The Methodists (1856) and the Baptists (1860)[16] came in the 50s and early 60s, and others followed in the 70s and early 80s. They were all expressions for evangelicalism with the characteristics Bebbington had pointed out as *conversionism, Biblicism, activism, and crucicentrism*. So the Army came in on a wave of evangelicalism.

The Army did not register as a dissenter community when it came to Norway. The pragmatism towards issues such as registration and official status, which was evident in the founders of The Salvation Army, seemed to become part of Army heritage. In matters of church registration this pragmatism was clear and can be seen in the way the Army in different countries used any sort of registration just to be legally present in a country, and then to build up the Army in the same way as usual independent of registration.[17]

---

law contained a special paragraph (§24) that concerned rights and duties for the Jewish community. Jews had been given access to the country in 1851 and their religious freedom became secured by the law of 1845 concerning non-members of the State church. See Breistein, *"Har Staten bedre borgere?,"* 75–98.

The examples from the 1845 and 1891 legislation mentioned were relevant for the work of the Army. The open meetings were no problem for the Army as it wanted to reach the public anyhow. The fact that the age for resignation was lowered must have been helpful for the Army considering the number of very young people attracted to its ranks. The possibility of registration as dissenters was never pursued therefore the removal of the clause concerning the oath and the right to perform legal weddings in a dissenter community was not relevant. If a registration was ever considered these issues might have been part of a consideration. There are no documents to indicate that it was even considered. The paragraph concerning the Jewish community just shows the scope of religious freedom and the religious pluralism developing within the country.

16. Breistein, *"Har staten bedre borgere?,"* 60–61.

17. It was quite interesting to see how the Army in Finland during the Russian Empire was registered as a housing association, 14 July 1898, then later as a foundation, 31 July 1941. In Russia before and during the revolution it was registered as a publishing house publishing the War Cry. The officers were registered as War Cry sellers. After the re-entry into Russia in the 1990s the registration was as a faith community (Local Community of the Evangelical Christian church "The Salvation Army" (Armija Spasenija) in Leningrad 28 March 1991). The army had to be registered town by town (at least three places) in order to be able to get an all Russia registration. In Norway the army was registered as a housing limited company 8 March 1899. It has since 1995 been registered as an organization. In 2005 a Salvation Army faith community was registered. In the beginning in Denmark the Army was registered as a commercial and limited company. 27 January 1970 it got the status of faith community by the right to perform weddings in accordance to the Law of Religion 1969. In Sweden the Army was registered as a non-profit organization in 1883, by that it was possible to publish *Stridsropet* (The War Cry). Such an association could not own property and the Army registered as a Publishing Ltd. Company in 1893. Most faith communities in Sweden used to register as foundations and so did the Army in 1932. Due to the law on religion of 1951 it obtained the right to perform weddings in 1952. In 2000 when the separation

Registration did not really seem to influence the work. This indifference to legal status can be interpreted as an evidence of a very strong Salvationist identity and strong organizational structure. The mission and vocation were clear. It was paramount to stay within the law but as important to creatively use all legal means for mission purposes.

As part of the plan of expanding the work to Norway Hanna Ouchterlony sent an officer to Kristiania in August 1887 to explore the situation. An outcome was an important event for the starting process of the Army with the visit of William Booth to Kristiania 25 October 1887. The Free Mission Society's building was rented for this and the hall was filled with people. The gathering and William Booth's speech was more a lecture about The Salvation Army than a revival meeting.[18] The officer had contacted *Den Kristne Alliance* (the Christian Alliance) whose aim was the conversion of people. Four men especially were at the forefront, a Methodist, a Baptist, a Free Mission man, and a State Church member. They were independent craftsmen and small business holders, a bookseller, a watchmaker, a postmaster, and a tanner master. The tanner master and State Church member, P.Th. Halvorsen, became the most ardent supporter of starting Frelsesarmeen in Norway. He offered to build a house for Frelsesarmeen. The offer was accepted as an answer to prayer and the building process started for a new building with an address in Grønland 9. That the economic support came from an owner of industry with an interest in evangelicalism was not new for the Army. The supporters of the Booth family and the Army's work in England had the same background, perhaps on a bigger scale, but initially the supporters belonged to the same segment of society.

On 22 January 1888 the new building was finished and the official opening of Frelsesarmeen took place. Hanna Ouchterlony with the rank of Commissioner[19] was now the leader of both Sweden and Norway. The British Staff Captain Albert Orsborn with his wife were to be local leaders in Norway under her supervision. They stayed until the autumn when another Englishman, Charles Sowton, took the same position under her

---

between State and Church was inaugurated the Army registered as a community of faith 1 January 2000.

18. Norun, *Med Kjærlighetens Våpen*, 24–25, Petri, *Hanna Cordelia Ouchterlony*, 336.

19. Commissioner is the highest rank after General within The Salvation Army. She was the first woman outside the Booth family to be given the rank. Norun, *Med Kærlighetens Våpen*, 27.

leadership.[20] By the end of 1889 the number of corps was twenty-seven.[21] The Army's paper *Krigsropet* (The War Cry) was published 17 May 1888 in Norwegian. The first months the Swedish paper *Stridsropet* had been used.

How much the solid doctrinal correspondence course received by Hanna Ouchterlony had filtered down to new soldiers and officers is uncertain, but looking at the names of the first Norwegian officers and their contribution to Army faith and practice could indicate that they had received a profound grounding. Whether such an influence came from Hanna Ouchterlony's leadership has not been possible to verify, but at least the result could point in such a direction. Carl Breien, who started his officer training aged 19 in April 1888, can stand as an example. He was a journeyman baker and son of a baker. He gave evidence of a profound doctrinal foundation in writing and his ministry had a long lasting effect, not only for Norway, but for Denmark and Indonesia. He served several years in Denmark as a Divisional Commander. On one of his train journeys he met Vilhelm Wille, a doctor from Køge who belonged to the Home Mission. In their conversation they discussed baptism, especially infant baptism, a theme Dr. Wille had been concerned about. Carl Breien explained the Army's position towards the sacraments, especially baptism. This conversation led to soldiership for Vilhelm Wille and his wife Marianne in Køge corps, and later to officership with a lifelong missionary service in Java as a specialist in eye disease building up an eye hospital that is still functioning today.[22] Breien's writings and his songs testified also to the grounding in Salvationists faith[23].

---

20. The Norwegian history books lists both Orsborn and Sowton as territorial leaders. This is not correct according to the information given by Petri. She refers to correspondence between IHQ and Hanna Ouchterlony concerning this issue. In her biography of Ouchterlony she had access to her papers and interviews with her. The letter of Memorandum, Hanna Ouchterlony asked William Booth for in order to prevent misunderstandings, stated that she had the overall leadership. She had responsibility for property purchase or refurbishing, finance, commissioning of cadets to officership, acceptance of married couples to cadets or officership and significant changes in the work where opinions differed. Petri, *Hanna Cordelia Ouchterlony,* 347. The first legal document covering Frelsesarmeen is from 1892. It described the Army's mission and structure and was signed and sealed by William Booth 25 March 1892. It supports that Norway was not an independent territory until 1892 as such a document would be made for an independent territory.

21. Territorial commander, *Annual Report* 1889.

22. Wille, *Korstog i Køge* and *Lys og Mørke*.

23. His song: *Kom, Gud med kraftens ånd* (God come with the spirit of power) nr.364 in *Frelsesarmeen sangbok (Salvation Army songbook)* gives the essence of Salvation Army holiness teaching. His song: *Hør din frelser kaller* (Hear the call of your Savior) nr. 266 in *Frelsesarmeens sangbok* gives the essence of the Army's understanding

A change in leadership came when Hanna Ouchterlony left the leadership of Sweden and Norway in 1892 for a special task in the USA to research, visit, and organize the Scandinavian work there. It was developing fast. The leadership of Norway now became independent of Sweden as the British Colonel Richard W. Wilson took over the leadership. The work had spread to most parts of Norway and grown extensively with 61 corps as a result. The holiness crisis marked these two years. It was grounded in misinterpreting the concept of freedom from sin as an outcome of sanctification. It caused a split between officers and soldiers with losses of both soldiers and officers as a result.

In 1894 Hanna Ouchterlony returned as leader of Frelsesarmeen in Norway. Within a week of her arrival she announced that she would arrange special holiness meetings every Thursday in Oslo.[24] Because of the holiness crises she was warned not to do this, but she was adamant to go through with it to heal the wounds and to give proper holiness teaching. It became an important tool to keep the Army's holiness teaching clear of extremism or repression. Apart from her teaching and mature leadership a number of initiatives in the Army's social work characterized her six yearlong second period as a leader of Frelsesarmeen. Frelsesarmeen was struggling financially. In spite of that she managed, both with her business skills and the use of her personal connections, to raise funds for a number of new initiatives—a hostel for "fallen" women providing for work and training, crèches, hostels for homeless men in Kristiania and Bergen, six new slum stations on top of the ones already operating, and shelter for unemployed men. In her last years the Army's missing person's bureau was started in 1897 and the Army's salvage vessel, *Catherine Booth*, was built. It was planned to operate among the fishers in Lofoten and along the Finnmark coast and was ready to be set afloat in January 1900. By the end of her time in leadership, Frelsesarmeen had spread all over Norway. The time of pioneering and of movement formation was over when Hanna Ouchterlony left Norway in 1900. She had been in the leadership position of Norway for ten of the twelve years of movement formation and pioneering.

Salvationist faith—Lutheran practice

As the time of pioneering and movement formation ended in 1900, Frelsesarmeen took up the challenge of translating the Doctrine book. Evaluations of which edition to translate must have been made, as Norway chose differently from the other Nordic countries. The obvious choice would have

---

of salvation.

24. Petri, *Hanna Cordelia Ouchterlony*, 357.

been to translate the newest English edition, but Frelsesarmeen did not go for such a solution, most probably because there were other factors than just a translation to take into consideration. These included the possible practice among soldiers in relation to infant baptism and the consequent membership of the State Church. Also, it would be as important to show that the Army was not hostile to the sacraments, even though the interpretation of them differed. The officers at large still abstained from having their children baptized and had severed their own membership of the State Church, but changes were on their way.

It could be expected to find a clear Lutheran influence on Salvationist faith concerning the sacraments in view of the membership of the State Church, but the Norwegian doctrine book from 1901 gives an even more surprising impression with the little section on Baptism and Communion. The surprise was that the Army in Norway translated the very first doctrine book from 1881 these years later, ignoring what had happened in 1883 when the Army decided to abandon the administration of the sacraments. Frelsesarmeen began its work in 1888 and had never acted outside of the 1883 decision. This first Norwegian translation of the Doctrine Book was most probably published in 1901.[25] It must have been a deliberate choice to include the section on the sacraments which was not a part of later doctrine books, and so going back to before the decision on non-observance regarding the sacraments was taken. This translation also served the purpose of showing that Frelsesarmeen was not hostile towards the sacraments as it had been accused of. The Doctrine Book of 1881[26] was a little catechism:[27]

> "What is the teaching of the Army on the subject of Infant Baptism?
>
> As a form by which the parents or guardians of children may consecrate and set them apart, and declare their intention of training them up for God and The Army

---

25. There is no publishing year in the book, but the first advertisement of the doctrine book appeared in *Krigsropet*, 21 September 1901. During the autumn there were several similar advertisements.

26. Booth, *The Doctrines and Disciplines of The Salvation Army*. It consisted of thirty-six short sections with a title for each. A number had the same title, but included different aspects of the theme. Section 26 gave an explanation of baptism and a comment on the Lord's Supper.

27. Petri, *Catherine Booth och Salvationismen*, 223 notes that it followed Cooke, *A Catechism Embracing the Most Important Doctrines of Christianity*, from the Methodist New Connection where William had been studying. Some of it was word to word. Green, *War on Two Fronts*, 43 refers to Field, *The Student's Handbook of Christian Theology* as the basic source. Both sources come from within Methodism. Cook's catechism was earlier than Field's. The sources show that *Doctrines and Disciplines* was based on general and basic Methodist teaching.

But what is the teaching of The Army on adult, or believer's Baptism, as it is called?

> Much the same. Only, in this case, the person baptised declares that he wishes it known that he is converted.

Does The Army consider Baptism as a duty that must be performed?

> *Decidedly not.* The Army only considers one baptism essential to salvation, and that is, *the baptism of the Holy Ghost.* There is one baptism. "One Lord, one faith, one baptism." Ephesians iv.5.

But was not baptism by water quite a common rite among the early Christians?

> Yes! And so was circumcision, shaving the head, washing the feet of the saints, and many other Jewish ceremonies, which were never intended to be binding on our practice and consciences.

Was baptism a ceremony prevalent in the Jewish Church?

> Yes: It was the rite by which proselytes or converts were introduced into the church.

What is the teaching of the Army on the subject of the Lord's Supper?

> When such an ordinance is helpful to the faith of our Soldiers, we recommend its adoption.

Is the ordinance of the Lord's Supper essential to membership of the Army, or to Salvation?

> Certainly not. Only a holy life, the outcome of love to God and man, attained and maintained by the power of the Holy Spirit, through faith in the blood of Christ, is essential to salvation."

This section illustrates that the sacraments were in no way central to Salvation Army belief or praxis. The value they were given was minimal and were closer to arguments for a non-observance than for an observance, but they were not hostile either. Especially when it came to baptism, the way *italics* were used to underline that the rite was not essential, and for showing what sort of baptism—the baptism of the Holy Spirit—that was important. The answer to question one gave the essence for an Army dedication and indicated that baptism was considered a dedication in line with the view of other Evangelicals. Baptism was a sign or a pledge, not something conveying grace in itself, but a ceremony that pointed to salvation conditioned by repentance and faith. Also the believer's baptism as in question two was placed in this category. It did not convey grace in itself, but was a testimony to salvation. Question three underlined that baptism was neither a duty to be performed nor a lasting commandment—only the baptism of the Holy Spirit was essential. The idea that baptism of the Holy Spirit would be contained within a water baptism was not considered at all. Question four is interesting because it made explicit what was implicit in question three. It compared baptism with a number of other rites among the early Christians that were temporal and not binding for future practice. All were considered "outward signs," but it seems as if they were not credited with the "inward grace." Looking at the number of questions, baptism had five and the Lord's Supper only two. The tone of the answers was more balanced in these two and there was no use of capital letters. The Lord's Supper was recommended if it was helpful, but it was made clear that it was neither essential to membership nor to salvation. As with baptism the Lord's Supper did not convey grace in itself. It might be helpful, but not essential. The holy life was stressed as essential. This was clear from the sections in the Doctrine book, the teaching on holiness was covered by eight of the sections. No other theme had so many aspects. It is difficult to view the Army's understanding of the sacraments as separated from its understanding of holiness or the holy life or sacramental life.

By choosing to publish this section these years later, Frelsesarmeen might have wanted to bring a Salvation Army understanding to infant baptism, as at least some, perhaps most Salvationists made use of in the Lutheran Church. The Army's understanding of the later dedication ceremony is reflected in the explanation. The dedication ceremony was introduced after the Army ceased to administer the sacraments. In Norway it became a custom at some stage for most Salvationists to bring the child to the Lutheran church for baptism and later on to bring the child to the Army for the dedication ceremony. This double blessing indicated a double allegiance. It was a strong allegiance, as Norwegian citizens brought the child to the State Church for baptism and staying within the tradition of family, friends, neighbors, and showing that they were proper Norwegians, even though they were Salvationists as well. It seems as if they brought with them the Army's understanding of baptism and gave a different interpretation of baptism from what was the Lutheran.[28] The other allegiance was to bring the child into Frelsesarmeen's fellowship and make the promise to be examples of what a Salvation Army soldier should be and bring the child up to belong to the Lord and be a faithful soldier in the service of God and Frelsesarmeen.

28. "Concerning baptism they teach that it is necessary for salvation, and that the grace of God is offered through baptism, that children ought to be baptized, as they through baptism are entrusted to God and pardoned by him. They condemn the Anabaptists who disapprove of infant baptism and profess that children are saved without baptism." Grane, *Den danske Folkekirkes Bekendelsesskrifter*, 51.

In her dissertation Breistein poses the question of the notion of the national and the Norwegian was bound to membership of the State Church, and therefore had an impact on the position of the dissenters in society.[29] Furseth, in her dissertation, mentions that, "discontinuity with the established religious tradition seemed to prevent movement growth."[30] Frelsesarmeen never demanded its soldiers to sever their bonds to the church. Reasons like these for not wanting to reject the membership of the Lutheran Church could have been in the minds of Salvationists, perhaps more implicitly than explicitly. Whatever the reasons, apparently there seemed to have been an unwillingness for Salvationists to be reckoned as dissenters legally. Perhaps the peculiarity and visibility of being a Salvationist was demanding enough for ordinary soldiers. To keep the bonds to the State Church would make them more like ordinary Norwegians. For Frelsesarmeen, with its mission driven focus, movement growth was absolutely central, but what happened seemed never to be due to an evaluation of what would benefit the Army most. The focus was to get people saved and to enroll soldiers for the continuation of the war.

The tradition of bringing the children to the State Church for baptism was not as usual among officers[31] in the early days as later on. This presumption is based on a diary from one of the Army's pioneers, Kristine Svendby (born Saksill).[32] In her diary from 1904–1914, written for her eldest son Fritjof, her last entry concerned his baptism, and that of his siblings, that took place two days before Fritjof's confirmation. She mentioned Fritjof's own wish to be confirmed. She also mentioned his enrollment as a soldier. Apparently the children had not been baptized as infants, so the baptism was connected to the confirmation that Fritjof wanted. Their personal choice of not originally baptizing the children reflected a more general attitude of officers at that time. From research into the addresses of officers' quarters, based on the census of 1900, it is clear that the officers in question, Ernst Wick with his family, Kristoffer Kristoffersen with his family, Henry Tandberg with his family, and Johanne Iversen were either stated as "Frelsesarmeen" or "left the church" or "no faith congregation." This probably meant that their children were not baptized. According to the census of 1910, all the mentioned officers now had the "s" for members of the State

---

29. Breistein, *Har staten bere borgere?*, 45.

30. Furseth, *A Comparative Study of Social and Religious Movements in Norway 1780s–1905*, 384.

31. It is only officers I have been able to trace. Traditionally there has been a difference between what choices the officers made and those of the soldiers. Officers and local officers would often make more radical choices than ordinary soldiers.

32. Skartveit, *Frelsesoffiser nr. 6*, 124–25.

church, while two other officer families, Martin Andersen's and Jens Klingsaid's, were marked with "no faith community" both in 1900 and 1910. A gradual change must have happened during these years. The last evidence is from Dr. Theol. Sverre Norborg[33] who in his book tells how he and three of his siblings stood around the baptismal font for their baptism in Tøyen church. Their officer parents did not dare tell anybody in the Army about this. This could indicate that they did not consider it the done thing as they felt it had to be in secret in contrast to the Svendby couple who did not consider it a secret.

Breistein refers to problems Salvationists had with the State Church.[34] It is clear from the following that the Army's position on the sacraments was known. In the note she refers to *Norsk Lovtidende* 1890:29 concerning a letter from the Church Department to the bishop in Kristiania, dated 10 February, stating that children who were members of Frelsesarmeen, even if they belonged to the State Church, ought not to be accepted for confirmation unless they left the association. The reason being that, according to information, the Army did not consider baptism and communion as sacraments. If a minister exerted an influence on the children concerning this issue, the department had no objection to that as long as it did not happen by objectionable means or in an improper way. Another example was a letter from the bishop in Bergen from 18 February 1890, stating that members of the State Church that belonged to Frelsesarmeen should not participate in the Lord's Supper as long as they were members of this association. On 9 January 1902, a letter came from the Church Department stating that in the future there would be no reason to exclude members of the State Church who belonged to Frelsesarmeen from the Lord's Supper, or as godparents, as long as they had not made themselves unworthy or, as members of Frelsesarmeen, had rejected baptism and communion as sacraments. That such a letter came from the Church Department in 1902 could support the theory that the doctrine book from 1901 had included this section on the sacraments in order to show that the Army was not hostile to the sacraments. It might have resulted in the letter from the department. The letter shows as well that if the Army's teaching concerning the sacraments was known, it was not kept a secret. The rejection of Salvationist State Church members must have been more widespread than the previous two examples show as the Church Department took up the case. The letter of 1902 could be seen as an opening. Salvationists were no longer automatically rejected from participation in the Lord's Supper, but they were expected to abstain

---

33. Norborg, *Seksti selsomme år*, 38.
34. Breistein, *Har staten bedre borgere?*, 115 note 240.

from rejecting baptism and communion as sacraments. The first doctrine book might have supported the Salvationists in their use of the sacraments. It did not reject the sacraments, but gave another interpretation. The interpretation might not have pleased the Lutheran bishops, but for an ordinary Salvationist it could be interpreted as a support, at least not a rejection

The pioneering officers appear to have been grounded in the Army's position to the sacraments and to have had a critical stance toward the Lutheran view of baptism as the example of Carl Breien's train journey shows. Whether that led them to abstain from having their children baptized, as in the case of the Svendby couple, or to interpret baptism in the State Church in Salvationists terms, is uncertain. Perhaps the wish of Fritjof to be confirmed indicated an initial trend for the young people of Frelsesarmeen, a trend that necessitated baptism of the children. This first doctrine book also came at an important time for the nation, as it was towards the end of the union time with Sweden and at the final stages of nation building. Kristine Svendby in her diary regrets that, as a woman, she could not vote, as this was a matter of great importance.[35] National feelings seemed to be rather intense with a great pride in being Norwegian. The decisions concerning membership of the State church can be interpreted as Salvationists wanting to be proper Norwegians, perhaps to signal this by regaining membership of the State church for those who had left the church and to baptize their children. The change seemingly had to do with nationality, with a strong allegiance to the nation, to the state, not with a change towards a Lutheran faith. Another reason for it happening at this time might have been that Salvationists, after the Army's initial period of pioneering and movement formation in Norway, had reached another level of status in society and therefore wanted to be more like other Norwegians belonging of the State Church and using the rituals of baptism and confirmation. In fact Salvationists seemed to make the same choices as other ordinary working class people did: to have a nominal membership of the State Church using the rituals of baptism, confirmation, wedding and funeral.[36]

It could be argued that Frelsesarmeen kept the tradition of The Salvation Army from before 1883 alive, not by administering the sacraments within the Army, but by making use of the sacraments in the State Church and giving them a Salvation Army interpretation. In this they overlooked the essence of the Lutheran belief, but their rationale for doing this might

---

35. Skartveit, *Frelsesoffiser nr.6*, 109–110.

36. Agøy, *Kirken og arbeiderbevegelsen*, 245 mentions that most working class people had their children baptized and confirmed in the church in spite of the agitation against Christian practice that came from the leaders of the Labor Movement published in their press. See also 252 and 254.

have been that they considered the State Church as an expression of a civil religion. To be accepted as proper Norwegians they kept the membership that included them in this institution and their children were baptized in order to belong and not be different from other Norwegian children. As far as I can see there was a parallel in Salvationists' attitude to the church to Ludvig Hope's ideas. He was a contemporary who considered the Norwegian Church as the religious service of the State, an organized and legal institution.[37] He illustrated his attitude by his well-known formulation concerning the church: "It is a scaffold we stand on while we are building the church of Jesus Christ." The Salvationists were making use of the church as a legal institution, as a scaffold they stood on as Christians and Norwegian citizens. To adhere to the State Church would help advance the Salvation Army's mission of salvation. Ludvig Hope's idea of the church as a legal entity, as the religious service of the State had some resemblance with the Salvationists' understanding and use of the State Church.

The Norwegian translation of the 1923 Doctrine Book with far reaching consequences

The change among officers from non-membership of the State Church to membership with the consequent double affiliation of Army/Church appeared to be firmly established in 1930 at the time when the 1923 Doctrine Book was due to be translated. This translation is remarkable because it excluded the appendix explaining the reasons for the Army's non-observance of the sacraments. The consequence was that generations of ordinary officers and soldiers had very vague ideas or were unaware of the Army's reasons for its non-observance until 1975, when the translation of the 1969 Doctrine Book was published that included the appendix on the sacraments. During all these years the influence of the statements of the 1901 Doctrine Book was present concerning the Army's view of baptism and communion, as it had been when these were still being administered within the Army. When it came to non-observance they had only silence concerning the issue in the Norwegian doctrine books.

It could perhaps be argued that Frelsesarmeen did not want to break what had become a tradition due to the 1901 doctrine book. A tradition that might have encouraged Salvationists to keep on using the sacraments in the State Church while giving them an Army interpretation. Frelsesarmeen of 1930 might not have felt it was ready to dissent so much from the State

---

37. Oftestad, "Fra 'forgård' til 'helligdom.' Folkekirken i Ole Hallesbys og Ludvig Hopes vekkelsesteologi," 100–103.

Church, as would be the case in an official document to advocate the Army's non-observance of the sacraments. Another interpretation could be that the leadership had sensitivity, a listening ear towards the Norwegian way of understanding church and Christian faith. It also included reflections on how Frelsesarmeen could best adapt to the culture. A link to such a listening ear could have included the celebration of 900 years for Saint Olav's fight and fall, as the focus of the St. Olav Celebration was to strengthen the State Church as a national symbol of unity on the background of a present crisis. The Norwegian people should gather in unity within the church.[38] Such a listening ear could be the case in spite of the TCs not being Norwegian.[39] In such matters they would most probably consult other Norwegian officers in order not to violate a successful accommodation. The reasons behind the decision are not possible to find, but the situation that it was excluded stands as a fact.

When it came to the content of the excluded appendix it was clear that forty years had passed and non-observance had become part of Salvationist church life so the Army internationally had to give reason for its position both externally as well as internally. The substance was not new, but the presentation of it was. The appendix was apologetic in style and nine pages long. The main point stated:

> "The Salvation Army does not observe Sacraments. It holds, in common with most other Christians, that they are not essential to Salvation."

Then it listed different reasons for the Army's attitude:

> "The religion of Jesus Christ is spiritual." It made a comparison to Judaism with its outward ceremonies and how they preceded the spiritual realities which Christ would bring. Examples from New Testament were stated—John 4:23, Galatians 6:15, and Romans 14:17
>
> a. "Christ's words, rightly understood, include no command for the permanent observance of any outward ceremony."
>
> b. "The fact that certain ceremonies were observed by some of the early Christians does not prove that all Christians ought to observe them."

---

38. Tønnessen, "*Et trygt og godt hjem for alle?*," 46–47.

39. The first Norwegian to hold that position came in 1941, Commissioner Joachim Myklebust. The TCs before that had been British, Swedish, and Danish.

c. "Sacraments are often a hindrance rather than help to those who use them, in that they lead people to rely upon outward ceremonies rather than upon Christ."

d. "The observance of Sacraments has been a frequently recurring cause of disagreement, bitterness quarrelling, and division among Christians."

e. "Sacraments cannot be, as some of their advocates claim, 'outward signs of inward grace,' for it is clear that some who observe them possess but little, if any, inward grace. It is equally clear that there are others who do not observe them who possess true inwards grace."[40]

There was an echo of both Catherine's and William's arguments. The overall statement of it not being essential for salvation is from William Booth's New Year's article as well as point e). The points of b), c), d), and f) are from Catherine's arguments and point a) is the overall underlining of the spiritual experience as the core of Christian life. These main points show that no substantial new insight had been achieved during these forty years of non-observance.

The TC in 1930 was Commissioner Karl Larsson, who was Swedish by nationality. He had served in Finland with responsibility for the work in Russia and in Russia itself a short time during the Revolution. At the time of World War II he took charge of the Army's work in occupied continental Europe from Sweden. In his diary from the 1930s he told about a female corps officer who had been asked to baptize a child and participate in a funeral within the State Church, as the vicar lived far away and the officer was close at hand.[41] This gives a glimpse of the situation upon which he made his decision. Karl Larsson also wrote some very comprehensive articles on The Salvation Army's view of the sacraments in his time as the TC. They were published in *Frelsesoffiseren*.[42] The articles were comprehensive and more in depth than the appendix in the doctrine book. They had a local Norwegian flavor in the examples. It might have been Larsson's way of compensating for the lack in the Doctrine book and it was certainly a solid compensation. However solid it was, its circulation was limited and not accessible, neither for the public nor for the soldiers. Not many would turn to copies of old officer magazines, so they were time limited as well. In contrast to this the doctrine book had to be taught at the training college for officers and in

40. *Handbook of Salvation Army Doctrine* 1923, 168–69.

41. Karl Larsson, *Under ordrer*, Vol. III 48–49.

42. *Frelsesoffiseren*: No.11 November 1931, no.1 January 1932, no. 2 February 1932, no. 4 April 1932, no. 5 May 1932, no. 6 June 1932.

preparation classes for soldiership so what was included and excluded in the book had lasting influence. It was quite unusual to ignore a vital part of a doctrine book authorized by the General in a hierarchical system as is the case with The Salvation Army, apart from an unusual procedure of publishing a book in translation where a part is omitted without mentioning this in the foreword or anywhere in the book.

The other Nordic countries had Lutheran state churches as well, therefore a search into the policy of the Army on this matter would be relevant. It revealed a different policy from that of the Army in Norway. In Finland the translation of the 1923 book came in 1929 with the appendix on the sacraments included. It seems to be the first Doctrine Book published in Finnish. The beginning of the Army's work in Finland was dominated by the Swedish language and Swedish speaking officers,[43] so the Swedish editions could very well have been the foundation the first years. In Sweden the first Doctrine Book was from 1904 and a translation of the 1900 edition without the section on Baptism from 1881 edition. The translation of the 1923 book was published in 1926 and had the appendix on the sacraments included. In Denmark the first translation came in 1899 and was similar to the 1892 edition without the section on baptism from 1881. In 1914 a translation of the 1900 edition that began with the eleven doctrines was published. Then in 1924 the translation of the 1923 edition was published with the appendix on the sacraments included. As can be seen only Norway decided to include the little section on baptism from the 1881 edition in its first doctrine book and to omit the appendix on the non-observance of the sacraments from the 1923 doctrine book in the 1930 translation.

Conclusion

The issue of working class people and working class culture as the locus of Frelsesarmeen did not change during these years. The Army stayed close to the working class and changed as the working class changed. Frelsesarmeen had published the 1901 book with the Army's original view of baptism and communion. It could serve as a guide to interpret the practice concerning the sacraments of ordinary Salvationists and officers, a practice the Army did not take up internally, but through the State Church. This could be seen

---

43. The Army's pioneers in Finland belonged to the Swedish speaking educated classes and some to the aristocracy as was the case with Constantine and Maria Boije and Hedvig von Hartman who were the central figures as the pioneering officers, but many other names as Björkenheim, Nicolay, Wrede, av Forselles and Hissinger from the beginning reflect this situation. Könönen, *En Arme på marsch*, 34–48.

as a wish to combine Salvationist identity with a proper Norwegian identity. The other important evidence was the letter from the Church Department in 1902 lifting the ban on Salvationists for communion and as godparents. Internationally it is interesting that Frelsesarmeen in a way took up the position before 1883 and carried that tradition with it until 1975 when the translation of the Doctrine Book included the appendix on the non-observance of the sacraments. In order to hold on to the original position the leadership of Frelsesarmeen decided to leave out the appendix on the sacraments in the 1930 translation. It is also remarkable that Norway was the only one of the Nordic countries to go down that line, even though the situation with the Lutheran State Churches was similar in the other countries. By these decisions they kept a Salvationist faith, but adhered to a Lutheran practice. These decisions concerning the doctrine books of 1901 and 1930 laid the foundation of significant factors for the process towards registration. It was the situation of double membership that became an obstacle for registration as a person could only be a member of one church. It also indicates why Frelsesarmeen did not register during all these years. It had found a way of accommodating itself by its soldiers' nominal membership of a powerful state church in order to secure members. It kept Salvationist faith, but adhered to Lutheran practice.

Chapter 4

Changes and Challenges from the wider Norwegian Society and Frelsesarmeen's Response to These

FROM ITS BEGINNINGS THE Salvation Army developed as it responded to what happened in society. Its birth was connected to the plight of the working class poor as a response to their religious as well as their social situation. Frelsesarmeen carried this characteristic mark with it as it advanced its work in Norway. It is interesting to see that this mark was still there during the years from the 1950s to 1975, which are the focus for this chapter. As society changed the original accommodation into Norwegian society seemed not to be as important as it had been. There were new challenges that not only had an impact on ordinary Norwegian citizens, Salvationists included, but also on society's institutions such as the State Church. There was a search for defining one's identity both among people and institutions. It also seemed as if Salvationist identity needed to be strengthened and redefined in view of new challenges. These new challenges influenced Frelsesarmeen in such a way that it started to consider its own legal situation. Registration as a faith community had been of no interest from the Army's beginning in Norway until the early 1970s, when it came forcefully on the agenda.

The creation of the welfare state based on legislation passed through parliament during the fifties was the essential impetus for the new social order developing in this period. The welfare state was built on solidarity within the population, a solidarity expressed through the fiscal policy of the state supported by political ideas as expressed in the social-democratic governments that were in power during these years. Based on the legislation of the fifties the welfare state developed highly professional social services throughout the sixties. The seventies saw the peak of this development. The fact that areas which had previously been dependent on the initiatives of private organizations such as Frelsesarmeen were now considered a public duty influenced Army policy. It made some of the Army's social work redundant. The traditional work of the Slum Sisters, for instance home care for elderly and dying people, domestic help for elderly, and families with special needs, became areas covered by local authorities. The Slum Sisters continued and found new needs that were not covered by the public authorities, or traditional areas where the social security net was not fine enough, but still statistics show a decrease in the numbers of stations.[1] A substantial part of the Army's Social Services were institutions. These were run by social officers who had developed their skills in social work through apprenticeship and not formal social studies. This became a challenge as a number of social officers had to get the relevant formal education on top of their officer education, mainly to be used in social institutions to meet the demands from the public authorities. It made social officers into professional social workers. It proved more difficult to change from pastoral work in a corps to social work at an institution and the other way round, as their particular skills were needed within social work. The interchange between leading a congregation and leading a social institution that had been fruitful for both kinds of services happened less often in this new situation. The changes were also the impetus of the practice of employing professional social workers, who might not have other bonds to the Army than their professional life. The connection between corps and social institutions became looser. That development became much more visible in the eighties and onwards as the numbers of officers diminished.

Norwegian society experienced great changes within employment in the years from 1961 to 1973 as industry was booming, resulting in export on a great scale. The rapid growth in industry demanded a larger work force and a growing number of married women replaced domestic duties with work in industry and commerce. The percentage of married women in paid work rose from 10 percent in 1960 to 24 percent in 1970. This significant change influenced the voluntary work many of these women had done for the Army in the local corps as local officers or youth—or social workers. Working women was nothing new in the Army, but the change from the fifties, where most married women had domestic work at home, to the situation of the new industrial boom made voluntary work more difficult to manage. Most soldiers tried to involve themselves in the work of the corps as much as possible, but with the dual tasks of home and work it became

---

1. In 1969 there were 27 stations, in 1979 there were 20, in 1990 there 13, in 2004 there were 4.

increasingly difficult for married women soldiers to give as much time as they used to.

A substantial number of the population moved from the countryside to smaller towns or cities to work in industry. In 1970 one million people more than in 1950 lived in towns and cities.[2] This had an effect on the Army's outpost work, which diminished during the 1970s. An outpost was a place where Frelsesarmeen held regular meetings away from the corps. Some outposts had their own soldiers, but most often those who attended were friends of the Army. The meetings could be held in a prayer house, a school room, a farm, an institution, and sometimes the church especially for concerts. The level of activities differed, but a general schedule would be that officers and sometimes soldiers visited the place, went from door to door with *Krigsropet,* or collecting money for the Army's work during the day. Late afternoon there might be a children's meeting and then an evangelical meeting at night. Depending on the distance back to the corps the officer/soldier would be billeted with Army friends. The work had great influence on Frelsesarmeen's status in the country as belonging to everybody. A number of officers had during the years been recruited from the outpost work and many young people had linked up with the local Army corps, when they moved to towns for further education.[3] The migrants from the countryside and the married women alone could not meet the demand for workers during this period of growth in the economy. A greater number of immigrants started coming to Norway to meet the need for workers. A discovery of a major oil field Christmas Eve 1969 made Norway into an oil producing nation.[4] The changes during these years affected nearly all spheres of life for ordinary people, so attitudes, hopes, and expectations altered because of great transitions in economy, work prospects, family life, mobility, greater equality between the sexes, and fundamental changes in society at large. Because of this growth Norway had the highest economic growth in Europe in the years 1974–1980. This new adventure, with such a promising prospect of the future for the nation, changed people's expectations and hopes for a future with unending riches. The public investment in expanding the welfare state with new hospitals, schools, universities, and more extended social benefits was very high and so was consumption by the population due to a substantial rise in income. The national economic growth was reflected in the private economy of the Norwegian people. There was money to buy goods, as for instance a car. The infrastructure changed

---

2. Furre, *Norsk Historie 1914–2000*, 189–92.
3. Lydholm, . . . *Teaching Them,* 85–99.
4. Furre, *Norsk Historie 1914–2000,* 224.

with new roads and tunnels. For the Army this also had an influence on the outpost ministry.

As immigration enforced a faster development in pluralism, the television, which was introduced in 1960, resulted in a common culture of entertainment that challenged traditional religious and pietistic attitudes. The challenge influenced Frelsesarmeen people's pattern of entertainment as well as statistics of attendance in meetings. This situation was reflected in the reports to IHQ from the TC as these two examples can illustrate. The 1972 report from Commissioner Sture Larsson explained the situation thus:

> "The attendances at public meetings are unfortunately 2,000 down per week. This means a decline of some 5,000 during my three years in Norway, i.e. 17.5 percent. I cannot put my finger on any particular cause for this, except that no doubt the rapid spread of television has taken some of our fringe adherents from us."[5]

During the sixties a youth culture of its own with a strong influence from English/American pop industry developed. The influence of this could be seen in Salvation Army pop-groups. The educational system was reformed and revitalized and a growing number of youngsters were able to pursue a higher education. In 1968 new universities opened in Trondheim and Tromsø and the following year a number of district institutions of higher education opened. The influence on the Army of the focus and quest for education was the opening of Jeløy Folk High School in 1974 in order to give Army young people, as well as youngsters in general, a year for personal development and new insights such as IT-technology. Jeløy was at the forefront with education in this technology and the IT-technology of Jeløy was used in the work of Frelsesarmeen's Commission of 1975–78. In September 1977 a conference-and-study center was opened on the Jeløy campus to further the education of officers and soldiers.

The growing number of students made the need for reforms visible. The students disagreed with the reforms the authorities wanted. The antiauthoritarian protests coming from the students inspired the youth culture at large. The protests against authority became a serious quest for democracy in different institutions, not only within the educational system, but on a wider scale involving society at large. The influence of this can be seen in the agenda of Frelsesarmeen's Commission of 1975–78 and its outcome. Not only young people united in protests, but also women, having entered the work force in greater numbers, protested against matters of inequality as for instance differences in wages. They gathered to work for equality

5. Territorial Commander, *Farewell Report* 1972, 2.

between the sexes in the public sphere as well as in the private. In Norway the Women's Liberation Movement developed mainly during the seventies and the focus was not only equality, but also liberation from oppression seen in structures of society. In the State Church the first woman was ordained in 1961.[6] Women's Lib influenced women officers to evaluate if the equality that was inbuilt into the Army's system also functioned in reality. Married women officers especially started to point out the gap between the ideal and realities. These debates were most prominent in *The Officer* and the issue was taken up in international commissions,[7] but also came to the surface in Norway.[8]

The general secularization of people and society had influence, because it meant that the traditional way Frelsesarmeen worked in order to reach out to people in the towns and outposts through indoor and outdoor meetings did not get the same response as earlier. The message seemed not to be as relevant for people's lives as the resonator for a message of salvation/conversion had lost its base. The general secularization affected a number of ordinary people so they turned away from a belief in God and from practicing their faith by attending places of worship, or fulfilling the religious routines of everyday life such as devotions or grace before a meal. This could also include ceasing to interpret their lives, their moral, spiritual, and religious experiences in the light of the values of the Christian faith. This challenge started a discussion of how to evangelize in such a situation among British officers. The inspiration came from USA in the secular city debate.[9] A British officer, Fred Brown, took up the discussion and connected it to his job as a corps officer in Regent Hall in London.[10] It showed that the challenge was felt and discussed, not in theoretical terms, but in practical ways. The following quotation from Charles Taylor describes the situation as it had become in the main period of this research, the seventies, and onwards:

> "From a society where belief in God is unchallenged and indeed, unproblematic, to one in which it is understood to be one opinion among others, and frequently not the easiest to embrace" . . . or "a society in which it was virtually impossible not to believe

---

6. In principle it had been possible for women to be ordained according to legislation concerning civil servants from 1938, but there was a schedule connected to the law stating that women ought not to be ordained in case the local church was against it. No women were ordained until Ingrid Bjerkås in 1961. She was nearly 60 years of age and had the urgency and courage to be a pioneer. Schjørring, *Nordiske folkekirker i oppbrud*, 200.

7. Hill, *Leadership in The Salvation Army*, 262–68.

8. Solevåg, *Likestilling i Frelsesarmeen?*

9. Callahan, *The Secular City Debate*.

10. Brown, *Secular Evangelism*.

in God, to one in which faith, even for the staunchest believer, is one human possibility among others."[11]

Salvationists were not immune from the general secularization either. They, too, experienced that belief in God was not "the easiest to embrace" among the different options of philosophies of life. Because of these changes it seemed as if Frelsesarmeen turned attention towards its own values, structures, and identity. During such a process the question of registration as a faith community became a feature. These examples give an indication of a society in process of rapid changes that had an impact on people's lifestyle, economy, values, attitudes, and beliefs as well as on the development within Frelsesarmeen.

The years leading up to 1975 within Frelsesarmeen

In the years preceding the decision to form a working group to look into the Army's situation and identity as a faith community, a change took place. A random look into the Annual Reports to IHQ[12] for 1949 and throughout the fifties reveals that the focus was very much on statistics and the rather vast numbers of people attending Salvation Army meetings. For example, the 1949 report mentioned that about 2 million people had attended the Army's indoor meetings during the year (1948). Then some attention was given to the condition of the country, economy, commerce, transportation, etc. In the following years a similar focus was present with an added emphasis on descriptions of evangelical campaigns, special youth outreach, and the like. In the reports from the sixties the emphasis changed. There was more concern for the organization as such a focus on the officers' situation, the social officers' need for more specialized education and training, the burden of too many duties for the field officers that could take the attention away from their work as evangelists and shepherds, as ministers. In 1962 Commissioner Westergaard came to Norway as Territorial Commander. He was Danish with an international upbringing and service and very much influenced by the British/International Salvation Army. In the report of 1963 he wrote:

> "Soul saving is not easy—although there is always a fairly ready response to Mercy seat appeals. A more ardent and realistic consciousness among officers and soldiers of the Army as a separate

11. Taylor, *A Secular Age*, 3.

12. A Territorial Commander will send an annual report on the state of the territory every year to IHQ. Via the Europe Zone the report will go to the General and Chief of Staff of the international Salvation Army.

movement, a separate people with a special mission and with specific characteristics would spur on to more and better attempts at soldier-making, corps organization and all the other things inherent in our function as the Salvation Army."[13]

This wish to strengthen Salvationists' identity as a faith community reflected in the report was characteristic of Kaare Westergaard's period as TC. Most importantly he wrote about the Army's stance on the sacraments both in an article in *Krigsropet*[14] and in an interview given to *Alle Kvinders Blad*. These articles alerted the interest of a number of the newspapers. The first one to give attention to this was *Morgenposten* on 13th March 1964 with the heading: "The Salvation Army stance on the sacraments." Other papers followed[15] and it gave rise to quite an intense debate. It was a debate most Norwegian officers would rather have been without and were not really dressed for. The reason for this situation can be found in the policy concerning the translations of the doctrine books into Norwegian with the result that the teaching on this matter had been limited, if present at all.

During the congress in June 1964, a conference was called that included leading officers from all spheres of work. The theme concerned the possibility of Norwegian officers performing funerals and wedding ceremonies. The actual situation was that officers did not lead such ceremonies in their corps, they were performed by other pastors, mostly Lutheran. Often a Frelsesarmee wedding ceremony would take place in the Army hall the following day or later the same day. In this way a number of Salvationists had two ceremonies. The conference decided to send a letter to the minister of the Department for Church and Education. The letter was sent on 26 of July 1964 and described the Army's position as a movement with the majority of its soldiers having a dual membership, one in the State Church, or a free church, and one in Frelsesarmeen. The letter mentioned that there was no intention presently to seek registration as a free church, but asked if it would be possible for Frelsesarmee officers to conduct committal service for its soldiers, and for certain officers in special leading positions to get the legal right to conduct marriages of its own officers and soldiers. A copy was sent to the Oslo Bishop, Johannes Smemo.

The actual reply to the matter was sent on 21 of January 1965. It stated that the members of the State Church could only be buried by a minister in the church. There were no rules concerning persons outside the State Church. Concerning weddings, the legal right to perform weddings was the

13. Territorial commander, *Annual Report of* 1963.
14. *Krigsropet* nr. 12, 21 March 1964, 6.
15. *Østlandets blad*, 9 March and 6 April 1964.

responsibility of the Department for Legal Affairs, but as matters were now, church weddings could take place 1) in the State Church, if the couple belonged to the church or if one of them belonged here and the other was dissenter, 2) in a dissenter congregation if the legal department had accepted the ceremony of marriage in that congregation, and a) if both parties or one of them belonged to the congregation, or b) one of them belonged to the congregation and the other to the State Church or was a dissenter from another free church. The Army's application was sent on to the Department for Legal Affairs. The reply from the department came on 7 May 1965 repeating that the legal right to perform church weddings only covered the two alternatives already mentioned. It was not possible to agree to other persons or organizations performing a legal wedding.

At a conference on 26 August 1965 for the leading officers the correspondence with the authorities was shared and a discussion took place. It was decided to write an article on the matter to *Frelsesoffiseren*.[16] The question of the Army's position, in case of changes in the law or if a new law was introduced, gave rise to a debate that ended in the decision to follow matters and repeat an application to the department if changes gave reason for that.

In Commissioner Westergaard's Farewell Brief of September 1966 to IHQ before leaving Norway he touched on a lot of things concerning the Army's position in the country, among these the question of obtaining legal status as independent church or religious movement. He then carried on:

> "The reason for this is constitutional and an outcome of the authoritative attitude and powers of the State Church over many years. Whereas it is now possible for us to obtain legal status and right as in the case with the Methodists, the Baptists and the Pentecostals in Norway today, it does entail that each individual member, or at least an agreed number, must cancel his connection (membership) with the Lutheran (State) Church, and it is rightly anticipated that few Norwegian Salvationists would be willing to do this [...] It is only correct to say that this situation causes no difficulties beyond an occasional irritation and there is not the slightest attempt from any authority to interfere with our administration. However, in this dual loyalty to church and Army lie the reason for a certain lack in the strength and sense

---

16. The matter was published in *Frelsesoffiseren* nr. 2 March/April 1966. The copies of the letters were followed by a short note saying that this was the situation, but the Army hoped there soon would be a solution on this question that was so important for Frelsesarmeen in Norway. All officers should by this be well informed.

of call as it directly affects us [. . .] the Army is a means of service more than a spiritual home."[17]

The Farewell Brief and the annual reports to IHQ expressed Commissioner Westergaard's own opinion that reflected his rootedness in the international Salvation Army and some difficulties in understanding or appreciating the Norwegian situation. Seen from an outside perspective it could be a natural conclusion on differences he had noticed from other places (and perhaps from another time). This explanation was given solely in view of the situation of double membership. He did not consider the problems arising due to changes in society, nor did he consider that dual loyalty was most probably the result of two different loyalties, that needed not exclude or weaken each other. The loyalty to the State Church was most probably not connected to calling or spirituality, it was based on national bonds, on being properly Norwegian. The State Church was the symbol of unity as a nation, of tradition, and of the history of Christianity in the country. Loyalty was to this national symbol of unity or to the civil religion of the state. The Army was a means of service, but it was certainly a spiritual home as well. Salvationists expressed their calling through their engagement in the Army. Looking at the statistics most Salvationists would be at the Army several times a week attending services, meetings and other arrangements such as practices (musical groups), study groups, or practical work. A Salvationist's sense of calling also included his/her everyday life at work and in the family. The loyalty to the State Church was expressed in the ceremonies of baptism (followed by an Army dedication), confirmation, wedding (followed by an Army wedding), and funeral. It was loyalties on very different levels. Even with these possible explanations, Commissioner Westergaard's point of looking at dual loyalty as a problem area that had to be dealt with or faced was important. In this time of change and with the effect of secularization, the focus changed also for Salvationists. It was more difficult to communicate the gospel to people, because the common ground for understanding basic Christian perceptions was eroding. Even so the problem neither concerned calling nor spirituality, but identity. It was exactly the need to strengthen Salvationist identity that the coming years' discussions and the decision to form the working committee of 1975 were to be centered around.

The report was written in 1966 at a time when concepts of spirituality and calling were challenged and in many ways regarded as outdated. The influence of secularization (through, for instance, the TV), the developing youth culture questioning tradition, authorities, and the like, would have influenced

17. Territorial commander, *Farewell report* 1966.

the Army as it influenced other churches and institutions. His comments showed that he was aware of changes in these two concepts, but his reasoning was too short sighted or convenient, at least it could not stand alone. The TC's reports to IHQ are not shared with others in the territory and it is the TC's own evaluation of the situation in a territory. It is read (scrutinized) by the General and The Chief of Staff and filed at IHQ. There will be a copy of the report at the TC's personal files[18] for the new incoming TC to read.

In 1969 Commissioner Sture Larsson arrived as TC. Sture Larsson's nationality was Swedish, but his service had taken him to all the Nordic countries, Denmark, Sweden, Finland, to continental Europe as leader in France, to South America and to administration at IHQ in London. He had the combination of a Nordic and international Salvation Army experience. The Leaders Conference took place in October. There was lots of business as usual, but a main discussion featured the Army's identity as a revival movement in a time of change when older officers through their experience had the old traditional view on revival, while the younger ones did not share that experience. The conclusion was to continue working to express the revival identity in a way that fitted today. The Army's organization and the wish for more democracy came into the debate. The Non-Conformist Act of 13 June 1969 was not discussed, but in the annual report to IHQ of the same year, the law was mentioned, especially the part with tax revenue from the state:

> "Sections of the press asked us if the Army in Norway would not take advantage of the financial benefit offered and declare itself a "free church". We have however not regarded this legislation as warranting such a step just now. A separation from the State Church should not be motivated on economic ground. Nor do we think the financial advantages would be so considerable. It seems however to be the general consensus of opinion amongst our officers that, if and when there is a separation of the church and the state in Norway, the time will have arrived for the Army to sever its connections with the church."[19]

It looks as if there had only been a superficial interest in the new law and that it had not been seen as relevant for the Army, not even with the prospect of economic gain. It is remarkable that finance should not play a role in decisions concerning registration, as finance was central for all the Army's activity and outreach in the country. One reason could be as stated: that the gain would be small in view of the expected small number who

---

18. The TC's confidential files are kept in the leadership office and are only accessible with the TC's permission. They are not kept in Frelsesarmeen's archives.
19. Territorial Commander, *Annual Report* 1969.

would register. It might reveal a fear of possible cost in Army membership if changes were propagated by using finance as a reason. It was the strong tradition of dual membership that would be challenged. The statement on separation of church and state showed itself valid as this was part of the reason why the working group of 1975 was inaugurated. Larsson referred to this as a consensus among the officers. It was not only his opinion or judgment of the situation, but a qualified statement based on input from officers. As TC he would travel all over the territory and visit corps and institutions. The tradition was that he would travel with the DC in the divisions. The conversations during these travels with corps officers, social officers, and divisional officers gave a TC a unique insight into attitudes and opinions especially among officers, but also among soldiers. Apart from the travels his position as chairman of the different boards where a question of this kind most likely would be discussed, gave him knowledge.

Reflections on the future of the Army's legal stance

The Non-Conformist Act of 1969 was crucial for all the free churches and had been the focus of work at the Dissenter Council for years, where Frelsesarmeen was present not as member but as observer. As Frelsesarmeen was not registered as a dissenter community, the interest in this work had been sparse and not a theme for consultations within the Army. However, Frelsesarmeen had to register according to this law if it registered as a faith community. The law was mentioned in connection with the possible financial gain by Larsson in 1969 in his annual report to IHQ. Frelsesarmeen's leadership was aware of the law, but it was not the passing of the law itself and the possibilities of the law that had any focus, but the possible separation of state and church and the implications the Army would draw if such a situation happened. In such a scenario different paragraphs of the law had a special interest for the Army. The change from being called a dissenter law to a law concerning faith communities in itself removed what had been experienced as discriminating. The word "dissenter" was removed, but as the law only concerned faith communities outside The Norwegian Church and not the church itself, it was in reality still a dissenter law. It gave, however, more equality to the faith communities than previously. It gave economic support to the faith communities according to the number of members in line with the support to the Norwegian Church. The greatest challenge for the Army was §8 of the law stating that nobody could be a member of a faith community and the Norwegian Church or two different faith communities at the same time. Dual membership was not possible.

There seemed to have been an expectation or a hope within Frelsesarmeen that an opening for dual membership would have been reflected in the law. Because of §8 the economic gain for the Army with economic subsidies for its members in case of registration as a faith community was not considered to be substantial. This issue was crucial for the Army. In the Farewell Brief of September 1966, Commissioner Westergaard mentioned the possibility of seeking legal status as a faith community already existing (due to the Dissenter Law of 1891), but the obstacle was that Salvationists had to cancel their membership of the State Church. The anticipation was that few Salvationists were willing to do that. The situation among Salvationists had most probably not changed during the three years until the law of 1969. The later results of questionnaires as well as the actual number of soldiers who resigned their membership of the Norwegian Church have shown that the issue of dual membership was crucial.

In the annual report to IHQ of 1969, which concerned tax revenue, Sture Larsson's comment was that financial matters should not be the reason for changing affiliation and that the financial advantage was not considered to be great. The right for faith communities to seek subsidies from the state and borough was dealt with in §19–20 of the law. The fact that the law opened up the possibility of a central faith community to be registered, and not only local congregations, was important for the Army in view of its central government. According to a survey from 1973 Frelsesarmeen had registered 11,680 soldiers and of these 11,516 were members of the Norwegian Church as well. 54 soldiers were members of the Pentecostal Church, 47 of the Methodist Church, 16 of the Baptist Church, 19 of the Free Mission and 1 was a Catholic. 28 soldiers had Frelsesarmeen as their only membership. The overwhelming majority had dual membership of Frelsesarmeen and the Norwegian Church. It seemed to be a situation most Salvationists were content with, even though there were some discussion on the matter of seeking registration as a church.

An illustration of such a discussion could be a letter from a young officer couple stationed in Vik i Sogn on 4 March 1974 to the leadership stating their dismay with the situation of dual membership of the soldiers. They saw the soldiers' loyalty towards the church as problematic and were considering their future as officers, if the Army continued this way and not as an independent faith community. By 26 March they received an answer from Colonel Carsten Solhaug who was the Chief Secretary. He mentioned the debate within the Norwegian Church, and that this was one of a lot of other reasons why Frelsesarmeen had to consider its own situation. He mentioned that over the last five years he himself had pointed out the need for Frelsesarmeen to think through its own situation, and at the same time raise its own consciousness about what was right seen from its origin, peculiarity, and mission in contemporary society. He didn't think the time was ripe for the Army to establish itself as an independent faith community yet, but to make things ready for such a situation would be fine. He mentioned that the Army met the six conditions in §14 of the Non-Conformist Act of 13 June 1969,[20] and none of these would cause any problems to fulfill as the whole organization of the Army had these areas included apart from voting rights. Unity within the Army, however, was very important and should not be harmed by a premature decision. He wanted to stress the extraordinary cooperativeness the Norwegian Church showed towards Frelsesarmeen in most places in the country. He wanted good cooperation with the church as well as with the free churches based on respect for them, but still it was important for the Army to be conscious of its own tradition and mission. The five years he mentioned covered the period from 1974 when he sent his reply and back to 1969. Even though he never mentioned the Non-Conformist Act of 1969 as a reason for his wish to form a working group, it could have had a decisive impact, at least the five years imply an influence of the law. However, the Reform Commission within the Norwegian church formed in 1965 also published its report in 1969 so the five years could refer to this report as well. In Solhaug's writings and decisions he himself mainly referred to the state/church relationship as the overall reason.

State/church status seemed to have been a theme that was not only followed, but discussed in different gatherings. A letter from 8 March 1973 from a local officers' council[21] signed by the 24 participants, contained a petition to the territorial leadership to form a group to look into the Army's position in case of a separation between church and state. There had been a lecture on the theme by Colonel Solhaug and a debate at the council. The reply stated that such a group might very well be formed, but first the Army wanted to follow the outcome and discussion of the Bishops' Council's meeting[22] on the theme.

---

20. His reference to §14 concerned six conditions necessary for registration as a faith community: 1) name and address of the faith community, 2) its creeds and doctrines, 3) its organization, activities and membership, 4) the members of the board, 5) name and sphere of responsibility of each spiritual and administrative leader, 6) the faith community's regulation with regard to its objectives, membership, voting rights, spokesmen, amendments to the statutes, and dissolution.

21. Local officers are soldiers with special responsibilities in a corps e.g. a treasurer, secretary, bandmaster. It is voluntary work, but the local officers are given authority in the running of the corps together with the corps officer.

22. The Bishops' meeting must have been *Utredningskommisjonen av 1969* under the leadership of Bishop Kaare Støylen. The commission concluded its work in 1973 with the recommendation that the church must have greater self rule. The secularization of the State and society made this important. The Norwegian Church was a

These are random letters, but they show that some reflection on the matter was taking place within Army circles around the country.

The work of commissions within the Norwegian Church

The commissions within the Norwegian Church seemed to be more in focus than the Non-Conformist Act of 1969 for Frelsesarmeen's leadership. The different commissions gave a background for what was explicitly mentioned as the main reason for actually forming a Frelsesarmeen commission, the possible separation between church and state. Apart from this main reason there was an echo of the mandate given to the Reform Commission of 1965 in the language Solhaug used for the need of an Army commission. The mandate to think through the situation of the church in the present society was what Solhaug repeated in his expression of the need to think through the Army's situation. The focus on identity was present in the Reform Commission as well as in the later Frelsesarmeen Commission. Solhaug seemed to have followed the work of the commissions within the Norwegian Church rather closely. The year 1969 was important for him according to the letter to the young officers in Vik i Sogn, and that year his reflections on the Army situation made him convinced that the Army had to think through its own situation thoroughly and preferably in the form of a working committee. The Non-Conformist Act of 13 June 1969 was a possible reason for his reflections. The other possibility was the report from the Reform Commission published in 1969.

In 1965 the Reform Commission was started by the 20th National Independent Church Meeting.[23] The theme of the meeting was: "People move—where is the church?" It was a discussion of a stronger identity for the church and a wish to better equip the church for mission. The mandate of the commission was to think through the situation of the church in the present society and evaluate the needs and possibilities for reforms that would empower the church for its task. The question of separation between church and state was not the main task. The report from the commission came in 1969. The most important suggestion was that a Church Meeting

---

community of faith and different from the state. Elstad, "Hundre års debatt on stat og kyrkje i Noreg," 7.

23. It is interesting to notice that this started in the same year as Vatican II ended with its fourth and last gathering in 1965. One of the eleven documents from the last gathering was *Gaudium and Spes* concerning the church in the world. Nr. 4 article in this document confirmed that the church had the duty of scrutinizing the sign of the times and interpret it in light of the gospel. It was a similar agenda as the one of the Reform Commission. McBrien, *Katolsk Tro gennem to Årtusinder*, 42 and 310.

should be formed with the responsibility and right to make decisions on behalf of the church, meaning that a substantial part of Stortinget's authority concerning church matters should be transferred to the Church Meeting.

On the basis of the report of the committee, and because of the general development in society, another committee was formed in 1969 to follow up on the work already done in view of the demands of the present situation. It should especially look into the relationship of state and church from a theological, social, legal, and sociological view-point, but it was stressed that the committee should not take a stand on any changes of the relationship between state and church. It should work with practical reforms as far as possible within the present state/church relationship. The final recommendations came in the autumn of 1973. It gave a critical evaluation of the juridical foundation of the present church order as there was a lack of coherence between the theological and legal understanding of the church. According to legislation the church was just a part of the state administration. The recommendation described the ecclesiological foundation of the church and concluded that the leadership of the church had to be based in the Christian congregation and in principle belonged to the church itself and not to any authority outside the church.[24] The whole question of a state religion as expressed in §2 in the Constitution had become an anachronism, as the reality was a pluralistic modern state with different religions and varied philosophies of life.[25]

The work of the commissions during these five years seemed to have strengthened Solhaug's conviction of the need for an Army commission. With the stress on ecclesiology in the reports from the committees and the concept of the Norwegian Church as a community of faith, he was aware of possible changes within the church that would make it difficult for Frelsesarmeen with its different ecclesiology to keep the close links to the church with double membership for most of its members. The influence from these commissions was more implicit than explicit when it came to give reason for forming a commission to look into Frelsesarmeen's registration. The result from the State/Church Commission was explicitly present when the Army's commission was formed.

---

24. Løvlie, *Kirke, stat og folk i efterkrigstid*, 102–111.
25. Oftestad, *Den norske statsreligion*, 263–65.

Challenges that made 1975 a crucial year

In 1975 two things happened that had an impact on the Army's decision to start the process of looking into its situation: First of all, the results of the State/Church Commission and then the resignation of Bishop Per Lønning.

The State/Church commission was a public commission inaugurated by the parliament in 1971. The seasoned Labor Party politician, Helge Iversen became the chairman. The reason for this public commission was to secure the interests of the state as well as the people. The church had formed two commissions, one in 1965 and the other to follow up in 1969. The report of the Reform Commission came in 1969 and was known, while the report from the follow up committee did not come until 1973. It was not fear of demands for separation between state and church that spurred the inauguration of the public commission, but a concern that the interests of both the state and the people could best be taken care of by a public commission. The mandate for the commission was to evaluate the overall system of state/church, how it was formed and how it worked and to give an account of different alternatives, if the relationship between church and state concerning organization should end. The basis for forming the commission, then, was not a general wish of a separation, but a growing demand for the state in its function as leader of the church to conform to the church's self-understanding. The core problem was, whether a modern state with its own interests could rule the Norwegian Church from the point of the church's own identity.[26]

During its work, letters were sent to other faith communities to get information concerning the relationship between the state and the faith communities as well as the structure of the faith community. Such a letter came to Frelsesarmeen 2 February 1973 and looked like a general letter similar to that sent to all faith communities. There were seven questions concerning statistics, rules for membership, process of voting, the structure in Norway, discipline, education of ministers, social institutions, mission, and economy, including support from the state and borough, support from members, support from abroad and, if possible, a total economic frame. The Army's answer was sent 21 March 1973 from Solhaug. It answered all questions, but the commission wanted greater details especially in the economic section concerning governmental support to social institutions. Supplementary information was given as well. The finance of the faith communities must have been a central focus for the commission, at least when it concerned the Army the commission wanted more details on questions

---

26. Løvlie, *Kirke, stat og folk i efterkrigstid*, 189–90.

of finance. The total picture of the faith communities would of course be revealed through the questions, so economy did not stand alone. Because of the questionnaire from the commission, the Army leadership became involved in the work of the commission and had a greater awareness about the work than might have been the case with the commissions within the Norwegian Church

The conclusion of the work came in March 1975. It made quite an impact that the majority of the commission in the final report recommended a transition from state church to a church with self-rule and with a relationship to the state similar to that of other faith communities. This result had not been anticipated. The report recommended how it could be done and stated why the majority had reached this result. The new church would be identical with the old one. The Norwegian Church would continue as a community of faith and keep its open character as a folk church. This would demand five alterations of the Constitution and several other changes in legislation. The church should be governed according to its identity as a faith community in contrast to a rule by Stortinget and local governments. The majority's recommendation was based on the principles of the church's own identity. The minority report was based on a pragmatic view of the church.[27] Most important for the minority was the overwhelming support from the Norwegian people to the church and the conviction that the State Church was the best to guard religious freedom and tolerance. Another argument was that a separation between state and church could very well lead to several different faith communities. The report was circulated for a public hearing in November of 1975. It was sent to church councils, local governments, ministers, bishops, different councils, the two theological faculties, organizations within the church, and so on, for consideration and comments. Parliament's decision and announcement came in March 1980 declaring that the state church system should continue presently, but that the parliament should be challenged for a decision before the end of the century.[28]

In March 1975 Colonel Solhaug was appointed as TC[29] in the same month as the result of the commission was published. During his time as CS he had worked on the question of the Army's situation in case of a separation

27. Oftestad, *Den norske statsreligion*, 276–77.

28. Løvlie, *Kirke, stat og folk I efterkrigstid*, 193–95.

29. Commissioner Karsten Anker Solhaug (1914–2012) was Norwegian, served most of his time in Norway apart from a three months period as CS in Denmark and some years earlier on Iceland. He had very great influence on the development of Frelsesarmeen as he served as CS from 1968–75, then as TC from 1975–81. It was a long spell in his home territory.

between state and church. He had strongly recommended a working group to look into the matter to be formed. He was convinced that in light of what was going on the Army had to look into its own situation and decide what to do. A new urgency had arisen to get the work going by the recommendation from the commission. Another important thing happened that added to the urgency. Bishop Per Lønning resigned on 29 May 1975, the same day as a new law concerning abortion that gave the woman the right to abortion under certain circumstances was passed through Stortinget. Lønning saw a dilemma between §2 in the Constitution—that Evangelical-Lutheran Christianity was the official creed of the Norwegian State—and this legislation on abortion. The state was violating the right of the unborn life instead of protecting human life and value. The church as a state church was left with a dilemma of loyalty. The bishops had given a united document with comments on the draft bill when circulated from the Ministry of Church affairs. Lønning argued that for him, personally, the dilemma of being a Bishop in the State Church and therefore closely linked to the State that passed the law could only be solved with his resignation as a bishop. It was a consequence of his long resistance against such a law. He asked his colleagues of ministers and bishops not to follow him and resign. He felt it was a personal call he had to obey.

Solhaug saw what had happened as a sign of wider perspectives, as an expression of the strained relationship between church and state at the present time. He saw it as a development that would eventually lead to a separation between church and state. The Army had to think through its own situation. "We would be irresponsible if we did not evaluate how we should react when and if the Norwegian Church gained a different status than as a state church."

Soon after Solhaug's appointment as TC he wrote an article[30] explaining why the matter had to be dealt with. The heading of the article was: "The State/the Church/The Salvation Army." In the article he mentioned Lønning's resignation as it seemed that the matter of the relationship of church and state had a new urgency, because of his resignation as a bishop in the Norwegian church as a consequence of the law on abortion that had been passed through parliament. It was not the issue of abortion as such, but the debate on abortion and especially Lønning's resignation that stood as a symbol of the difficulty of the State/Church relationship, with legislation being passed through Stortinget that was opposed to fundamental Christian values and beliefs. How could the Norwegian Church continue as a

30. Published in *Frelsesofficeren* July 1975. Solhaug shared the article by reading it for the officers in an officers' meeting during the annual congress in June before it was published.

state church when there was such a clash of values between the church and Stortinget that functioned as the head of the church on behalf of the King. The Army was aware of possible changes ahead in the relationship between state and church because of the whole situation.

In the article, Solhaug expressed his personal view concerning the best timing for the Army to establish itself as an independent faith community. That would be when the state and church separated. It was not his aim to provoke that, but to think through the Army's position. He mentioned the situation with most Salvationists being members of the Norwegian Church as well as of the Army with the strength and weakness of that situation. He was not calling for a debate on this issue as such, but on the issue of how to act in a situation of a possible separation between state and church. Solhaug did not explain why a separation between state and church made the situation urgent. A possible reason why the separation of state and church became so decisive for Solhaug could be found in the concept of civil religion implicitly viewing the State Church as a sort of civil religion. The reason is that it seemed unproblematic for Solhaug that Salvationists had a double membership—Frelsesarmeen and the Norwegian Church as long as it was a state church, while in his opinion it became problematic if the state and church separated. This statement of his gained a widespread acceptance as a valid reason or a sort of *Kairos* in the coming years, but it was never supported by any explanation or reason for it being so.

Conclusion

The influence of the period challenged Frelsesarmeen's traditional way of accommodating itself within the Norwegian society. The values, mission strategies, and generally accepted way of working were facing changes. The effect of secularization and social upheavals, changes in work life, a developing youth culture, and a change in traditional gender roles made the quest for identity come into focus. This situation had its effect on Frelsesarmeen and its soldiers and questions about the Army's mission and mode emerged. Internal matters became a focus and a search for identity, a specific Salvationist identity for this time in history began. The compromises of the past of accommodating itself in relation to the State Church seemed not as important any longer, because much greater issues such as secularization were at stake that could undermine any church. Registration as a faith community seemed no longer just to be an unimportant matter without relation to Frelsesarmeen's identity. It became linked to this new quest of seeking and strengthening Salvationist identity. The letter from the young couple in

Vik i Sogn as well as the letter from the local officer's council suggest a wider awareness of this altered situation. The statistic of Salvationists' membership of the Norwegian Church and other churches gave a realistic view of the situation as it was presently.

In 1969 The Non-Conformist Act was passed through Stortinget. It was the year Solhaug mentioned as the time, when he became convinced that the Army had to look into its own registration in case the state and church separated. The law influenced Frelsesarmeen's considerations concerning registration, because it was the legal foundation for registration as a faith community. During the coming years §8 became decisive for Frelsesarmeen's reluctance to seek registration. The report from the Reform Commission also came this year. It had a greater focus on church identity and mission of the Norwegian Church than had been the case earlier. In a situation with such a focus the difference between the Lutheran Church and Frelsesarmeen would become clearer. In particular, the church's belief in the sacraments as constitutive for being a church in comparison to the Army's non-observance of the sacraments would be difficult to ignore. Letters and other papers from the confidential archive reveal that Solhaug considered Frelsesarmeen to be a church, because it functioned as such for its members and it had a strong identity in its doctrines and structure.

The outcome of the work of the State/Church Commission was important, as was the resignation of Per Lønning, because it illustrated a situation of bonds between state and church that in Solhaugs' view could not last. In the article "The State/The Church/The Salvation Army" Solhaug expressed his personal view concerning the best timing for the Army to establish itself as an independent faith community. Solhaug never gave a reason why the separation of church and state was so decisive for Frelsesarmeen. Solhaug took up the issue twenty years later in 1993 when he opposed the forming of the second committee Frelsesarmeen's Church Commission, and repeated his argument that the right timing for Frelsesarmeen to register as a faith community would be when a separation between state and church happened.

The result of the influences from the commissions, especially the recommendation from the State/Church Commissions of a separation between state and church as well as internal considerations within Frelsesarmeen was that Frelsesarmeen's Commission was formed, commissioned, and started its work at the end of 1975.

Chapter 5

The Work of Frelsesarmeen's Commission 1975–78

ON THE BASIS OF the events leading up to the crucial year of 1975, Solhaug planned to form a forum with a wide representation from within the Army for debate, comments, and suggestions, not a fast-working one, but one that would work in depth. The idea of such a forum expressed a new development within the Army's hierarchical system, a development of more consultation with a stronger influence from soldiers and officers alike. It could be interpreted as Frelsesarmeen's answer to the quest for democracy.

In the article, "The State / the Church / The Salvation Army" Solhaug stated that as the law was now, the Army could gain recognition as a church at any time without any difficulties, but in his view the best timing would be in connection with a separation of church and state. In the middle of the article explaining why the matter had to be dealt with, he had a small paragraph that expressed another very important motive he had for starting this process. He wrote: "There is something that I am fully convinced about. Our consciousness about Salvationism ought to be raised and as far as possible we must be aware of its possibilities and how it can express itself in practice in the future." This statement is supported by a letter he later wrote to Commissioner Dahlstrøm[1] where he stressed the need for Salvationists to occupy themselves with their own identity and status: "We are not so sovereign in The Salvation Army that we can preserve our identity and our distinctive character long term if we ourselves are not supporting a process of self-awareness." It was the Army's identity he wanted to be explored in fact the same as the Reform Commission was asked to do for the Lutheran

---

1. The letter of 24 August 1976 was an answer to a letter from Dahlstrøm who apparently protested against the questionnaires of the FA-Utvalget (Dahlstrøm's letter is not preserved in the files).

church. Solhaug also mentioned that there would be a new edition of the Doctrine book for sale at the end of the year and hoped that the study of the doctrines would be widespread. He felt that the situation demanded this to be taken seriously. This doctrine book signaled a new direction as it was the first time the Army's non-observance of the sacraments was explained and published in Norway in an official doctrine book. This showed, firstly, that the time when Frelsesarmeen was hiding its position for its own members as well as for the public was over; secondly it also indicated that Solhaug prepared the way for registration as a faith community by having a full account of Salvation Army doctrines and positions, and by this supported a process of self-awareness.

The leaders' conference 16–18 September 1975 decided to appoint a commission to investigate the issues of The State / the Church / The Salvation Army.[2] On 9 October a letter was sent to the soldiers and officers whom the TC wanted to appoint to the working group. The letter stated that the mandate of the commission was "to come up with investigations that can be the basis for making a decision about The Salvation Army's registration as an independent congregation." It was emphasized that the mandate was not to take decisions, but to analyze the situation for decisions to be taken. The commission was not expected to be a fast working commission as the task might take years to be completed. It seemed to be of utmost importance to get this group started and get it to work as he mentioned that the group might have its first meeting before Christmas. The urgency of the matter, even though it would not be a fast working group, was proved as the first meeting was already called on 6 December 1975. The State / Church commission's majority and minority recommendations were on the agenda and were evaluated and debated, but not Lønning's resignation as a symbol of the difficulties of a state church. A focus which all the members supported was a wide analysis of the possible impact of registration as an independent faith community and a general evaluation of advantages and disadvantages. The international perspective had to be considered as well as a local perspective. Present at the first meeting were Commissioner Solhaug, the CS Colonel Sven Nilsson, and the commission. It had fourteen members, of these seven were officers from different fields of work,[3] six soldiers of these fourteen were local officers, and a former soldier who presently was at MF

---

2. Leaders Conference, *Minutes* 1975.

3. The Field Secretary, the Editor in Chief, the DC from North Norway, 4 corps— and social officers, the secretary was Captain Fred A. Solli, corps officer in Namsos.

Norwegian School of Theology.[4] The chairman, Bernhard Slettholm,[5] was a Sergeant Major, a central local officer position. The representation from different places in Norway was fair and the number of officers and soldiers was equal. The secretary was an officer. However, there was no gender equality as only four out of fourteen were women. In selecting the members of the commission the balance between soldiers and officers seemed to have been most important while the gender issue was less in focus. The most important matter on the agenda was a debate concerning an idea of sending a questionnaire to all Salvationists about their affiliation to the church and their use of its services. The importance of this debate was proved when the questionnaire, with its results, became a reality. An introduction into the Army's attitude towards the Free Church Council, the work of the council as well as the Army's observer status in the council, were also on the agenda. The main issues of the task were addressed in this first meeting.

The commission began the process of getting the information and insights needed to give an analysis of the present situation as well as of possible implications of future changes. It engaged in the task of finding important material and reflecting upon the findings in order to give the input needed for the leadership to make decisions. As an outcome of that the group became a study group as well, calling for papers on different issues. Papers were prepared by members of the group and others who were invited to give their paper and stay for a dialogue on the theme. These study / dialogue sessions continued especially on theological questions for the first four gatherings, then themes of practical matters were predominant in the following meetings, but it was still in the study / dialogue form. The papers that were presented covered these themes:

- Our faith and that of the Church. A comparison.
- Frelsesarmeen in ecumenical perspective
- Frelsesarmeen and the Norwegian Church, an evaluation with background in the previous paper.
- Frelsesarmeen's identity and ecclesiology

4. Hans Arne Akerø. At the time he was research assistant at MF Norwegian School of Theology. He has since been a vicar for eighteen years, worked at the Bishop's office in Oslo and at the department for education at the Clergymen's Association. In 2010 he became section leader at the Church Council's Section for Worship and Culture. Curriculum vitae for Hans Arne Akerø.

5. Bernhard Slettholm had been an officer for six years. Later he worked as a journalist in *Folkets Fremtid*. He was a member of Oslo local council for twenty years with membership of the social committee. In Hellerud, a part of Oslo, he was leader of the School and Culture Committee.

- The situation of officers (numbers and prognoses of the future in recruitment)
- The future prospects of the social work with Frelsesarmeen as an independent congregation
- Frelsesarmeen and democratization
- Financial factors

These papers were printed in the final report, but from the minutes it is clear that there were a number of other papers presented.

Even though Frelsesarmeen's Commission was not expected to be a fast working commission it certainly kept focus on the main agenda and got down to work intensively. Two of the most important issues—seen in retrospect—were the main features of the second meeting 5 and 6 March 1976. Firstly, it was decided to send out the questionnaire mentioned at the first meeting. The questionnaire and the process around it were very thorough and it became an instrument that gave a workable tool for the soldier's attitude and practice all over the country. Jeløy, the Army's folk high school, had been opened in 1974 and was still new. It was at the forefront of IT-technology and that capacity was used to work on the material from the questionnaire. Secondly, what became influential was the paper professor Nils Bloch-Hoell[6] gave at this second meeting. The title of his paper was "The Salvation Army in an ecumenical connection." His paper was printed in the final report. In his paper he went straight into what he considered the core of the matter: that the Army on the one side considered itself a revival movement and refused to be a church, and then the question of whether the Army in reality already was a church. The central issue of his paper concerned the problem of the Army's stance towards the sacraments. Concerning the Army's non-observance of the sacraments, his main sources were six quotations from an interview with William Booth in 1895. There was no reference to where the interview took place or was printed, whether it was from a Norwegian paper in connection with one of William Booth's visits to Norway or a translation from an English interview. Block-Hoell referred to the interview with the comment that this interview most likely was known by the group. That could support a Norwegian interview, but by research at the National Library there was no such interview. However,

---

6. He was the first Professor in Ecumenical Theology at the Theological Faculty of Oslo University in 1969. His doctoral thesis from 1956 concerned the Pentecostal movement in Norway. In it he had a section on Methodism as well. He was the only one outside the Army to present a paper.

the interview appeared to be the one written by Sir Henry S. Lunn in 1895.[7] His record of the interview was colored by his own disagreement with the Salvation Army on this matter. This was obvious when his record and the original six points from the interview were compared. He used a mixture of paraphrasing and direct quotations, but in both he missed out on what were the most important issues. Two examples can illustrate this. Concerning point five he quoted one of the sentences of a longer paragraph in this way: "This has made us say that as circumcision doesn't apply, so baptism is nothing." The original sentence was: "This leads us to say that as circumcision is nothing, so baptism is nothing—but the keeping of the commandment of God." He simply stopped in the middle of a sentence that cannot be split up without the meaning getting lost. "Keeping the commandment of God" was the main issue. The other example was that he missed out the conclusion of the interview, which was as important for the issues he was dealing with in his paper—the ecumenical situation. It also had importance for his later reference to the newly published Norwegian Doctrine Book (1975). The remembrance at every meal of the suffering of Christ and at every bath of the cleansing of the purifying blood of Christ, which illustrated the moving of the rituals from sacred acts to everyday life, from sacraments to sacramental living. This was vital for any understanding of Salvationists' faith and practice. Block-Hoell wondered if these 80 year old arguments were still relevant. His opinion was that the Army's understanding of the sacraments and of Christianity itself was spiritualistic meaning that material things and physical phenomena in themselves did not really have spiritual significance. He did not expand his definition further. A main point in his paper was the danger of spiritualistic Christianity, which he considered The Salvation Army's non-observance of the sacraments to indicate. He mentioned examples of similar spiritualistic understanding from church history, from the time of the reformation, those who denied baptism to be of any value, and those who warned against giving the same authority to the Bible as had been given to the pope, a warning against a bible pope. He took the example of the Quakers, whom he considered distinctly spiritualistic with their non-observance of the sacraments and not even with the Bible as the highest authority, but the inner light. He was glad that the Army at least had a dogmatic faith in the authority of the Bible even though it might be an expression of fundamentalism.[8] The problem was not the Army's Bib-

---

7. Lunn, "The Salvation Army and the Sacraments."

8. From the Doctrine Book which Bloch-Hoell had consulted, it is difficult to regard the Salvation Army's view of the Bible as an expression of fundamentalism. Concerning the nature of biblical inspiration it stated: "The doctrine of the inspiration of the Scriptures does not mean verbal dictation. Such a theory leaves out of account the

licism but its spiritualistic understanding. He felt that issue was the core problem in an ecumenical perspective. The Army was active and easy to cooperate with in ecumenical matters and was a member of the WCC even with a representative in the central committee. The Army was exemplary in its ecumenical will to cooperate, its warm humanity made cooperation possible and joyous. Still the problem was there. The Faith and Order meeting in 1937 felt it was necessary to point to the practice of the Quakers and The Salvation Army in connection with the sacraments. Even though the meeting didn't state exactly what these serious difficulties were, he was sure it was spiritualistic Christianity that was behind the statements. The fear that an understanding of Christianity without the sacraments would spread was the real danger. Another source he referred to was the appendix of the newly published doctrine book, plus *The Sacraments—The Salvationist's Viewpoint* from 1960, from which he had got the impression that the tendency in the theory and praxis concerning the sacraments had gone in a negative direction. His question was if that was correct. It was no wonder that Bloch-Hoell felt a negative trend, as nothing had been in the former doctrine books. In his conclusion he firstly repeated what he as a Lutheran ecumenical Christian considered problematic, and then evaluated how he considered the Army:

> Frelsesarmeen contributed to propagate Christianity without the sacraments. The neutral attitude could go in a negative direction if Frelsesarmeen established itself as an independent faith community.
>
> As Frelsesarmeen was functioning at the present moment it was generally appreciated by other Christians and church families, because of its social work among people the established churches found it difficult to communicate with or had neglected, as well as its evangelism among the same groups as a supplement to the churches. Frelsesarmeen was easily incorporated within ecumenical settings and an example for other Christians by its Franciscan like ideal of self-denial and happy Christianity. It was a wake up call to the churches. That was its worldwide mission.

It was not an easy task for the commission to debate his lecture. Firstly, because his attitude towards the Army's practice if it considered a church registration was rather forceful. He was using the word danger in

---

human element in the composition of the Scriptures—for example, differences of style and though-forms, divergencies in accounts of the same events. It would also involve the need to ascribe finality to stages of revelation which are incomplete." *Handbook of Doctrine*, 17.

connection with propagating Christianity without the sacraments. He even called the practice without the sacraments false doctrine and false practice, even though the churches in his opinion would hardly consider the Army heretical. The reason was that one should be cautious about labelling anybody a heretic (not that he didn't consider it in that way). The examples from the interview could hardly be corrected, as none of the commission had the original document and most probably didn't know it. There had not been much teaching concerning the Army's non-observance. To this it must be added that he was considered a theological authority representing both the theological faculty as well as the Norwegian Church. In spite of this there was a debate between him and the members of the group. The debate at the meeting focused on the sacraments, especially infant baptism, not on the ecumenical situation. It stayed within the Lutheran setting as different members asked about the church's teaching on children who had not been baptized. There was a little about Frelsesarmeen's dedication ceremony versus baptism, but no substantial discussion on the Army's position. There seemed to be an attempt to move the dialogue to the Army's development from movement to church, but there was no further debate on this in the minutes, neither did the minutes indicate a discussion on his points of a spiritualistic theology,[9] or any answer to his question whether the Army had gone in a negative direction in its attitude to the Sacraments. His paper was not really designed to open up a debate; it might rather have been a confrontation had the members felt they had the arguments needed for this. The evaluation of the paper happened at the fourth meeting half a year later. Here three of the members had prepared reflections on Bloch-Hoell's paper. These concentrated on the question of whether the Army should register as an independent faith community, the relation to the global Salvation Army, and the position of churches other than the Lutheran in a global perspective. The sacraments were mentioned in connection with the Lutheran definition of a church "where the gospel is taught purely and the sacraments are administered rightly" as the foundation. There was no discussion of the Lutheran definition of church, whether there could be other definitions of church. As the group apparently accepted the Lutheran definition as the only valid one, the discussion centered round the question of how the Army could regard itself as a church without the sacraments. There was no conclusion as they seemingly didn't have any alternatives to the Lutheran defini-

---

9. It was unfortunate that such a discussion didn't take place. It would have cleared the apparent confusion of what it meant. References to it appeared in the report of the Commission in 1978 and again in the report from Frelsesarmeen's Church Commission in 1996. Both commissions connected this to the invisible church and not to the pneumatological foundations of the Army.

tion. On the basis of Block-Hoell's paper it was taken for granted by the commission that the relationship to the Norwegian Church would develop negatively if Frelsesarmeen registered as an independent faith community. The reason for this was given with Block-Hoell's argument that it would propagate Christianity without the sacraments and thus be considered to propagate false teaching. If Frelsesarmeen abstained from registration things would continue as they were presently.

The influence of this paper on the final recommendation seemed to be rather profound. The threat of being considered heretics might have surprised or even shocked the commission and that might be the reason why the scenario he painted was not questioned. They might have been uncertain of how to argue the matter in light of the absent teaching of the Army's position. His paper was printed in the final report of Frelsesarmeen's Commission 1975–78 and was referred to in Frelsesarmeen's Church Committee's report eighteen years later in 1996. In a way it was surprising that this was the case as his paper could have been passed in silence, but as it was included there must have been an interest within the commission to have this rather stark warning against registration.

Input from American Salvationists and smaller communities in Norway

Two issues were on the agenda of the third meeting 24 June 1976—the observance of sacraments among Scandinavian American Salvationists and attitudes to registration in smaller communities in Norway. Both issues became influential. The practice of Scandinavian American Salvationists gave inspiration to introducing confirmation. The results from the smaller communities were very different from the results of the questionnaire coming in later, but it gave an indication of the differences within the country. The sacraments and the Army's ceremonies and symbols as well as the ecumenical situation continued to be part of the debate with papers and discussions. Very early on the suggestion came up concerning the idea of introducing a confirmation ceremony in the Army. The work on that continued and so did the process for funerals to be Army funerals led by an officer.[10]

At this third meeting the commission had invited Captain Esther Olsen, who had previously been leader of the Scandinavian corps in Brooklyn, to speak of the tradition in this corps concerning ceremonies and

---

10. The papers on these two questions were presented and discussed at the sixth meeting, 15–16 April 1977.

sacraments. The Army[11] at some stage decided to introduce infant baptism in the Scandinavian corps (there were several in different locations). The ritual from the Lutheran church was used, but the ceremony was simple just using a wash basin for the water. It was underlined that this act did not have significance for salvation. Apparently the Army's dedication ceremony was used as well in the same meeting. It was common to have both Godmother and Godfathers at both events. The Love Feast was quite common among Salvationists there. When the Love Feast was celebrated on Maundy Thursday people regarded it as the Lord's Supper even though it was a Love Feast.[12] The elements used were Altar wine and Jewish biscuit or wafer. This differed from a Love Feast in Europe, where the elements would be bread, juice, or fruit, but the Love Feast was never practiced a lot neither in Scandinavia nor in the rest of Europe. The Scandinavian corps had confirmation as well, based on one to two year's teaching centered upon the Bible, Salvation Army doctrines, Orders and Regulations for Salvationists, and Church History. Baptism or dedication was not a condition for participation in the confirmation ceremony, as the meaning of confirmation in the Army was to confirm your faith, not the baptism. Esther Olsen mentioned that American Salvationists looked upon the Scandinavian corps' practice with a bit of suspicion, as if they were not real Salvationists. For the working group the lasting influence from the insight coming from the Scandinavian American corps was to further the work of introducing confirmation in Frelsesarmeen.

In the same meeting that the American scene was presented, one of the members of the group gave a paper on his research on the attitudes of soldiers in smaller communities concerning the question and consequences of the Army's possible status as a registered faith community. His research was done in Vik, Sandal, and Stord. It showed that 99 percent of the soldiers would prefer the situation to stay as it presently was, only 1 percent wanted Frelsesarmeen to register as an independent faith community. On the questions concerning the situation if the Army became a registered faith community and the consequences of having membership in one church alone, the answers divided into three groups: 1) A group who in such a situation

---

11. It is uncertain who "the Army" was, if it was at Territorial Headquarters or at some other level. It would be unlikely for the Territorial Headquarters to make such a decision as the American Army saw the Scandinavian traditions as odd according to Esther Olsen. It could have been on the level of the leadership of the Scandinavian work.

12. Love Feast: "Reflecting its Methodist heritage, as love feast in The Salvation Army is a meeting for public testimony that is generally accompanied by partaking of bread and water as a sign of unity, mutual confidence, and goodwill. The practice is of great help when there are special needs for renewed harmony in the corps." Merritt, *The A to Z of The Salvation Army*, 353.

would feel forced to leave the Army, but reluctantly and with great regret. The reasons for such a decision were the close bonds to the church in the small community, the tradition in the family of belonging to the church for many generations, and the sacraments. Most of them had not known the Army's position towards the sacraments, when they were enrolled as soldiers, but were now aware that there would be no administration of the sacraments in Frelsesarmeen as a registered faith community. 2) A group, who would decide to stay as soldiers and have the Army as their only church, stressed that they would only leave the Norwegian Church reluctantly, as they considered it as a symbol of unity among the Christians in the small community. Because they considered the Army as their spiritual home they would stay, even though they wanted things to continue as they were presently. 3) A group who didn't know what to choose. Both the church and the Army were precious to them. They hoped this situation would not occur and that things would remain as they were. The paper didn't state the percentage of these three groups, if they were equal in numbers or which had the majority. It was clear that none of them wanted any change. As a reflection of the doctrinal basis for these answers, the paper stated that the soldiers expressed clear Salvation Army teaching, for example in connection with baptism. They considered it as a blessing of the child similar to the dedication ceremony. They clearly confessed salvation through faith, repentance and conversion (rebirth). They did not agree with the importance the church gave to the sacraments, but neither might they have agreed with the Army's non-observance. They were simply not familiar with the Army's teaching concerning the sacraments. The paper also touched upon the practical consequences of registration as an independent faith community. The focus was the situation at the outposts concerning the different places the Army normally held its meetings. The churches and prayer houses showed great hospitality in the present situation, but the question arose whether this would be altered in the case of registration. The situation of renting the schools should not be affected by a possible registration. The paper was valuable for the dialogue, in so far as it drew a picture of the situation in the smaller communities, both the soldiers' attitudes and the practical situation, as the majority of the committee came from the Oslo area. The outposts had been extremely important all over Norway for the Army's work since the beginning of the century with the largest number of outposts in the 1930s. Now, in the 1970s, the work was dwindling for a lot of reasons, such as migration to towns and cities, because of the booming industry, but the outposts were still an important part of the work for the smaller corps such as the ones that had been scrutinized. It would have been valuable had there been some information indicating the method used for gathering this data as for instance the question of written questionnaires or dialogues, if it was done individually or in groups. It became important as results from the official questionnaires differed a lot from these results.

The findings from the Commission's questionnaire

By the fourth meeting on 1 and 2 October 1976 the results of the questionnaire had been gathered and worked through at the IT-system at Jeløy. In spite of a continuing dialogue on theology, the main focus changed to more practical matters. First of all, the commission delivered a request for the leadership to contact the Commission on Justice in Stortinget to explore the possibilities of a change in the Non-Conformist Act of 1969 in order for the Army to be able to get the right to officiate at weddings and committal ceremonies. The commission wanted to see what sort of influence Frelsesarmeen would have on the decision-making authorities without being a registered faith community, as this would be a marker for the necessity of being registered as a faith community. To have these two ceremonies within the Army had long been a wish as could be seen in the correspondence from 1964. It was obvious that the commission wanted to find other solutions than a registration as an independent faith community. The main part of this meeting was used in evaluating the result of the questionnaires. The commission could look at graphs and percentages as a tool for an overview of the situation in the country. The deeper analysis of the results became part of the continuing work. It was crucial for the recommendation of the commission to evaluate the results of the questions even though these results did not give a clear cut answer to the decisive question of whether or not Frelsesarmeen should register. There were eleven questions in the questionnaire with different options and small boxes to cross and no possibilities for longer written answers. The questions were:

1. Gender (male/female)
2. Age (14–18, 19–25, 26–40, 41–60, over 60)
3. Where in the country do you live? (Eastern part, South/West, Mid-Norway, North-Norway)
4. Where are you a soldier? (Outpost, village corps, corps in a town)
5. Is there a corps officer at your corps? (Yes/No)
6. Position in Frelsesarmeen (Bandsman/songster, local officer, ordinary soldier, officer)

7. How often do you attend meetings in Frelsesarmeen? (Once or more weekly, 1–3 times monthly, seldom, never)
8. Do you attend the church? (Just at baptism–confirmation–weddings etc., now and then, regularly)
9. Do you attend meetings in other churches? (Regularly, seldom, never)
10. Do you receive the Lord's Supper? (Regularly, seldom, never)
11. Do you want Frelsesarmeen to become a church? (Yes, no, don't know)

The questionnaire was answered by 2576, around 70 percent women and 28 percent men. The percentage according to age was: 35 percent over 60 years, 36 percent between 41–60, 19 percent between 26–40, 6 percent between 19–25 and 3 percent between 14–18. The highest number came from the Eastern part of Norway (about 42 percent), the lowest number came from North Norway (about 9 percent). Most of the answers came from corps in towns and most with corps officers (90 percent against 8 percent). Concerning the position in the corps 44 percent were ordinary soldiers, 19 percent bandsmen and songsters, 14 percent local officers, 14 percent officers, 8 percent had a dual position of local officers and bandsmen/songsters.

The frequency of attendance showed that 76 percent came to the Army once or more weekly, 13 percent 1–3 times monthly and 8.5 percent seldom. Men and women's attendance was equal, but there was a difference when it came to age, 93 percent of the young (14–18) and 70 percent of those over 60 were present once or more a week. There was a difference in activity in the different parts of the country, 80 percent in the eastern part and 68 percent in northern part attended once or more weekly, the southwestern part 74 percent and middle part 75 percent had the same attendance. The group made the obvious note that the activity simply was higher in the cities than in the villages and at the outposts.[13] The high attendance of once or more a week was seen from 59 percent of the soldiers, 92 percent of the local officers, 88 percent of the bandsmen/songsters, 87 percent of the officers. (The group noted that both active and retired officers were counted under the same heading).

Attendance in the Norwegian Church showed that 32 percent would be there for baptism, weddings, confirmation etc., 61 percent now and then and 4.1 percent regularly. There was no clear difference between the sexes, but of those who went regularly more men (5.1 percent) that women (3.8 percent) were in that group, while more women (63 percent) than men (55.3

---

13. At the outposts there would seldom be weekly meetings, more likely biweekly or monthly or quarterly. The outpost attendance shows only 17.3 percent of once or more a week.

percent) were in the group who attended occasionally. The age groups differed very little and the same with the groups according to geography. The outposts showed a much higher regular attendance (18.4 percent). Attendance in other churches showed that 4.3 percent went regularly, 71 percent seldom and 22 percent never. The difference between the groups was not significant apart from the outposts where 29.6 percent went regularly. Concerning participation in communion the questionnaire showed 7 percent participated regularly, 54 percent seldom and 35 percent never. Women participated a little more than men, the older more than the younger, north of Norway more frequently than eastern Norway, the outposts more than corps.

On the main question of Frelsesarmeen becoming legally registered as a faith community a majority of 38.2 percent said no, 35.1 percent said yes and 26 percent didn't know. A comment by the commission was, that among those who had not decided might be some who waited for the development of the state/church relation to be clear before they made a decision. More men (45 percent) than women (32 percent) voted for a registration, the younger—all groups up to 60 (43.4 percent, 49 percent, 43.4 percent, 37.6 percent) more than the older (25.5 percent). Northern Norway had a higher vote for (47 percent) registration than the rest of the country (34 percent, 34.1 percent, 33 percent). More officers (46.2 percent) voted yes than ordinary soldiers (30.4 percent), local officers and bandsmen/songsters nearly the same (37.9 percent and 37.6 percent). Concerning outposts, villages, and towns the votes in favor were 27.6 percent, 30.8 percent, and 36.6 percent.

It was clear, that none of the groups exceeded 50 percent in favor of registration. There was a majority of *no* votes even though the *yes* and *no* groups were close. The difficulty was the 26 percent who didn't know what they wanted and the reason why. Did they want to wait and see what would happen in the state/church relationship or did they consider the question irrelevant? Another problem might have been, that the state/church relationship would be relevant for the *no* group as well. Would a different situation have altered their vote? In such quantitative research as this these questions are not answered, only the basic facts of the situation. Less than a quarter of the soldiers answered the questionnaire. How much of this was due to failure in the delivery of the questionnaire, and how much was a reflection of Salvationists' lack of interest in the question of registration? A weakness of the questionnaire was that the officers were not divided into active and retired. With 46.2 percent of all officers in favor of a registration an expectation based on the actual registration in 2005 could have been 60 percent to 70 percent "yes" votes among active officers and 10 percent–20 percent among the retired.

Concerning the relationship to the Norwegian Church and to other churches the percentage that attended on a regular basis was very close, 4.1 percent for the State Church and 4.3 percent for other churches. The percentage of those who seldom attended was 60.8 percent for the Norwegian Church and 70.8 percent for the other churches. These figures showed an ecumenical spirit, but not that the relationship to the Norwegian Church was especially close. It didn't correspond with the figures for membership mentioned earlier with 11,516 having double membership of the Norwegian Church and Frelsesarmeen out of the total of 11,680 soldiers. The membership of other churches was very small and didn't explain an attendance in other churches as close to the attendance of the Norwegian Church. An explanation to the fairly high attendance in the other churches could have been that the charismatic movement was at its peak during the 1970s. This movement affected all denominations, the Army included, and created a number of gatherings for equally minded people from all churches. Had the survey been during the 1960s or 1980s these figures might have differed.

The relationship to the Norwegian Church rested on the rituals. 31.6 percent attended only for baptism, confirmation, weddings, etc. Younger participants had a higher percentage than people over sixty. The figures concerning communion did not reveal a clear relationship to the State Church. Even more it didn't state in which church people participated in communion, which had been important because the figures for attendance in the Norwegian Church and other churches were so close. 7 percent participating in communion on a regular base was not overwhelming, but it was bigger than the 4.1 percent who attended the State Church regularly. It could be that the 4.1 percent of those attending the State Church and the 4.3 percent in other churches put together would explain the higher percentage. There might have been an overlapping between the two groups, and that some of them attended both the Norwegian Church and other churches regularly. The Lord's Supper was important for a smaller percentage of the soldiers and officers, and more than half (54.4 percent) of all participated seldom, but did participate, while a third (34.9 percent) never participated. The old Salvation Army's interpretation: "When such an ordinance is helpful to the faith of our Soldiers, we recommend its adoption" might very well have been in focus for Salvationists partaking in the communion, as there had mostly been silence on the issue in the following years. Communion did not count for the strong bonds to the Norwegian Church, but rather baptism, confirmation, wedding, and funerals made up the relationship. Of these rituals Frelsesarmeen was planning to introduce confirmation and was working with the possibility of gaining the right to perform weddings and Christian funerals. This left baptism as the sole important bond to the church. Traditionally this ritual had confirmed them in being true Norwegian citizens. The more profound reason could have been a confirmation of belonging to the ordinary fellowship within the smaller communities and an adherence to family tradition going back many generations. The survey revealed respect and veneration for the Norwegian Church. It seemed that many considered the Church as the symbol of Christianity in Norway, a symbol they wanted to support and certainly didn't want to weaken. The commission identified the church as the spokesperson for Christendom in the country.

The results of the survey of the small communities were strikingly different from the rest of the country. The two surveys were in no way identical, and the result from the smaller communities that 99 percent wanted things to stay as they were gave a totally different picture of the situation. The reason might be found in the very different approach between a small survey that could have been based on individual interviews or interviews with a whole group and then a professionally conducted questionnaire where all data had been worked through via IT technology.

The commission concluded and recommended that the survey should not be decisive for the final decision, as the *yes* and *no* groups were so close and the reasons behind the *don't know* group were unknown. The results would be used as a guide in the main conclusion from the group. The data from the questionnaire was also used in comparison to the results from Tor Wahlström's questionnaire from Finland to interpret the Norwegian situation.

Tor Wahlström's dissertation and its influence

Tor Wahlström's dissertation concerning The Salvation Army in Finland as a community of faith was referred to throughout the discussions of the commission as well as in the final report. The commission had wanted him to come to Norway and present some of his research, but they did not succeed in this. Part of his dissertation, 35 pages, was copied and distributed to the members. It concerned the questionnaires he used and the results from these plus part of his conclusion. Some of the members had read the whole dissertation.

The main subject of the dissertation was the Army as a faith community, and the goal was to reach a definition of the Army that described its essence both from a confessional and sociological viewpoint. It was based on empirical research of groups of officers and soldiers all over the country. Wahlström went into dialogue with published works on the Army from different Finnish theologians and with sociologists of religion such as Ernst Troelst, Max Weber, and Bryan Wilson. He analyzed the difference between church and sect and found a number of notae ecclesiae within the Army, but even so he especially looked at all the different signs of what specified sects sociologically. He looked at the descriptions that would place the Army as a sect and all those that didn't. The ones that didn't fit seemed to be in majority. He then analyzed the concept of religious orders and made a comparison between the Jesuits and the Army, especially a comparison between the Constitution of the Jesuits and Orders and Regulations for Soldiers. The similarities between the two were striking.[14] There had been accusations against William Booth for reintroducing Jesuitism, but there was no evidence that he actually ever had read the writings of Ignatius Loyola.[15] Wahlström pointed to the similarity of reasons for the founding of the two. Often new sects and orders had arisen due to schism, but that was not the case with either of these. His conclusion from the research was:

> The Salvation Army in Finland is an integrated part of the international movement, and at least in this country appears as an order within the universal church. This order regards it as its task to operate as a revival movement, especially among people who are estranged from Christianity and the church, to encourage holiness among the Christians, and to perform social work anywhere the need of society and human distress appeal to the Christian conscience for help.[16]

Several times in the dissertation he used the term Lutheran Salvationists, but not in his conclusion as he pointed to the fact that The Salvation Army could not be linked to any specific church as a religious order.

Of special interest for the working group were the different results from his empirical research. Concerning the sacraments he had posed two questions: "Do you regard the sacraments as a) necessary for salvation, b) enough for salvation?"[17] His conclusion from the results was that Salvationists had a Salvation Army attitude to the sacraments, but in practice they acted as Lutherans. Concerning infant baptism and the dedication ceremony he asked if the parents should only bring the child to be dedicated in the Army or bring it both for baptism and dedication or just bring it for baptism in the church. Three quarters of the Salvationists that answered wanted the child to be baptized (most of these wanted both ceremonies), only a fifth felt that the dedication ceremony was enough. Concerning the Lord's Supper he felt that the result proved his expression of Lutheran Salvationists.[18] A

14. Wahlström, *Frälsningsarmeen i Finland som trossamfund*, 58–59, 90–97.
15. Sandall, *The History of The Salvation Army*, Vol II, 31–32.
16. Wahlström, *Frälsningsarmeen i Finland som trossamfund*, 212.
17. Ibid., 71–74.
18. Ibid., 183–91.

number of corps would go as a group to the Lutheran Church on Maundy Thursday for communion, other places the officers and soldiers would attend the communion service privately. His conclusion of this research was that 90 percent of the Salvationists had participated in communion within a three-year period.

In his research he had a question concerning church and state as there was some work being done in Finland for a separation between the two. The first question concerned the attitude to such a separation, whether Salvationists regarded this as desirable, regrettable, or don't know. A difference between officers and soldiers appeared, as 41 percent of the officers considered this as desirable and only 27 percent of the soldiers, concerning the term regrettable 58 percent of the officers and 64 percent of the soldiers sympathized, and finally the don't know box only got 1 percent of the officers and 9 percent of the soldiers. The next question concerned the situation if church and state separated. Should the Army register as a free church or continue with the present arrangement? 36 percent of the officers wanted registration as a free church and 64 percent would continue as it was presently. Of the soldiers 25 percent wanted a registration and 74 percent to continue as usual. The research of interest for Norway concerned confirmation. Wahlström explained in the questionnaire that the Army in Sweden and Denmark had a confirmation ceremony preceded by teaching and confirmation camps, which the Army's young people chose instead of the confirmation in the Lutheran church. He underlined that the confirmation was without communion. The question was whether that would be fitting in Finland. For this question he had separated the officers into active and retired and then the group of soldiers. The active officers were divided between 51 percent for confirmation and 46 percent against, 22 percent of the retired officers were for and 75 percent against, while 50 percent of the soldiers were for and 47 percent against. The soldiers and the active officers were very close. The next question concerned funerals and he explained that the committal service in Denmark was conducted by an officer, while it in Norway was conducted by a Lutheran minister. His question was what was most appropriate: officer or minister? The results from active officers were 53 percent for an officer and 45 percent for a minister. 14 percent of the retired officers were in favor for an officer and 83 percent for a minister. 56 percent of the soldiers preferred an officer and 29 percent a minister. In this question the "don't know" group of soldiers was bigger than the other two. The last question concerned weddings, if the Army in Finland should pursue legal rights to perform weddings. 56 percent of the active officers answered yes, and 39 percent no, 22 percent of the retired said yes and 75 percent no, while 70 percent of the soldiers answered yes and 25 percent no.

The majority of both active officers and soldiers were in favor of an officer gaining a priestly function, the soldiers even more than the officers. Wahlström had a lot of other research questions, for instance the Army's holiness teaching compared to Luther's "simul justus et peccator," or the Army's attitude and praxis in connection with alcohol and tobacco. The majority showed a clear Salvationist faith and attitude.[19] The situation of interpreting the sacraments in Salvationist terms was present here as in Norway. The doctrine books had been translated faithfully to the original English version throughout the years, so Finnish Salvationists had known the Army's position all along. Their use of the sacraments did not rest on ignorance of the Army's position, but on a deliberate choice. As the Lutheran church in Finland was a national church as well as in Norway some of the same reasons for baptizing the children were present here, reasons for belonging and to be true Finnish.[20] There was a difference when it came to communion. Even though the questionnaires were different between the research in Norway and the one in Finland, the number of Salvationists in Finland who participated in communion seemed to be far greater. The Lord's Supper was received in the Lutheran church rather than in other churches as might have been the case in Norway. Wahlström's definition of Finnish Salvationists being Lutheran Salvationists can be defended, especially on the grounds of their participation in communion and because of the answers to the question of separation between state and church, if that were to happen. The vast majority wanted the Army to continue as it was and not seek registration as a church.

The research revealed that the bonds to the church in Finland were stronger than in Norway. Here the situation concerning the church was more like a civil religion, as Salvationists' nominal membership was not so much connected to the Lutheran faith as to the state institution with all it symbolized of citizenship, unity as a nation, and the unity of nation and Christianity with the long tradition as a Christian nation. The Norwegian Salvationists could be called State Church Salvationists instead because it was the church as an amalgamation of state and church they adhered to. In spite of growing pluralism in the country, most Salvationists still considered membership of the Norwegian Church as part of their national identity as proper Norwegians. It was the possible separation between state and church

---

19. Ibid., 183–91.

20. The difference in the situation is that the Orthodox Church in Finland also has a national status (there were orthodox Salvationists as well). Even though the Lutheran Church is dominant and Wahlström calls Finland the most Lutheran country in the world, the situation with two national churches makes a difference in national identity. It is possible to be Finnish without being Lutheran.

that gave the impetus of forming the commission. It seemed inconceivable for the Army that Salvationists should keep the affiliation to the church if it was not a state church. The affiliation was not so much to the Lutheran part as to the state part. The situation in Finland was different, because a separation between the two would not alter the allegiance of the majority.

There were two particular main differences between the Army in Norway and in Finland that could give some explanation to the difference in the affiliation to the Lutheran church. The most striking one was the much larger percentage of women[21] in the Army in Finland. The other was the figures of those coming new into the Army as the only ones in their family. In Finland the percentage of newcomers was around 76 percent, in Norway it was 65 percent. For both countries the vast majority came from a Lutheran background. For both countries a good number of the first generation Salvationists had parents who had attended church regularly, so they were not strangers to the church. With such a large percentage of first generation Salvationists and with no demand from the Army to sever their bonds to the church, the affiliation to the church could very well linger on, not only as a nominal membership, but also as more active participation as for instance in the Lord's Supper. The vast number of women would support a more active participation in the church as women are often the ones maintaining the cultural and religious traditions of the family.[22] The connection between the Lutheran church and the Salvation Army in Finland can be illustrated through the visitation of the bishops. Wahlström mentioned in his dissertation that a bishop generally would visit Salvation Army institutions in his district during his visitations. When a new TC was appointed in Finland he would visit the different bishops when he/she was visiting the Army work in the Cathedral towns. This was hardly a general praxis in Norway as can be seen from an article in *Krigsropet* from 20 March 1976 concerning Bishop Kaare Støylen visiting *Elevator*, the Army's industry home during the visitation in his diocese. The article presented two photos and a longer report of the event. It illustrates that it has been done in Norway, but also that this must have been a special occasion, a rare one as it was featured so prominently in the paper.

The commission didn't find the definition, religious order, a comprehensive definition of the Army's identity, but that it could define the actual function within Finnish and Norwegian Christendom. In Norway the Army

---

21. I made research in Finland in 2004 based on a questionnaire sent to all officers to uncover original recruitment of the Army and membership in other churches. In Norway I conducted a similar questionnaire in 2009. The results of the Norwegian questionnaire was published in Lydholm, . . . *Teaching them*, 83–99. Around 60 percent answered in both countries.

22. McLoad, *Religion and the People of Western Europe 1789–1970*, 28–35.

had functioned as a lay organization within the Lutheran church without sharing the Lutheran confession and without hampering the contact with the international Salvation Army. They reflected on the fact that the appendix on the Sacraments had been absent from the Norwegian translations of the doctrine books, while it was always part of the Danish books, and posed the question whether this was because the Army did not want to sow discord and therefore refrained from marking itself as a church. They argued that Norwegian Salvationists were not as influenced by Lutheranism as Finnish Salvationists were, but that the definition religious order could be defended in Norway as well, especially seen in historic retrospect.

Wahlström's research seemed also to be influential internationally even though his dissertation was written in Swedish. The General of the time, the Canadian Clarence Wiseman wrote in the international Officer Magazine in 1976 an article: *Are We a Church?*

> "There are Salvationists in some parts of Scandinavia who up till now appear to have little difficulty reconciling membership in a State church with membership in the Army. It must be said that this duality has in no way diminished their devotion, but it does raise an important question: should the Army in such circumstances be looked upon as a religious order?"[23]

Later in the article he resumed the idea of an order and stated that if this concept and an association to the State Church had allowed people to keep loyal to the Army they should be considered part of the composite picture of the Army, as long as the movement possessed freedom and autonomy to maintain its identity and function. He stressed the grace of flexibility without surrender of essentials as a gift by the Holy Spirit, and identified the Army as "a permanent mission to the unconverted and a caring social movement," which in some places assumed the features of a religious order. He stressed that various aspects existed within the shape of an Army and concluded the article with the question: "Can all these elements be subsumed under the generic designation 'church?'" The commission also referred to this article in their papers.

The final report of the commission

After much evaluation, discussion, and study, the commission delivered the final report to the leadership on 6 May 1978. The report consisted of

---

23. *The Officer* 1976, 435–41.

11 chapters that presented the main papers from the group's research into different issues.

The first chapter gave a short historical view over the relationship between Frelsesarmeen and the Norwegian Church, stressing that the Army never demanded its members to resign their membership of the church in contrast to the free churches. It showed a relationship that spanned the bridge from confrontation to cooperation. It stated the renewed awareness within the church of the significance of the sacraments, and a greater awareness among Salvationists of the foundations of their faith. The question was posed whether that situation would create a greater distance between the Norwegian Church and Frelsesarmeen. It concluded with the remark that, in spite of the Army not being registered as an independent faith community, it was regarded as such in many quarters. This small chapter ensured that the historical situation (especially the fact that the Army never had demanded its soldiers to resign the membership of the church) would be part of the considerations before a decision was made.

Chapter three contained a short comparison between the faith of the Army and the faith of the church. It was based on Salvation Army doctrines and the Symbolic Book of the Norwegian Church. It stressed the basic doctrines that united the Army and the church and showed the difference concerning the meaning and use of the sacraments. It concluded with a reference to the Army's holiness teaching. It did not develop this nor did it make any comparison with the Lutheran "simul justus et peccator" like Wahlström had done in his questionnaire in Finland. In the same chapter Bloch-Hoell's paper was included. His paper was followed by an evaluation of the possible consequences of remaining as an organization or establishing the Army as a church. The evaluation was made on the background of Bloch-Hoell's paper as it was considered representative for the Norwegian Church. Visually it is striking that the explanations and presentations concerning "remaining as an organization" was twice as long as "establishing the Army as a church." The opposite could have been expected as the present situation was well known. The evaluation of the first point concluded that a possible separation between state and church could result in a stronger demand for orthodoxy within the Norwegian Church. Such a development might prove difficult for Salvationists. Within the church the positive relationship with the Army most probably would remain if the situation stayed as it was. The short evaluation of the second point was based on Bloch-Hoell's paper and stated that the relationship to the church would alter and aggravate negatively. The reasons for that statement were that the Army would promote a non-sacramental praxis and that would be considered a heresy from the church. It would be necessary to mark its distinctiveness towards other churches, a situation that would lead to competition especially with the Norwegian Church, where confrontation would be inevitable. The intensity of this would depend on the climate within the church. The final point was that revival thinking would recede into the background. The conclusion of the paper recaptured the present good relationship with the Norwegian Church, based on the possible reason that the Army was not an independent faith community. If the Army established itself as an independent faith community a number of divisions between the Army and others would occur, some collaborative projects might suffer. The ecumenical situation internationally would remain as it was, but whether or not that would be the case within the country would depend on the wish of other churches to continue to cooperate with the Army. The group found it essential to further Christian unity and to strengthen the bonds between the Army and the established churches. The Chairman, Bernhard Slettholm, doubted that the ecumenical situation could be considered a recommendation for preserving the present situation. He agreed that there might arise some divisions between the Army and the Norwegian Church, but that the relationship to the free churches most probably would be strengthened. Frelsesarmeen had always shown goodwill for ecumenical work, any division would come from the other side. Long term he doubted there would be any harm for the Army.

The main conclusion from Frelsesarmeen's Commission was at the end of the report, but already here the conclusion was clear. This evaluation of the two different options was not treated equally. It presented a positive image of the present situation as long as separation between state and church did not occur. The option of registration as an independent faith community was presented rather negatively. It didn't take into account the Army's fine heritage in the country for ninety years based on the Army's work, not on Salvationists' membership of the Norwegian Church. It disregarded the fact that ecumenical relationships normally were based on independent churches and the fact that the Army's mission, theology, and praxis would not change. The previous ignorance of the Army's position towards the sacraments within the Army would disappear anyhow, as the Doctrine Book with the appendix on the sacraments had been published two years earlier. The chairman's balanced view in contrast to the group was present in the final conclusion as well.

Chapter 4, concerning Salvation Army identity and ecclesiology, had long term influence, as extracts of this were included in the report from the 1993–96 committee. It was strongly influenced by Bloch-Hoell's paper. Its main point was to argue for the invisible church as the theological foundation for William Booth (because he did not have any teaching on the visible church according to the writers of the paper), and to stress that he had an ecclesiology of the spiritualistic type. The writers also claimed that Booth was ecumenical and had a strong wish that the Army should be undenominational. The main point from this was that the Lutheran influence was not as strong in the Army in Norway as was the case in Finland. This was based on the findings from the questionnaires. Wahlström's thoughts of the Army as a religious order could be relevant for the Army in Norway as well. The paper was well over six pages, which included a couple of pages on early Army history and was marked by lack of proper sources, both historic sources as well as doctrinal. The part concerning the invisible church appeared as statements rather than arguments. However, it was part of the final report and some of the statements were carried over to the 1993–96 report.

The appendix included documents and correspondence, including a report of a meeting on the 13 of April 1977 between Bishop Støylen, Commissioner Solhaug, Bernhard Slettholm, and Tor Martin Ødegaard from the commission. The meeting was followed by correspondence between the Bishop and Commissioner Solhaug. The agenda of the meeting concerned funerals and weddings, and the Army's wish to gain the rights to perform these ceremonies. Concerning funerals there was no great hindrance and a commission was already working on the legislation concerning weddings. If the result of this work was a civil ceremony followed by a blessing in a church, the Army would be equal to other churches. The question of confirmation was discussed as well, and the Bishop could not see any difficulty there, but would want cooperation between the church and the Army. It was stressed from the Army side that there was no wish of any confrontation with the church. The reason for wanting to perform these ceremonies was based on the wish to raise the individual soldier's consciousness about his/her belonging to the Army, for in reality Frelsesarmeen functioned as a faith community. The Bishop expressed an understanding for these thoughts and concluded with the wish that Frelsesarmeen would not pursue a registration as an independent faith community, but added that this decision of course belonged to the Army. The fact that such a meeting took place and that a minute from the meeting was printed in the final report together with the correspondence with the Church Department showed how important it was for the Army to ensure that no actions or decisions would hamper the relationship with the Norwegian Church. Frelsesarmeen acted as if it needed a sort of approval from the church. The little delegation's own interpretation of the meeting was printed in the minutes: "The meeting was very positive seen from Frelsesarmeen's point of view. We were confirmed in the fact that the Norwegian Church regards Frelsesarmeen as an equal brother in the Christian fellowship. The church does fully accept that a number of its member's regard Frelsesarmeen as their spiritual home." The equal brother is perhaps difficult to spot, rather a patronizing bishop's advice and kind interest, as if Frelsesarmeen had been part of the Norwegian Church and the Army acting according to this.

The report ended with the main conclusion signed by eight of the members and a minority conclusion signed by the Chairman and two other members. The main conclusion stated:

- that the reasons for registration as a faith community were not weighty enough to recommend such move at the present time.
- a recommendation for Frelsesarmeen's situation to be continually evaluated in relation to other churches, to the authorities and within the Army itself. The question should be revisited if/when the state and church separated, as this would create a new situation for the Army.
- that Frelsesarmeen should engage in raising self-awareness within the organization for example by an increased focus on education in all the aspects of Army life and by introducing confirmation.
- that Frelsesarmeen should engage in a continued dialogue concerning its identity as either church, movement, sect, or order.
- that Frelsesarmeen should further develop its relationship to other churches and Christian organizations.
- finally, that most important for Frelsesarmeen was to stay a revival movement.

The minority conclusion recommended that Frelsesarmeen should make clear that in principle it should seek to become registered as a faith community eventually, in order to strengthen Salvationist identity. The reason why the minority group would not recommend Frelsesarmeen to register as an independent faith community at the present moment was: firstly, the difficulty in manning corps with officers, and, secondly, that the questionnaire did not give a clear-cut answer. The commission wanted to wait and see a clarification on the relationship between the state and the church. Otherwise the group agreed with the main conclusion.

Conclusion

The final report that summed up the work of the commission was printed and distributed, not only to the leadership and board members of different boards at THQ, but to all corps in the country. It made public all the material that could become the basis for dialogues and discussions at a local level. Articles in *Frelsesoffiseren* referring to the report showed that it had been read and reflected upon. The work of the commission printed in the final report became influential not only for the time being and the immediate debate in *Frelsesoffiseren*, but also for Frelsesarmeen's Church Commission 1993–96. When this was formed it was decided to build on the final report of 1978 for theological matters and concentrated on legal matters and different models of registration.

The leadership decided to follow the recommendations of the report and did not pursue registration as a faith community[24], but agreed to put measures in place in order to strengthen Salvationist identity. The national situation concerning the State/Church relationship had settled since the decision to form the working group had been taken. The result of the hearing from the State/Church Commission was that the vast majority wanted to keep the State Church. With this clear result the question was settled at least for the time being. With this development the question was not as urgent for the Army leadership now as at the time the working group was formed, as the main reasons for starting the commission were the possible separation between state and church as well as the wish to strengthen Salvationist identity. Both of these issues were addressed in the final report from the commission. The recommendations on both issues were followed up by the leadership.

The whole process of forming a commission, sending out a questionnaire with an appeal for debate, and as the work progressed a continual reference to the findings in *Krigsropet* and *FA-Kontakten* signaled a new style of leadership within Frelsesarmeen, a leadership that wanted an informed debate on these vital issues. This was also evident in the fact that the final report was distributed so widely. It reflected to a certain extent what was happening in society in the quest for democracy in different institutions and the various efforts to gain the right to be consulted.

In the interim period between the two commissions, Frelsesarmeen's Commission 1975–78 and Frelsesarmeen's Church Commission 1993–96, new challenges came that demanded attention, but the overall recommendation of strengthening Salvationist identity stayed as a central matter both for responding to new challenges as well as a follow up on the specific recommendations.

---

24. The Annual Report to IHQ covering 1977 referred on the first page to the changed situation: "The final word in regard to the question of disestablishing the Lutheran Church as the State Church of Norway has not yet been said, but it is more and more obvious that the outcome of the lengthy discussion will result in a near status quo in the relation between the State and the Lutheran Church. This development has had its influence on the findings of our commission on the State/the Church/The Salvation Army. This unexpected turn of things does not create the same basis as expected for registration of The Salvation Army as a separate denomination in this country."

Chapter 6

Developments in the Interim Period 1978–1993

THE PERIOD BETWEEN THE two important commissions: Frelsesarmeen's Commission 1975–78, and Frelsesarmeen's Church Commission 1993–96, was an interim period that proved to be of great importance for Frelsesarmeen's development towards a registration as an independent faith community, as well as being a link connecting the work of the two commissions. In this period the outcome of the first commission and the development on the basis of the report can be detected. This development opened up the way for the second commission of 1993–96. Even the heading of the second one—Frelsesarmeen's Church Commission—indicated a development. During these years the Army acted upon the recommendation from the Commission 1975–78 to strengthen Salvationist identity in different ways. One of the important issues for strengthening Salvationist identity among the young people was the ceremony of confirmation. Another influence upon the Army coming during the 70s was the wish to have a voice in decisions, to have democratic rights. The commission recommended a greater focus on democratization and the outcome of this will be considered. The financial status of the officers became an issue, because statistics showed that the numbers of officers and cadets were declining. This situation was reflected in the recommendation of the minority of the commission. Modern music coming out of the youth culture became a focus within Frelsesarmeen's youth work as well as its mission, and the introduction of modern musical styles helped the younger generation to build a Salvationist identity and stay within the fellowship instead of being estranged from Army worship life. The introduction of a new kind of membership, adherents, that did not demand commitment to a certain lifestyle as was the case with soldiership, was a tool to include both young and old in Frelsesarmeen without the demands of soldiership.

One result of the final report of the commission was a number of articles in *Frelsesoffiseren* on the Army's status as a church. The *Officer* had an ongoing debate on the subject during these years as well. Important for this issue was the engagement the Army internationally had in giving input to the Lima document, *Baptism, Eucharist and Ministry,* from the World Council of Churches. The response the Army gave to WCC was translated and published in Norwegian.[1] The process influenced the Army's theological debate and resulted in the publication of a Salvationist Ecclesiology.[2] Within Frelsesarmeen the period revealed a growing ecumenical involvement. This was not only a sign of a stronger Salvationist identity as a church, but also reflected an influence of the international Army's ecumenical engagement as participation in the process concerning BEM.

Influences from society upon Frelsesarmeen

During the 70s and into the 80s traditional industry faced years of crisis and, in some cases, closure. As the situation within agriculture, fishing, and shipping industry was serious as well, the outcome of all these changes was that smaller communities, depending on, for instance, mining, were dissolved as people moved away. The loss of jobs within industry was 100,000 between 1980 and 1982.[3] This happened parallel with the growing oil industry and the growth in public services that created a number of new jobs. Nevertheless, it was a time of unemployment and transition for a large part of the population with a growing number that could not manage all the changes. The expanding welfare state took over and provided a livelihood for these people through different benefits such as sick benefits, unemployment relief, disablement pension, etc. The transition within society, the improvement in economy, the increased possibility of getting hold of alcohol and drugs meant that a number of people developed alcohol or drug abuse.[4] Such developments in society influenced Frelsesarmeen's social services. It meant reforms within its alcohol-rehabilitation work, building new rehabilitation centers upgrading older hostels to rehabilitation centers. There

---

1. *Dåp, nattverd og embete*, Limadokumentet, Frelsesarmeens svar.
2. Needham, *Community in Mission*.
3. Ohman Nielsen et al., *Norvegr*, Vol. IV, 219.
4. Furre, *Norsk historie 1914–2000*, 302. According to Furre there were 50 percent more people in 1980 that were registered at the centers for temperance that ten years previously.

was a renewed focus on rehabilitation. It had been the aim of the old hostels as well, but in the balance between care and rehabilitation, more targeted and professional rehabilitation developed. Fretex, Frelsesarmeen's recycling industry, also developed rapidly around the country to create workplaces. Not only were social services rebuilt and upgraded, but officers working in rehabilitation had to get further education within these specific areas as well as in leadership skills. At the same time the number of professionally trained employees grew substantially. This expansion, both in activities, education, and employees, meant that the bonds to the local corps in the area were loosened. If the employees were soldiers they would be the bridge between corps and social institutions together with the officers who led the institutions, but with employees without any adherence to the Army, apart from their work there was no such connection. Throughout the late 80s and 90s, a number of employees took over leadership positions as well because of the lack of officers, with the outcome that the gap between corps and institutions became greater in some places. The development of rehabilitation and other areas within social services also resulted in a number of soldiers choosing social services as their professional career.

In spite of serious challenges in society, the overall expectations, as well as the actual experience for a large part of the population, were a comfortable life with a growing income to cover more than bare necessities. This change in the economy of ordinary people became a challenge for the Army. The challenge came because the increase of the officers' living standards in no way followed the average welfare increase. The Salvation Army had an international system of paying its officers an allowance and not a salary, which Frelsesarmeen also adhered to. The allowance was based on a frugal lifestyle and was designed to cover the necessary material needs. Housing was part of the allowance as officers lived in the Army's officers' quarters—flats or houses of a modest standard. The financial status of the officers became an issue as this was considered a possible reason for the declining numbers of officers and cadets.[5] The result of the declining numbers was that it became increasingly difficult to man corps and institutions in the country. An issue that was not discussed in connection with the diminishing number of officers and perhaps not realized was the clash of values going on in society. There was a focus on individualism, on what would benefit the individual the most, on loving oneself as the most important. This was illustrated by popular self-help books of American origin, for instance books by Wayne

---

5. The situation can be viewed through The Annual Reports to IHQ as for example 1986, 1: "We have lost 11 officers this year" and from 1987, 1: "We have lost 17 officers this year." The annual Report did not state the officers' economy as a reason, it only stated the figures.

D. Dyer.[6] It was contrary to the traditional ethos of the nation and certainly contrary to the Army where the ideal was to deny oneself through a simple life style and to love others, to dedicate ones' life to this ideal.

Another issue coming during the 70s that influenced Frelsesarmeen was the wish to have a voice in decisions—to have more democratic rights. The students, with their fight for influence at the schools and universities, were not the only ones aiming for democratic rights. Throughout the 70s a vital part of the Social Democratic program was to gain influence for the workers on the workplace, as well as a demand from Stortinget (Norwegian Parliament) for elected people into the boards of the banks. Democracy in the workplace did not survive into the 80s, while the representation in the boards of the banks went through in 1977.[7] The right to be heard, to be consulted, and to be elected to boards was not only the wish of students and workers, but also concerned the Norwegian Church. These matters of gaining the right to be consulted or having a voice in decisions taken on all levels became an issue for Salvationists as well. The commission 1975–78 had this on their agenda. Within the Norwegian Church this development was marked by a process of democratization. One of the reasons for forming the Commission in 1975 was the State/Church Commission's recommendation of a separation between state and church. The result of the hearings within the different councils and institutions of church and society concerning the recommendation was that the large majority did not want a separation between state and church, but rather reforms and greater self-rule within the church. The Government accepted the consequences of this in 1981 and proposed the following: The State Church should continue, but elected church councils should have a greater say in church affairs. The Diocesan Assembly should be legally confirmed, the Diocesan Councils should be extended to have responsibility for the appointment of ministers, catechists, and others and a Church Assembly would be formed. The Church Council (The Diocesan Common Committee) which had been legally instituted in 1969 should be elected by the Church Assembly. The changes within the Norwegian Church were passed through parliament in 1984.[8] As can be seen the influence upon Frelsesarmeen concerning having a voice in decisions and planning came from a wide sector of society.

Music in connection with youth culture became an important challenge for the Army as well. It started in the 60s influencing the Army

---

6. His books were published in Norwegian translation in the beginning of 1980s. Ohman Nielsen et al., *Norvegr,* 230.

7. Furre, *Norsk historie 1914–200,* 246.

8. Ibid., 299.

internationally with new music and musical styles. The Army's response both internationally and nationally in Norway came during the 60s, but the long lasting effect or broader effect of this change came during the 70s and early 80s. It concerned communication and identity within the younger generation. Music had been central since the Army's beginning, if not essential to Army life. It was not only important in worship and evangelism, but music also became a vehicle for Salvationists identity and developing this through active participation. The different musical groups created bonds of fellowship and means of service for Salvationists. Music had relevance in all settings also in teaching sessions like the confirmation classes.

The ceremony of confirmation

The reason for the commission's recommendation for introducing confirmation was stated as strengthening Salvationist identity by improving the teaching of the young people. The teaching would be centered on Salvation Army theology, history, and ethics instead of Lutheran teaching and influence coming through confirmation in the Norwegian Church and, through this, highlighting Frelsesarmeen's own values and own identity. By introducing confirmation, Frelsesarmeen prepared the way for later registration by making a greater distance from the church. As the majority of Salvationists had the double allegiance of baptism in the church and dedication in the Army, the tradition for many had been that baptism was followed by confirmation in the church and dedication by a possible soldier's enrollment in the Army. Not all Salvationist children were enrolled as soldiers, as the enrollment demanded quite a lot of a fourteen year old,[9] therefore an increasing number of Salvationist children were enrolled some years later at sixteen or eighteen years of age, if at all. As confirmation was a cherished tradition among ordinary Norwegians[10] with a large majority of the youngsters being confirmed, the Army kept the close bonds to the youngsters by introducing it, and by this avoided a stronger influence from the church at this age. It was both a wish to strengthen Salvationist identity and to keep the young people within Frelsesarmeen. By introducing the ceremony of confirmation Frelsesarmeen gave Salvationist youth the chance of adhering to this vital rite without having to seek it in the Norwegian Church.

9. See the Soldier's Enrollment Appendix II.

10. The percentage of youngsters being confirmed was 89 percent in 1980, 85 percent in 1985, 81 percent in 1990. Even though it seemed to be falling 1 percent every year the percentage was still high. Schmidt, *Endring og Tilhørighet*, 67.

The first issues of *FA-Kontakten* (Salvation Army Liaison), a small photo copied paper from the Leadership to Frelsesarmeen around the country, reflected the work of the commission as the debate concerned the possible introduction of confirmation as a Salvation Army ceremony. The first to write on the issue[11] was Tor Martin Ødegaard, a member of the commission. The following paper[12] published four articles, one signed by six persons. Three of the contributions were negative towards the idea, because the Army had its own teaching system already in place with junior soldier's and corps cadet's lessons[13] and its own ceremony, the soldier's enrollment, which was possible from the age of fourteen. Confirmation was new and not a natural part of the Army system. The other argument was that confirmation and baptism belonged together, therefore to introduce confirmation in Frelsesarmeen would be to take the ceremony out of its context. However, the debate did not continue, as no comments were published in *FA-Kontakten* concerning these matters which could have been expected in light of their relevance. Behind the protests might very well have been an uncertainty of how this would fit in and how it would be interpreted. When confirmation eventually was introduced it looks as if the whole issue must have had greater support than was evident from *FA-Kontakten*. The fourth letter was from the CS, the Swedish Colonel Sven Nilsson, writing a short history of confirmation within the Army. He mentioned that the Scandinavian corps in USA for years had included confirmation as part of Army life as well as the Army in Switzerland and Germany doing the same. The Army in Sweden had started confirmation in 1964 using a booklet build upon teaching material from the Army in Switzerland. As the commission had recommended the introduction of confirmation it was on the agenda and discussed at the Leadership Conferences of 1979 and 1980. It was also on the agenda for all officers' courses during the spring of 1981 with information of the teaching material. The first official confirmation was held in April 1982 and the first confirmation camp for two of the divisions was held in February 1984.[14] *Krigsropet* from 1982 up to 2005 shows that the number of participants at the confirmation camps was growing. From being held at divisional level they changed to territorial level for all the youngsters preparing for confirmation. The fact that *Krigsropet* prominently placed

---

11. *FA-Kontakten* third quarter of 1976 (There was no page number as it was just four A4 pages).

12. *FA-Kontakten* fourth quarter of 1976.

13. Corps cadets from the age of thirteen followed a six year study program writing monthly lessons concerning the Bible, doctrines, Salvation Army history, etc. They had weekly gatherings and were actively engaged in the corps' program.

14. *Krigsropet* 14 June 1982,19 and 2 April 1984, 19.

photos and reports from confirmations, as well as from the confirmation camps, shows that it was considered an important Frelsesarmeen event. Not only Salvationist youngsters were confirmed in the Army, but also young people engaged in Army youth activities who had no Army family background. Some of the parents supported an Army confirmation because the children of their own accord had chosen to belong to one of the Army's youth groups. They wanted to acknowledge that Frelsesarmeen had become their children's church. The prominence of the confirmation, as reported in *Krigsropet*, could be a signal of Frelsesarmeen's wish to proclaim its identity as an independent faith community able to offer this important rite of passage. Another aspect was the connection to national identity in the Norwegian Church. The majority of the girls wore a *bunad*, a national costume at their confirmation. This underlined that confirmation was not only a rite of passage happening within the faith community, being celebrated within the family, but also a bond to the nation, a strong signal of being Norwegian. This could be compared with the soldiers' enrollment, which used to happen at the same age as confirmation, with the young people dressed in uniform as a testimony of being in somebody's service. By wearing a uniform, the youngsters represented Frelsesarmeen and their faith, but with no connection to being Norwegian. The uniform would be more a signal of dissent from than belonging to ordinary Norwegian life. The introduction of confirmation had the result that young people growing up in the Army and involved in Army youth activities considered Frelsesarmeen as their church. It was an important step towards registration as an independent faith community, because the Army identity was being strengthened through the ceremony and Frelsesarmeen's youth felt connected to the majority of Norwegian youngsters. They were not dissenting, but belonging.

Getting a voice in decisions and planning for soldiers and officers

By introducing the ceremony of confirmation the Army took hold of a strong tradition within the country and made it an Army tradition. During these years Frelsesarmeen also tried to open itself to influence from contemporary society. An influence from society at large was a demand of greater democracy and being part of decision making. Democracy as such could not be combined with the Army's hierarchical system, but it was possible for boards and councils on all levels to open up to allow soldiers and officers a voice in decisions and planning. This development proved to be crucial for the development of Frelsesarmeen during these years. Decisions grew more in line with the wishes of ordinary soldiers and officers. The input from members of different councils gave an insight to changes going on in peoples' lives, to their thinking and attitudes, and to how they wanted to express their faith. This made the leadership more aware of what was going on among the Army's people than had previously been the case.

Democracy was on the agenda for the Commission 1975–78, but not dealt with at length. The main reason for this becoming a minor subject for the commission was that the process to give soldiers and officers a voice in decisions and planning was being done by another committee and developed parallel with the commission's meetings. The concern for democracy or the quest for more participation in decision making was picked up straight away from the agenda of the commission by the TC. The Army's hierarchical system had not given itself to democracy, and an outcome of the system had been that it had fostered passivity, not in engagement in meetings or in activities, but in debate and decision making. Active participation had not been encouraged, but in the years from 1975 to 1977 a structure of corps councils, divisional councils,[15] and a territorial council was formed. The membership of these councils was not based on election, but appointment and consultation by the corps officer, the DC or the TC. The first Territorial Consultative Council[16] had its opening meeting 4 and 5 March 1977. This was one way of meeting the quest for the right to be consulted. Another was a new paper *FA-Kontakten* published in the first

---

15. A Corps Council dealt with policy, strategies, program, and finance. The members would be the local officers who formed the membership council plus two or three representatives from ordinary soldiers. The representatives would be exchanged every second year to get a wider group of soldiers into the corps council over a period. The corps officer would always be the chairman. The frequency of meetings depended on the corps—monthly, bimonthly, or quarterly.

A divisional council would primarily deal with program and strategies. The membership would be corps officers, local officers and ordinary soldiers. The divisional commander would always be the chairman. The meetings would be quarterly. An effort was made to secure younger people a place in both councils.

16. *Offiseren* 1977 no 3, 50–52. The Territorial Consultative Council had a representation of officers, local officers and ordinary soldiers. The TC was chairman and the CS deputy chairman. The secretary would be an officer appointed by TC. At least one of the officers as well as one of the local officers and one of the soldiers had to be women. It had 15 members. The divisional councils should suggest representatives for the territorial council. The membership would be for a period of two years, but half of the first council would be there for the first three years in order for the exchange of members to be every year with half of the council each time. The agenda would depend on matters arising as people were free to send in suggestions for the agenda. Otherwise it would be matters arising within the territory, but never individual personnel cases. The council would meet twice a year. TC would give information of how suggestions had been followed up. The files of the Territorial Consultative Council.

quarter of 1976[17] for soldiers in Frelsesarmeen, with an invitation to send in articles and letters for debate and reflection. There were a number of other publications[18] apart from *Krigsropet* and *Frelsesoffiseren* that might have filled the need for communication and debate earlier on. The long term interest centered around the corps councils and divisional councils. They were local and the issues on the agenda closer to people's lives and perhaps more relevant. An important issue for all three councils was that the culture of debate was developed and encouraged. A movement towards more democracy than was the case with the councils mentioned came with the Army's youth organizations. The democratization of Salvation Army Scouts and Girl Guides started in 1977, with calling for a national session for election of board members and leaders. These sessions were held every second year. In 1982 the structure of the overall youth work, FAU (Salvation Army Youth) was reorganized and national sessions were held every second year with direct election of leaders and board members. The development of democratic processes, which the young people became trained in and got used to, influenced corps, divisions, and the Army as such. This did not mean that democracy was introduced into Army structures, but that the boards and councils in practice became more than consultative at least in some places. An officers' forum was started officially in 1994,[19] but there must have been another sort of officers' forum earlier as there are minutes from a meeting during the congress of 1992. The minutes were published in the September issue of *Frelsesoffiseren*. According to the line of direction for this official officers' forum the members were to be elected among all officers. There had to be seven members of the forum, three corps officers, two social officers, and two THQ officers. They were elected for a period of two/three years and could be re-elected once. The chairman was elected by the forum. Neither the TC nor DCs or any other head of department could be elected. The forum would gather three times a year and in connection with the yearly congress all officers would gather for discussion and election of the members for the forum. The forum was meant to be a consultative council with no executive power. The aim was to open up a space for dialogue

17. It consisted generally of four A4 pages, sometimes of six. It was published quarterly and continued until 1989.

18. *Den unge soldat* (The Young Soldier) was published until 1993. Then another paper *Juniorposten* for children followed for another ten years. The paper concerning music *Menn-Meninger-Musikk* was published from 1964-1970 and the paper concerning social work *Faklen* stopped in 1970. *Krigsropen* made a change in 1970 in order to incorporate both music and social work.

19. Letter of 12 December 1993 to all officers from the TC, Commissioner John Ord. Attached to the letter was the line of direction.

concerning conditions for officers, ideas for the Army's mission methods as well as being an instrument of strengthening communication between officers and the leadership of the territory. The forum has been active ever since. Looking into minutes of meetings the agenda developed mainly in the direction of practical matters, such as study leave, work hours, housing, allowances—a lot about work conditions, and not so much concerning the Army's mission.

The whole development of councils, boards, and forums met the demand from soldiers and officers alike for having a voice in planning and decisions. It did not change the Army's hierarchical structures officially and could not as the structures were based on international rules and regulations, but it influenced the way leadership was performed from a more authoritarian leadership to consultative leadership on all levels. The advent of this newer culture of debate, discussions, and decisions within the Army on a wider scale than previously can be seen as an important aspect of advancing a stronger Salvationist identity.

The Army's personnel situation concerning numbers of officers

However positive the influence of councils and boards was, it did not alter the critical situation of officer personnel. The decrease of officers happening during these years was a concern for the Army at large and especially for the Army's leadership who had the responsibility of appointing officers to all the different positions in the territory. There were not enough officers to man all corps, institutions and THQ positions. A growing number of positions were filled by employing civilian employees, meaning that they were not officers. Civilian employees very often were soldiers, but quite a number had no affiliation to the Army apart from their work. A similar situation was shared by the Army in the other Nordic countries. According to Hugh McLeod it was a situation shared by virtually all churches in Western Europe:

> "From about 1967 the Churches were in a state of crisis in most parts of western Europe. There was a general decline in church attendance, many churches lost members, large numbers of priests were resigning, and there were few newcomers to take their places."[20]

There were varied reasons behind the crisis, but most of them originated in the growing secularization that affected Salvationists as well as other

---

20. McLeod, *Religion and the People of Western Europe 1788–1970*, 135.

citizens. Free time or leisure time was spent differently than was previously the case. Television, for instance, opened up a number of cultural inputs through film, theatre, and debates that gave voice to very different values from the traditional pietistic Christian values, that had been the horizon for most Salvationists. With such a variety of values the interpretation of moral, spiritual, and religious experiences became more diverse. They would still interpret life in view of the Christian faith, but the scope for interpretation was wider than before due to the diverse influences. Added to this was a growing focus on all the material possibilities that were within reach due to the general rise in living standards. An officer's prospects, however, did not include great material options as it was based on a frugal life style. The dwindling number of officers became a challenge for all Army activities because the officers were the ones initiating new activities in the corps according to the needs of the town as well as visiting ordinary people at their work places or in their homes. This had its roots in the covenant and ordination of officers.[21] It was more an ordination to the world than to Frelsesarmeen, meaning that a lot of the officers' work focused on the town or district as much as the particular corps. The Army's presence and its work in the local district would simply be diminished by a deficit of officers.

The commission worked with statistics of officers over a period of time and argued that registration as a faith community depended upon an adequate numbers of officers to pastor soldiers in corps and outposts all over the country. The minority highlighted this issue as a reason for not supporting registration at the present time. The Commission continued to work with this issue. It made a forecast for the years 1978-1982 based on the numbers of the previous years. In the forecast they estimated fifteen new officers yearly summing up to seventy-five new officers. A more secure forecast was the sixty-two officers entering retirement during these years. On the basis of the percentage of previous years they estimated that forty officers would leave officership. That would give a decrease of twenty-seven officers all together. The group estimated that the lack of the twenty-seven could be compensated by ex-officers returning to officership and employment of more civilians. The actual statistics[22] for the five years shows a decrease in active officers of fifty-eight, which included the new officers coming in. The estimate had been twenty-seven. As the number of cadets/new officers had been higher than estimated (81 instead of 75) the number of officers leaving officership had exceeded the prognosis. Looking into the

---

21. See Appendix III and IV.

22. The Salvation Army Year Books 1979-1994 (The statistics are based on the previous year).

statistics of the whole interim period, the number went down from 440 officers in 1978 to 290 in 1993, a decrease of 150 officers. The forecast proved to be too optimistic for the five years and the situation did not improve for the whole period—on the contrary, it worsened. The commission had also looked at the figures of officers leaving the work from 1942 to 1961, most probably based on a questionnaire indicating the reasons why officers in this period had left. Reasons were varied, but the majority had left due to health problems or marriage. An officer could only marry another officer. If an officer married a non-officer (even a soldier) they had to leave officership. Other reasons were too heavy of a workload, inadequate allowances, lack of education for the increasing demands on officers, or loneliness. The commission gave suggestions for changes that could better the prosperity for officers, such as better housing, allowances, and more settled work hours. As far as possible posting young officers to isolated places should be avoided. The Army had not changed its policy towards officer personnel concerning allowances and work hours at the same speed as conditions in society at large. The difference between conditions for ordinary people and officers grew wider. Another challenge was the uproar against authority and the demand for having a voice in decisions that had a wide appeal in society. Even though the Army introduced different councils and boards the authoritarian system that really affected officers' lives was neither addressed nor challenged. Whatever the reasons for individual officers leaving or for the lack of interest in pursuing officership as an option, the statistics gave a clear message of decline. This became a permanent challenge in the years ahead as the situation did not change, on the contrary it grew worse. The work on recruitment and democratization focused on the Army's system in order to update it so the system itself should not be the main hindrance. An outcome of a focus upon recruitment of young people for officership was to build new premises for the training college. The new school for officers was opened 12 September 1983. As the cadets' training was based upon two years of living in a community while having the teaching and practical training within this setting it most probably made sense for the leadership to address these practical issues. It was moved from central Oslo to Asker and placed in beautiful surroundings. The housing for the cadets changed from rooms on a corridor to independent flats in small houses. An update on the actual training was introduced as well.

It was important that Salvationists were able to identify themselves with Frelsesarmeen instead of feeling estranged from it, but more had to be done to address the development of Salvationist identity in a changing world. Music had been extremely important through the Army's history for identity building, both through participation in musical groups as well as the use of music in personal and corporate worship life, therefore modern music styles were another area the Army examined.

A development for strengthening identity through new musical styles

The challenge of dwindling numbers of officers and young people pursuing officership as a choice of career was added to the challenge of keeping the youngsters who grew up in the Army's children and youth sections within the Army. Many left the Army during their teens. Confirmation was one way of trying to keep them and teach them, another was to look into the general youth culture and see what could be adapted into Army life in order for the young to feel included. Reorganization of the youth work to include democratic processes was an option pursued, and so was an evaluation of musical styles. This was a different way of strengthening identity. The introduction of new musical styles had not been part of the commission's work, but music had traditionally played an important role in Salvationists' community life. Not only was music a great part of worship, both within the corps as well as in the public, but the musical groups were also important vehicles for fellowship, identity, and belonging among Salvationists. In order to strengthen identity for the younger Salvationists, as well as responding to youth culture at large, effort was made to incorporate modern music into Frelsesarmeen. As mission was at the very heart of Salvationism, the focus on contemporary music also served this purpose as well as strengthening the identity.

Historically the Music Hall style cherished by the British working class formed a pattern for congregational singing and music within The Salvation Army. This style followed the Army as it settled in Norway. The lyrics were American/British evangelical hymns as well as Wesleyan hymns or original Salvation Army songs. British brass banding was transferred to Norway as well and incorporated into the Army here. Salvation Army composers both British and Nordic wrote music for bands that at this time had become traditional tunes. Klaus Østby was a Norwegian pioneer within Army music and called the "father of Army music in the North."[23] Very early on in Norway songwriters appeared among the pioneering officers, for example Carl Breien and Henry A. Tandberg.[24] String-bands were a special Nordic feature, choirs that were accompanied by guitars, piano, double bass, and mandolins

---

23. Norun, *Med Kjærlighetens Våpen*, 143–45.

24. Ibid., 135–37. According to John Bjartveit from Frelsesarmeen's archive, Carl Breien published around 130 songs and Henry Tandberg around 100. The best ones according to Bjartveit had melodies written by Klaus Østby.

and violins as well. The lyrics and the music for string-bands were originally Scandinavian, mostly written by the Army's own people.[25] The bands and string-bands characterized Frelsesarmeen's worship at in-door meetings and services as well as at open air meetings. In Sunday schools the young peoples' bands and string-bands played and sang as the adult bands and string-bands did in worship services. Brass bands especially applied to bigger corps, while string-bands were present in smaller corps as well. By the 1960s and 70s this had become old tradition and it appealed not as strongly to the young people as it used to. Youth culture in society was influenced by American/British pop music, and that inspired Army young people to form song groups with drums, electronic guitars, double bases, and piano, occasionally brass instruments as well, for instance trombone or cornet. The first one to appear in the late sixties was S-team that was inspired by the British Salvation Army pop-group the Joy Strings.[26] S-team traveled to different corps in Norway as well as to the other Scandinavian countries. Other groups coming after were Happy Soldiers and Joy Friends.[27] In 1982 NSB (Norwegian Salvationist Band) started. It became the most popular of these bands in its inspiration and influence on Frelsesarmeen's youth as well as other youngsters. It traveled on several tours in Norway to visit Frelsesarmeen's corps and to participate in youth music festivals. Because of the Army's transnationalism tours abroad were arranged not only to the Nordic countries, but also to France, Nederland, New Zealand, and New York.[28] In order to encompass different contemporary music styles, musicals became

25. The string-band tradition was very strong in Sweden and quite a lot of songs came from there. In Norway Klaus Østby gave out collections with songs written by different Norwegian writers, Hjalmar Hansen gave out collections with his own songs for string-bands from 1944 and onwards. Both Carl Breien and Henry A. Tandberg also wrote songs for string-bands. Bernhard Fjærestrand was another songwriter writing both for congregational singing and for string-bands. From the 1980s and onwards many Danish songs were used for string-bands all over Scandinavia. The lyrics were written by Anne-Lise Silfverberg and the music by Erik Silfverberg. They picked up a more modern rhythm. In Norway their songs were published by Frelsesarmeen's Music Department.

26. The Joy Strings was the first Salvation Army pop group that really became influential across the Army world and quite famous in Great Britain outside the Army. It started among cadets and officers at the International Training College in London in 1964. It soon hit the headlines of the British Press when it played in a cabaret show in the 'Blue Angel' night club in London in March 1964. It had already appeared in different well-known programs on TV. It toured different countries including Norway and in that way initiated similar groups. Coutts, *The History of The Salvation Army* Vol. 7, 169–70.

27. Norun, *Med Kjærlighetens Våpen*, 148–49.

28. Hagen, "NSB-en orientering," 6–8. The group appeared on Norwegian TV as well as publishing five LPs.

a popular feature in Salvation Army music life. They also started in England when two young officers, John Gowans and John Larsson,[29] were asked to write a musical for the Year of Youth 1968.[30] Jeløy Folk High School took up the challenge to perform a Gowans/Larsson musical every year from 1975 and onwards. The pupils toured with these musicals to different places in Norway as well as in Sweden and Denmark. From these performances divisions were inspired to take up the idea of performing musicals. Some of the songs from the musicals became loved hymns in Salvation Army worship and later appeared in the official songbooks. Notwithstanding, the traditional style with brass bands and string-bands continued during this period as the dominant musical expressions in Army worship, but the influence from contemporary rhythmic music and the musicals could be heard in the music written, chosen, and played by these groups as well. By modernizing the traditional style, as well as introducing contemporary music, the Army avoided Salvationists feeling estranged from Army worship as well as helping strengthening Salvationist identity among the younger generation.

Reaching over from contemporary music as a vehicle of Army identity to ecumenical theology, as will come in the next section, is quite a step, but it is not as wide as it might look at first because both music and reflection upon the Army's own theology/ecclesiology through the ecumenical challenge concerned the soul of the Army. The Army's engagement in both these areas was important during these years in finding and developing Salvation Army identity in a changing world. The process of the BEM document inspired the Army world to study its own tradition in comparison with this document. It resulted in a stronger focus on Army identity.

The Salvation Army's response to BEM (the Lima Document)[31]

For a number of years, the Commission on Faith and Order within the World Council of Churches had studied the issue of Baptism, Eucharist, and Ministry in order to reach a sort of consensus among churches that eventually would result in hospitality among the churches in connection with the

---

29. John Gowans wrote the lyrics and John Larsson the music. Later both of them became Generals. John Gowans was General from 1999–2002 and John Larsson followed him from 2002–2006. *Salvation Army Year Book* 2013.

30. The first musical *Take-over-bid* had its first performance in the autumn of 1967. Later they wrote *Hosea, Jesus Folk, Spirit, Glory,* etc. These were some of the musicals known in Norway. Norun, *Med Kærlighetens Våpen,* 220.

31. WCC, *Baptism, Eucharist and Ministry.*

Eucharist. It also hoped to further the understanding and respect between the churches for different views, as it tried to interpret different traditions in a way that the common denominator would stand more clearly. In 1982 it published the result of the work done, in popular terms called the Lima Document. It was considered to be a discussion paper, and as such it was sent out to member churches asking for responses to the work.

The Salvation Army took up the challenge and formed a study group at International Headquarters in London. The group made a draft that was sent to Army territories around the world asking for responses to the draft document. The official response from the Army was given in 1985[32] and five years later the response was published, including responses from twenty territories and individuals as well as giving information of the actual process.[33] In Norway a small commission of three people was asked by the TC, Commissioner Martin Högberg, to read and comment on the document.[34] The document was translated and published[35] as was the case in most territories. The Salvation Army had been actively engaged in the World Council of Churches as one of the founding members since its beginning in 1948. During the 1970s and 1980s a growing ecumenical awareness was seen in different churches, and for Norway the inauguration of Norwegian Theological Dialogue Forum in 1983 could stand as an example of this. Even though the Army was engaged in ecumenical dialogue, the reason why the Army internationally actively engaged in responding to the document on such a wide scale as was the case might be found in the General of the time. General Jarl Wahlström was Finnish and the younger brother of Tor Wahlström,[36] whose dissertation was dealt with in the previous chapter. In Jarl Wahlström's speech to the High Council 1981, as a nominee for generalship, he pointed to the fact that a general should find the "balance between denominationalism and ecumenism": "Whilst constantly guarding the Army spirit and strengthening the Army's profile, he must have an open mind and a sincere will to co-operate with Christians of other Churches and movements to maximum degree."[37] The maximum degree could partly give the answer for the Army's engagement in the process. It could be added that

---

32. IHQ, *Baptism, Eucharist and Ministry*.
33. The General of The Salvation Army, *One Faith, One Church*, 1–3.
34. Norun, *Med Kjærlighetens Våpen*, 234.
35. *Dåp, Nattverd og Embete*, Limadokumentet, Frelsesarmeens svar.
36. Jarl became General from 1981–86. As a young officer Jarl Wahlström served as Chaplain to the Finnish armed forces during the Winter War November 1939 to March 1940 as well as the War of Continuation July 1941-September 1944 against the Soviet Union.
37. "High Council 1981—Speeches of nominees," 2.

Wahlström had a concern for developing Salvation Army theology. Another reason could be to signal to the WCC that the Army had not altered its support for the WCC in theological matters in spite of its change from member to observer in 1981.[38] The Lima document was on the agenda[39] for the International Leaders Conference in Berlin in 1984. Such a conference was chaired by the General. Territorial Commanders from all territories around the world were present. All Commissioners (a number of these were TCs while others were in the administration at IHQ) would be present. Each general had at least one International Leaders Conference during his/her term of office. To place the issue of the Lima Document there signaled the utmost importance of the matter to all Army leaders, meaning that the issue could not be ignored at a national level. Item one on the agenda dealt with the Army's identity and ecumenical relationship, and the study of the Lima text gave an opportunity to deal with these. The most important outcome of the process was what it added of new input to Salvationist identity. The quest to strengthen Salvationist identity was not only a Norwegian one, it concerned the international Salvation Army as well.

The Norwegian translation followed the original English document fairly accurately for the main part of the document, but it omitted individual sentences and paragraphs plus the whole conclusion.[40] The conclusion con-

38. From 1948 the Army had full membership and since 1981 the affiliation was as a Christian World Communion in a fraternal relationship. This new unified international status differed from membership of the council by separate national churches of each denomination. It gave the Army an observer status like the Roman Catholic Church in contrast to full membership. The reason for the change of status can be found in the WCC's economic support through the Program to Combat Racism to different liberation movements in Africa, especially the grant to the Rhodesian Patriotic Fund led by Joshua Nkomo, which became the last straw. The problem was not a program to combat racism, but that the grants were given without any requirement of accountability, "on trust as evidence of total commitment". The Army's attitude was that this was too naive as the money could be used for other purposes. In Rhodesia especially a large number of Salvationists were killed, both expatriates as well as Rhodesians. The number was between four and six thousand according to Brown. The Army considered the economic support to be an expression of a political standpoint. The Army's exit from WCC as a full member was challenged from within the Army itself when it happened as well as in the years ahead. From WCC a lot was done to avoid the change in status. The General Secretary flew to London to meet the General soon after and a group from WCC and from the Army was formed to negotiate the matter. Brown. *The Gate and the Light,* 229–243.

39. According to Wahlström the discussion was interesting and valuable. It did not lead to greater alterations in the draft document. The final document was delivered to the WCC in 1985. Wahlström, *En vallfartssång,* 166–67.

40. As a contrast to the Norwegian policy the Danish was different. The Danish translation was an edited document with the full conclusion. It stated that the document had been edited only to contain the main answers and then referred to the full document in English.

sisted of responses to four specific questions the churches had been asked to answer from the Faith and Order Commission. There was a pattern in the omissions. References to the Army's non-sacramental practice as having roots in New Testament or being in accordance with the Bible were omitted. The following from page two in the document could stand as examples: "The Army's founders were compelled to seek the guidance of the Holy Spirit in their interpretation of New Testament teaching on the sacraments of baptism and the Eucharist and on the ministry." This was translated": Our founders were gradually led to give up baptism and Eucharist." The word *led* might have been an interpretation of "seeking the guidance of the Holy Spirit," but the Norwegian translation avoided taking an interpretation of the New Testament into account for this decision. In the next paragraph the sentence omitted was: "This, we believe, is sound New Testament teaching" referring to the founders' decision. These two examples claiming a biblical base for the Army's non-sacramental practice could be seen in the light of a strong Biblicism. There would be differences of opinion within the Army concerning interpretation of the Bible both internationally and nationally as in Norway from a liberal to a conservative interpretation. Even though a belief in the inspiration of the Bible is stated in the first doctrine, a literal reading of the Bible has not been part of the teaching in Salvation Army doctrine books as can be seen in the chapter concerning the nature of inspiration in the 1969 Handbook:

> "The doctrine of inspiration of the Scripture does not mean verbal dictation. Such a theory leaves out of account the human element in the composition of the Scriptures—for example differences of style and thought-forms, divergences in accounts of the same events. It would also involve the need to ascribe finality to stages of revelation which are incomplete. The Holy Spirit does not deal with men as though they were machines; each of God's messengers retained his own powers and characteristics. It is, therefore, clear that not all parts of the Bible are inspired in the same way or in the same degree. The Holy Spirit endowed his messengers with insight to interpret for our profit the events through which God disclosed His will for men."[41]

There must have been an intention to translate the conclusion, as the Norwegian edition on page 6 in harmony with the document stated that the four questions posed to the Army would be answered in the conclusion. These four questions and the answers were an important part of the document. An interpretation of the Norwegian translation could be that the

---

41. *Handbook of Doctrine* 1969, Sec. IV, 17.

omissions within the document expressed the translator's own Biblicism or attitude. It might not have been noticed before the printing process as the document and translation had to be scrutinized in order to find them. But that the omission of the four pages long conclusion could have gone unnoticed would be unlikely. The TC was Norwegian, Commissioner Einar Madsen,[42] so the reason for not publishing the answers to the four questions could have been based on considerations he felt important as a Norwegian. Frelsesarmeen's response in Norwegian was published in 1986, eleven years after the translation of the doctrine book that included the appendix on the Army's reasons for its non-observance of the sacraments, so this issue was not hidden any longer. Madsen might not have wanted a discussion concerning the sacraments, which this could release, and could not see the need for further reflections on the theme. He had to arrange for translation and publication of the document, as this was an issue of importance for IHQ he couldn't just ignore. A natural focus for debate could be the answer of maintaining the need for a witness "to the freedom of God to bless his people even outside the traditional sacramental means of grace." As the teaching of officers and soldiers up to 1975 had excluded the non-observance of the sacraments at least in regard to teaching from the doctrine book, the TC might have judged that the majority was not ready for such a discussion or he simply did not want this discussion to surface. Such an interpretation could be founded on basis of Frelsesarmeen's policy of translating doctrine books from 1901 to 1975 concerning the sacraments. It could point to a subtle conflict on the issue between Frelsesarmeen and The Salvation Army. The earlier translations might have been an expression of such a conflict, and this might still have been the case in spite of the 1975 translation. As a Norwegian Einar Madsen would be alert to such a possible conflict.

The Salvation Army's response to the Lima Document was "in the nature of an explanation, an apologia, and above all a witness to the experience granted by the Holy Spirit to many Salvationists of succeeding generations and differing nationalities."[43] In the introduction the respect for denominations who uphold sacramental observances was expressed together with regret that the document ignored the views of non-sacramentalists. Throughout the response the Army clearly upheld its own position as it interpreted the different sections on baptism and Eucharist. It protested against the tendency to limit the boundaries of being Christians and the fellowship of God's people by sacramental language as for instance bap-

---

42. Ejnar Madsen was a Norwegian officer that had solely served in Norway. He was TC from 1985-90.

43. Ibid., 6.

tized Christians or those baptized and then Eucharistic fellowship. It kept upholding the confession of the one faith as the essential mark, and that union among Christians was by virtue of union with Christ as God's people. There were comments on most of the points in the Lima document on what was helpful for further reflection as a Salvation Army and then protests or different interpretations based on Army doctrines. In the section concerning the Eucharist the connection between the Army's understanding of the meaning of the Eucharist and the doctrine of sanctification "as a positive experience producing the possibility of holiness in living" was referred to several times. The comments concluded the section by this statement: "For The Salvation Army, one of the outcomes of this study will undoubtedly be a re-emphasis on the significance of this doctrine."[44] The last paragraph of the section on ministry was the end of the Norwegian translation. It ended by claiming the right for Salvation Army officers to be accepted as part of an ordained ministry "through which God has been pleased to perform all the essential functions outlined in this section of the Lima text."[45] All ceremonies in connection with covenant-making, dedication, and ordination, commissioning and appointing of Salvation Army officers were attached in appendix 5. The other appendices were the doctrines, the articles of war in connection with swearing-in of soldiers, the dedication of children. None of the appendices appeared in the Norwegian translation. The four questions that needed response in connection with the Lima text were:

1. The extent to which The Salvation Army can recognize in the Lima Text the faith of the church through the ages.
2. The consequences which The Salvation Army can draw from this Text for its relations with other churches.
3. The guidance which The Salvation Army can take from this Text for its worship, educational, ethical, and spiritual life and witness.
4. The suggestions The Salvation Army can make for the on-going work of Faith and Order as it relates the material of this Text on Baptism, Eucharist, and Ministry to its long-range research project "towards the common expression of the apostolic faith today."

Concerning question 1) The Army could easily respond to "the faith of the church as distinct from the traditional observances of the churches." It underlined that the Lima text had failed in making "the crucial distinction between the sign and the truth signified" as it ascribed "to the sacraments'

---

44. Ibid., 20.
45. Ibid., 28.

powers belonging to the Holy Spirit alone." It made clear again that The Salvation Army differentiated between apostolic faith and apostolic tradition and found that the binding together of the two in the text posed a problem. 2) It focused on visible unity as a proclamation of the common faith by word and life and, "that ecumenism lies in common faith and witness and mutual recognition rather than uniform church practices." 3) The Army had identified aspects of its own worship that seemed to parallel traditional rites and had examined its worship and ceremonies to ensure that the contents were "as spiritual and growth-producing as we claim." It maintained the need for a witness "to the freedom of God to bless his people even outside the traditional sacramental means of grace." The Army was convinced that it had the essential characteristics of the Body of Christ and that the "officers conformed to the pattern of apostolic calling."[46] 4) It stressed that the essential focus had to be Christian unity in faith. Faith had to be stressed as the priority of the commission rather than order. It underlined "our prime concern must be the production of a mighty force of Christ like people to carry the message of the church to the world in their life-style and character."

The process around the Lima text within the Army as well as its response had an impact on Army territories around the world, because it focused on the Army as a community of faith. The most important was the debate on ecclesiology that followed, especially when the Army published its book on ecclesiology in 1987 as an outcome of the process. A reasonable interpretation of the whole process with the Lima document could be that it became an inspiration to Frelsesarmeen for engaging more fully in ecumenical life in Norway.

Ecumenism in Norway

The active participation in ecumenical life was highlighted in *Krigsropet*. Already in 1983 when The Salvation Army internationally had started the process of preparing its response to the Lima text *Krigsropet*[47] published a full page of the Army's statement concerning its status as part of the universal church and its attitude to the debate concerning the Lima text. It was the essence of what later became the official response. It was clearly a new policy in Norway to publish its position on the sacraments and on ministry as widely as in *Krigsropet* which was distributed all over the country with

---

46. It mentioned that a clearer definition of Salvation Army ecclesiology and theology was being prepared. It was published two years later. Needham, *Community in Mission*.

47. *Krigsropet* 7 November 1983, 10.

most of the papers sold to the general public. It was not only a focus on The Salvation Army's attitudes, but also a focus on the WCC's General Assembly in Vancouver, where the Army gave the statement. The growing engagement in ecumenism from Frelsesarmeen was evident during this period. The involvement signaled a stronger wish to be counted as an independent faith community than might previously have been the case. The Army had been part of the Dissenter Council as an observer so ecumenism had not been ignored, but the engagement became more evident. An important development was the inauguration of the Norwegian Theological Dialogue Forum in May 1983, where the Army's representative was Commissioner Solhaug, who by now had retired as TC. In June 1984 *Krigsropet*[48] published a photo of the members with a presentation plus a short description of the three meetings there had been. This showed first and foremost that Frelsesarmeen was engaging itself in theological debate and as important that this was announced in *Krigsropet*. As part of the same development Frelsesarmeen was accepted as a member of the Free Church Council instead of being an observer. In an article in *Frelsesoffiseren*[49] the TC, Ejnar Madsen, gave an account of the situation. He stressed that the decision not to register the Army as an independent faith community according to the Non-Conformist Act of 1969 was still valid, but that the council now had an understanding of faith community that could include Frelsesarmeen as a member.[50] The acceptance of the Army's membership happened in February 1988. Madsen concluded the article by stating that any change in Frelsesarmeen's registration would be based on debate and consultation, but personally he did not judge this as relevant in a foreseeable future. Only if the development towards separation between state and church appeared

48. *Krigsropet*, 4 June 1984.

49. *Frelsesoffiseren* no.2 1988. Before the article appeared in *Frelsesoffiseren* it was sent out as an open letter in January. A letter of protest arrived from Commissioner Haakon Dahlstrøm on 29 January 1988. The full correspondence is not in the archive any longer, only the answer from Madsen to the first letter, but not Dahlstrøm's protest, and then two more letters from Dahlstrøm where he developed his arguments, but not the answers from Madsen. Dahlstrøm had been TC in Norway from 1972–75. Prior to that he had been TC in Finland and Nigeria.

50. The Army saw a possibility for full membership by presenting its doctrines, structure, its training and ordination of its officers as proof of the Army being a faith community. The statues of the council stated that faith communities could be members, but did not state that they had to be registered as such. By taking the initiative and proving its case Frelsesarmeen's identity as an independent faith community must have grown stronger at this time than previously was the case. The other free churches might not have identified with Frelsesarmeen as a fellow faith community before as the Army had to prove its case. The information concerning the process was given by Lt. Colonel John Bjartveit who was Frelsesarmeen's representative in the Free Church Council at the time.

in force again would a change in the Army's registration be considered. A letter of protest came from Commissioner Dahlstrøm. It developed to a correspondence. The essence of his long letters was his strong opposition to Frelsesarmeen's membership of the Free Church Council, because by this it would be part of the break-up of the saints. Support for the unity of the universal church was the overall issue. He quoted the Apostles Creed. His belief in the Holy Catholic Church, the Communion of Saints was central for his arguments. He seemed to consider the State Church in Norway as well as other national churches in Europe as expressions of the holy catholic church, but not the free churches. He had no difficulty with the different expressions of the Universal Church in Orthodox, Catholic, Lutheran, and even Methodist, but it had to be an expression for unity within national borders (apart from Methodists as they have never been an expression of a national church, but the Army originated from Methodism. That might be the reason for the inclusion). The free churches were to blame for a split-up of the saints. He considered adherence to the national church as an expression of unity among Christians, a Christian duty based on the Apostles Creed. Because of this he didn't want the Army to identify with this breakaway group as he considered the Free Church Council to be. For him unity was the most important issue. Added to this was respect for the historic role the Norwegian Church had fulfilled through a thousand years in Norway. Apparently Salvationists were not dissenters as long as they had a nominal relationship to the State Church. The nominal membership comes in because of his expression "hobby horses" about issues he disagreed with in the church. It might have been belief in the sacraments as notae ecclesiae he referred to as the Army didn't share that belief, and the differences between the Army and the Norwegian Church was evident in connection with the sacraments. He saw the Army as unbiased, independent, and autonomous with total freedom. The Army seemed to be of another kind than other churches, independent of anything. That was the situation in Norway. In countries without state churches or non-Christian countries it was natural that the Army was registered as an independent church. It seems as if membership of the Norwegian Church was not considered an allegiance of faith, because Salvationists according to Dahlstrøm couldn't have double or multiple allegiances. He consistently named the Norwegian Church as the State Church. The church as a state institution was implicitly present as well. There were no other written sources available that could support the views of Dahlstrøm from other Salvationists, even though he claimed that many agreed with him. There might have been other letters that have been lost, or people around him[51] having discussed the case, but not written any letters of protest. However, regarding the focus on Christian unity Dahlstrøm might be representative for a number of Salvationists as the unity aspect often have been voiced in other settings. In spite of whatever protest there might have been, *Krigsropet* published two months[52] later a rather extensive report from the yearly conference of the Free Church Council. This publication signaled a more active participation from the Army as a result of the membership. Another development published in *Krigsropet* appeared in 1993 with the establishment of The Christian Council of Norway. It was founded 14 December 1992 and its constitution stated:

> "The Christian Council of Norway is a fellowship of churches, Christian faith communities and denominations in Norway who according to Holy Scripture worship and profess God—Father, Son and Holy Spirit—as Creator, Savior and Giver of Life."[53]

The founding members were the Norwegian Church, the Catholic Church, the Baptist Church, the Methodist Church, and Frelsesarmeen. Other churches were planning to join, but needed a decision from their yearly conference. The Free Church Council continued in spite of this new council until the two councils amalgamated in March 2006 and Frelsesarmeen was present in both councils. The engagement in ecumenism as well as the publicity around it as part of Salvationist identity building could be interpreted as a step towards preparing itself and its members for registration as an independent faith community.

Articles in Frelsesoffiseren and The Officer concerning registration and ecclesiology

The whole process of the Lima text and the growing ecumenism resulted in a focus on Salvation Army ecclesiology. This became evident in articles in *Frelsesoffiseren* as well as in *The Officer*. Even though the debate was not intense it was present. The first Norwegian articles concerning ecclesiology and registration were published in *Frelsesoffiseren* in 1980. In three successive articles[54] Major Roger Rasmussen reflected on the Army as a faith

---

51. Dahlstrøm traveled extensively in Norway conducting meetings especially in the very north of Norway. The consequence of his protest was that he cancelled his planned travels. Letter of 4 February 1988.

52. *Krigsropet* 4 April 1988.

53. *Krigsropet* no 7 1993, 11.

54. *Frelsesoffiseren* 1980, no. 2, 30–31, no. 3, 50–51, no. 4, 70–71, 80.

community. The articles were mostly reflections on material from the report of Frelsesarmeen's Commission of 1975–78 especially Tor Wahlström's research, but also on an article from *The Officer*[55] as well as Army history books. Rasmussen stressed the mission focus of the Army and pointed to the founders' unease with established church order and the refusal to name the Army as a church. Rasmussen quoted the founder's saying "We are not a church-we are an Army" in connection with the unease of anything ecclesiastical. As a conclusion he came with his own comments on registration as an independent faith community based on his service in England and Denmark, where he experienced what it meant to be a church in its own right in legal terms. He preferred this option to the present Norwegian situation. The reason was the opportunity to follow the congregation in "the festive moments of life as well as in the days of sorrow." He considered Frelsesarmeen as on its way to such a situation and concluded with an encouragement for the Army to be a living and effective church. He could not see that Frelsesarmeen would be less of an Army by the changes he anticipated. In 1984 four articles appeared in *Frelsesoffiseren*[56] by Nils-Petter Enstad at the time the editor of the paper. The articles were an attempt to define Salvation Army ecclesiology on the basis of Wahlström's dissertation, Frelsesarmeen's Commission's report, Norwegian theological literature, and Salvation Army writers such as Frederick Coutts. These articles were well argued to a greater degree than any other articles in the paper on the subject. His main points were first and foremost to argue that the Army was an independent church because it was part of the universal church of Jesus Christ, a worshipping faith community, and an organized denomination with its own orders, structures and defined boundaries. It had a theology of its own and a clergy. The different articles addressed these five issues. Enstad did not take up the debate concerning registration as such, but a legal registration as an independent faith community would be the natural outcome of his arguments. In that way his articles were part of the debate concerning registration.

During the 1980s a debate in *The Officer* originated in the Army's answer to the Lima text. It concerned mainly the ministry section. The word, ordain, which had been introduced into the Commissioning Ceremony of Salvation Army officers in 1978[57] became the main focal point. It was the so

55. Coward, "A Hunger for Hell."

56. *Frelsesoffiseren* 1984 no. 1, 16–18. No 2, 26–27, 38. No. 4, 66–67, 73–74. No.5, 82, 85

57. The reason for introducing the word, ordain, into the ceremony was to express that SA officers' commissioning was similar to the ordination of ministers in other churches. It was based on requests from different territories. General Arnold Brown introduced it because of these requests. The wording became: "In accepting these pledges

called "churchy" implications of using the word that started the whole debate. An important part of the debate concerned officer identity, Army identity as a church, and the tension between being an Army and being a church. The historic skepticism dating back to William and Catherine Booth against all that looked or sounded "churchy" or ecclesial came to the open in the debate. In the October issue of *The Officer* 1985 Chick Yuill[58] from the British Territory opened the issue based on the Army's answer to the Lima text. He objected to officers being an ecclesiastical caste as he saw officership as a function within God's people and not as a caste of its own. He used the introduction of ordain as the visible expression of this new development. The debate continued through 1986 in the section of *The Officer* called "Postbag" with six contributions mainly from the British territory, but also from Brazil, Australia, and New Zealand. In 1987 the debate on ministry continued into 1988 based on an article by the British officer, Fred Hoyle.[59] In 1992 the articles and debate had moved onto the concept of being a church with titles such as "Do we Really Want to be a Church?"[60] "Denomination or/and Evangelical Society?"[61] or "Church or Churchy."[62] In 1993 the debate was back to ordination[63] only in 1994 to return to the concept of being a church.[64] The articles formed a debate as each referred to one or two of the other articles. Even though the situation of legislation concerning the Army was very different in other countries from the Norwegian, the quest for identity was equally present in the debates in UK, USA, Australia, New Zealand, Canada, and Brazil. The question of registration was not on the agenda in these countries. The double allegiance of its members as in Norway with allegiance to the Norwegian Church and the Army was not an issue. Still the question of how to be a church or the identity of the Army as a church was central. The resistance towards anything "churchy" or any use of ecclesial language came to the forefront, as did the tension between language stemming from the military metaphor and ecclesial language, increasingly coming into use in the Army mainly through ecumenism, was evident in the debate. The whole issue, both the one concerning ordi-

---

which you have each made, I commission you as officers of The Salvation Army and ordain you as ministers of Christ and his gospel." Lydholm, "Rites for commissioning/Ordination to Ministry in The Salvation Army," 411.

58. Yuill, "Reflections of a Corps Officer." *The Officer* 1985, 437–440.
59. Hoyle, "Priesthood and Officership." *The Officer* 1987, 549—552.
60. Raby (USA), *The Officer* 1992, 304–06.
61. Harris (Australia), *The Officer* 1992, 307–09.
62. Harfoot (USA), *The Officer* 1992, 420–22.
63. Robinson (Canada), "Ordained by God in Christ." *The Officer* 1993, 77–81. Brown (United Kingdom), "Ordained for Men." *The Officer* 1993, 81–83.
64. Harfoot (USA), "Church or Churchy." *The Officer* 1994, 221–26.

nation as well as the one concerning the question of being a church, revealed the continuing quest of finding a specific Salvation Army identity as a church, that made sense for Salvationists themselves while at the same time communicating within an ecumenical dialogue. From the contributions it was clear that the debate was widespread in different countries in the same period. The Army in Norway was no stranger to such a debate which was illustrated by the articles in *Frelsesoffiseren*. In 1998 *Salvation Story* and in 1999 *Salvation Story Study Guide* were published with a chapter called "People of God." It was the first time Salvationist ecclesiology was stated in the doctrine book. This was an outcome of the Lima process and the publication of *Community in Mission* by Phil Needham as well as the need the debate in *The Officer* had revealed for further focus on ecclesiology within the Army. The debate on ecclesiology and the stronger ecumenical involvement not only influenced people's attitudes and their Salvationist identity, but it also spurred on fundamental changes.

A new kind of membership as another step towards registration as an independent faith community

One of the changes that came in the wake of the debate concerning identity as a church was a new kind of membership. The introduction of confirmation was an important step in fostering Frelsesarmeen's young people, even though it deviated from following traditional Army programs concerning teaching and ceremonies alone. It was an attempt to reach out to youngsters who did not follow the traditional line of being enrolled as soldiers. It opened the door more widely for the youngsters to belong to Frelsesarmeen without having to commit themselves to a special life style and stricter rules. The next step on this road of widening the door for membership without demand of commitment to soldiership came with the introduction of adherents.[65] It

---

65. Adherents can be traced back to 1886. It was introduced in places where The Salvation Army was the only available church. Some people became adherents without being committed Salvationists. There are references to Salvation Army adherents in an article about prison work in *The Officers Review* January–March 1944, 9–12. It was a different context than adherents at local corps. In 1948, The Chief of Staff issued a Minute (1948 IA/25) re. Adherents of The Salvation Army, which stated: "It is not desired that the recognition of Adherents shall be adopted as a general policy, but only as agreed by the General for such territories where the system may be advisable." From 1950 and onwards, 'Orders and Regulations for Senior Census Boards' included an Appendix on Adherents which applied to territories where the General had approved the adoption of the Adherents' system. This was the historic background for Adherents. The General must have approved the system to be more widespread in the seventies when it became a common part of corps life in UK and in the eighties and nineties in the Nordic countries.

was aimed at people over the age of 15. It was a civilian membership of the local corps. It was announced and explained in *Krigsropet*[66] as a new avenue of membership. The rationale for introducing it was that a number of people felt they belonged to the Army, but were not ready to make the commitment as soldiers, and therefore without any formal affiliation. This was the official explanation, but the Army had always had friends attending its meetings and engaging in its work without this possibility. It might also have been connected to the dwindling numbers of new soldiers. Fewer people who came new to Frelsesarmeen wanted to commit themselves as soldiers, this reason also applied to the Army's own young people. The Army not only in Norway, but also in the other Nordic countries as well as in England realized that it became more difficult for people to pledge themselves to the soldier's covenant. Adherents would belong to the corps and could engage themselves in a number of activities as, for instance, social outreach. They would have access to Army ceremonies such as dedication of infants, confirmation, weddings, and funerals. The condition for membership was to be over the age of fifteen and to know The Salvation Army's doctrines. An adherent was expected to join in Salvationist worship as much as possible and to support the Army's work financially. The admission as an adherent would be marked in a public meeting with a short ceremony and a certificate of membership as an adherent. The years to come proved the importance of this new form of membership both in numbers[67] as well as in commitment to Frelsesarmeen from people, who previously would have considered themselves as friends of the Army, but now became adherents. For some the step to become an adherent started a process towards soldiership.

The introduction of this form of membership made room for people who wanted the Army as their faith community without the stronger commitment soldiership demanded. This membership was another step towards registration as an independent faith community. The image of Frelsesarmeen as a religious order mentioned in the final report of the Commission of 1973 could be sustained as long as the membership consisted of soldiers and officers committing themselves not only to Army belief, but also to the Army's orders and regulations concerning lifestyle. The broader scope of membership was a natural outcome of a development towards seeing itself as a church.

It started in Norway in 1989, in Denmark June 1989, in Finland in 1991, and in Sweden in late eighties (The Archive in Stockholm has not been able to give an exact year for the introduction, but states late eighties and by the latest early nineties).

66. *Krigsropet* nr. 16 1989.

67. The number of adherents in 2000 (based on 1999 statistics) was 637, in 2005 it was 1051, and in 2013 reveals a number of 1515. *The Salvation Army Year Book* 2000, 2005 and 2013.

Conclusion

The interim period was innovative, strengthening Salvationist identity by addressing the challenges which faced Frelsesarmeen from within its own ranks as well as from the wider society. This strengthened identity was the key factor for taking the question of registration up again in 1992 with the result that Frelsesarmeen's Church Commission was formed in 1993. The recommendations of the Commission of 1975-78 were followed up, especially the introduction of confirmation and the system of boards and councils on different levels giving Salvationists a voice in decisions and planning. Frelsesarmeen addressed structural challenges stemming from the Army's hierarchical system without being able to change the system itself. As part of an international denomination Frelsesarmeen could not make alterations to the system as such on its own, but could soften procedures by adding boards and councils for consultation. Final decisions would always stay with the leadership on the level matters were dealt with, but in practice the recommendations from the councils and boards would most often be followed. The introduction of confirmation and adherents departed from the stricter Salvation Army line where teaching programs such as recruits' classes for soldiership[68] resulted in committed membership with fairly demanding rules of lifestyle. It opened the door wider for people who wanted to adhere to Frelsesarmeen, but not to all the demands of soldiership. Both of them were steps on the way for the Army to be registered as an independent faith community. By these measures, the Army created both a more inclusive ceremony, confirmation, and a more inclusive membership, adherents. The work and report from the commission started a process of reflection on Army ecclesiology. This was further strengthened by the Lima Text and the wider involvement in ecumenical life. Membership of the Free Church Council and of the Norwegian Christian Council made Salvationists as well as other church members aware of Frelsesarmeen's identity as an independent faith community. For the younger generation the introduction of modern music into Army life influenced Salvationist identity that did not clash so much as it otherwise would have done with the youth culture they adhered to. It had an effect on all generations, because the development of the music used for worship and for musical groups reflected the general development of musical culture in the country.

In spite of the work done to improve conditions for officers' training and conditions for officers at large, the situation of recruitment of cadets

---

68. Earlier a number of young people were enrolled as soldiers at the age of 14. The enrollment could be seen as the Army's "confirmation" where the family would have a family party like other confirmation parties.

stayed as a challenge. The number of new officers stagnated and the total number of officers fell.[69] It became a constant challenge in the years ahead to staff corps and institutions with officers. What had been thought to be emergency solutions became permanent: closure of corps, officers leading more than one corps, corps led by the division, local officers leading corps on top of their jobs, leadership teams made up of local officers and soldiers etc. The will to find solutions meant that the number of corps closures was not as drastic as could have been anticipated.[70]

Discussion concerning registration as a faith community was present during the whole period as could be seen in the articles from *Frelsesoffiseren* as well as in the article that explained full membership of the Free Church Council. The decision not to register at the present moment in 1978 when the report came from Frelsesarmeen's Commission remained for the time being; the option was not closed. At the annual meeting of the Forum for Active Officers during the congress in June 1992[71] it was evident that the time had come for another commission to be formed to look into the question of registration as a faith community. A question came up for the Army leadership to reflect on. How would the leadership react, if a group of soldiers and officers who had no other church affiliation than Frelsesarmeen registered a faith community based on Salvationist teaching and principles as a preliminary arrangement, while they waited for Frelsesarmeen to register as an independent faith community. The answer from the CS was that it would not be received favorably. Instead he posed the question of whether the time had come for opening the discussion concerning church registration again. Some conditions for a possible registration were mentioned such as: a) no demand to leave the church would be imposed on people who were already members, b) officers being commissioned after the registration would be expected to be members of the registered faith community, c) an adequate time of transition would be given. The suggestion of opening up the work on registration was well received. A few months later in October 1992, the Leaders Conference decided to form a commission to look into registration. Frelsesarmeen's Church Commission was formed and started its work.

---

69. The statistics for 2000 named one to be ordained (2nd year cadet) and 226 officers, in 2005 nine to be ordained and 200 officers. *The Salvation Army Year Book* 2000, 175 and 2005, 194.

70. In 1975 the number of corps was 134, in 1993 it was 124 and in 2005 it was 116. *The Salvation Army Year Book* 1976, 1994, *and* 2006. (The statistics are based on the figures of the previous year).

71. *Frelsesoffiseren* September 1992, 9–10.

Chapter 7

Frelsesarmeen's Church Commission 1993-96

FIFTEEN YEARS HAD PASSED since Frelsesarmeen's Commission 1975-78 gave its report, years where the focus had been on strengthening Salvation Army identity. Now the time had come for further research into the matter of registration as a faith community. This time the main impetus for establishing a commission came from within Frelsesarmeen as could be seen from the meeting for active officers during the 1992 Congress. The fact that a group of officers was prepared to form a faith community on their own initiative, while waiting for Frelsesarmeen to register as a faith community, signaled impatience with the present situation and a strong wish for both action and response from the Army to this. While the main reasons for setting up the Commission 1975-78 came from outside the Army, especially the possible situation of a separation between state and church, this new commission was mainly based on internal pressure.

This new process towards registration as an independent faith community was a natural outcome of what had happened concerning Salvationist identity during the previous years. It could be viewed as an indication of a successful process of strengthening Army identity. A growing, but still small number of Salvationists,[1] had brought their membership of the Norwegian Church to an end and as a result didn't bring their children to the church for baptism, but chose the dedication ceremony as the only one. They had a single affiliation to Frelsesarmeen alone and not the usual double affiliation of Army and church. This group wanted Frelsesarmeen to register as a faith

---

1. I build the small number on the statistics of the first members who registered in 2005. There are no statistics that indicate church affiliation other than the one from 1973 used by the Commission 1975-78.

community, so that neither they themselves nor their children would be considered churchless in a legal sense.

Even though the decision to form Frelsesarmeen's Church Commission 1993–96 was spurred on by internal pressure and it was not the only influence. Another major influence came from international politics. The fall of the Berlin Wall and the collapse of the Soviet Union had a major impact on The Salvation Army internationally as the General of the time, Eva Burrows,[2] seized the moment and started a rapid expansion and pioneering of the Army's work in the former Eastern Europe.[3] Frelsesarmeen in Norway became involved in this expansion as it was asked to reopen The Salvation Army in Russia. The Army's work in Eastern Europe had been closed down in the years after the end of World War II, during the Soviet regime in Latvia, Estonia, Czechoslovakia, Eastern Germany, and Hungary. The Salvation Army in Russia had been closed due to "anti Soviet activity" on 27 February 1923.[4] The Army had only been in Russia from 1913–23 and mainly in St. Petersburg with some activity in Moscow. This reopening and pioneering involved different Salvation Army territories in Europe as they were given responsibility for pioneering the work. Germany (West) would expand to the former East Germany and later Lithuania (1998). The opening took place in Leipzig 16 June 1990.[5] The Netherlands would open work in Czechoslovakia in 1990, where the Army had been from 1919–1950, Switzerland would pioneer the work in Hungary in 1990, where the Army had worked from 1924–1949, Sweden in Latvia also in 1990, where the Army's presence had been from 1923–1948, Norway would open the work in Russia in 1991, and Finland in Estonia in 1995. The Salvation Army worked in Estonia 1927—1940. In the Soviet period Salvationists from Finland had been visiting former Salvationists in Estonia. It had to be private visits called birthday parties in order to get visas. From 1990 visits and preparations for the opening took place on a regular basis. This period of expansion widened the focus of the Army territories from national concerns to all these changes and challenges in a new world order. It gave new energy, optimism, and a broader view of the Army's work than the one of a declining European Salvation Army. IHQ delivered press releases and photos in order for the

---

2. Eva Burrows was elected General in 1986. She was in office for seven years, as the usual five-year period had been extended with two years. She was Australian, served for fourteen years in Zimbabwe (Rhodesia), and in UK. She was TC in Sri Lanka, Scotland, and Australia before her election to General.

3. Wickberg, "Det lysner I Øst." *Krigsråbet* nr. 19 1990, 6–7.

4. Copy of document (Protokol nr. 14) from Committee for Sects under the Central Committee 27 February 1923 in Moscow.

5. *Krigsråbet* nr. 12 1990, 11.

Army to be updated on the latest news. This was reflected in the national Salvation Army papers such as *Krigsropet* in Norway, where a vast number of articles appeared especially in the years 1991–1993. The secular press also took up Frelsesarmeen's engagement in Russia. Twenty-one different newspapers and two magazines from around the country had focus on this in feature articles.

The responsibility for reopening the work in Russia made a mark upon Frelsesarmeen. A number of people became involved in the gathering and transport of emergency help to Russia as well as in supporting different social outreach projects that were started. Norwegian officers, Lt. Colonels John and Bjørk Bjartveit, were sent to Leningrad (St. Petersburg) with the responsibility to open The Salvation Army in Russia. An American/Swedish couple, Majors Sven-Erik and Kathy Ljungholm, opened the work in Moscow. The Temple Band from Oslo crossed the border and gave concerts at the official opening meetings in Leningrad on 6 and 7 July 1991. Visits of new Russian Salvationists and officers to the following Norwegian congresses brought the vitality of a newfound Christian faith. It gave reason for excitement and fresh energy. This exchange between Norway and Russia gave a new perspective of the Army's work. The focus was on being an expanding Christian Church. The Army in Leningrad was registered as a local community of the Evangelical Christian Church "Armija Spasenija" (The Salvation Army) on 28 March 1991.[6] When re-opened the Army registered in the different countries in the former Eastern Europe similarly to the one in Leningrad. Due to the transnationalism of the Army Norway had never been isolated from influences from abroad, as there had been lots of contact over the borders and Norwegian officers had brought news from the countries they worked in, but this was closer. It was combined with all the political changes going on in the former Eastern Europe. This focus became relevant for Frelsesarmeen's work as well. The awareness of expansion and growth was renewed as well as Frelsesarmeen's identity as a church.

An influence from society at large was the digitalization of people's daily lives. PCs became part of people's homes similar to the TVs in the 70s. Around a million had access to the internet at their place of work in 1998, nearly half the working force. The same year it was estimated that 1.7 million Norwegians had access to the internet either at work or at home. The mobile telephone became widespread as well.[7] Very early after the

---

6. It was authorized by the legal administration of the Executive Committee for the town Leningrad. The situation in Russia was that the Army in each town had to register. An all Russia registration could be sought when there were five local registrations. Such a registration was pursued and achieved in 1999.

7. Furre, *Norsk historie 1914–2000*, 322.

introduction of the internet the international Army started making use of it for sharing information.[8] It installed Lotus Notes to connect the Army world through e-mails. It opened up for personal contacts to the Army in different countries and for quick and current information. A new wave of influence came into Frelsesarmeen from the international Salvation Army. The internet became a vehicle for the flow of news from the work in the former Eastern Europe and the rapid growth of the Army in these countries. Registration and recognition as a church in the reopened Salvation Army in these countries might have had an influence on the officers who were impatient because of Frelsesarmeen's slow process towards registration as an independent faith community.

Frelsesarmeen's Church Commission 1993–96

The outcome of the crucial meeting for active officers during the congress of 1992 was one reason for starting Frelsesarmeen's Church Commission. The final report from the commission stated the reasons for this new commission by describing three groups of Salvationists that felt a need for the Army to have a legal registration as an independent faith community:

> A group with affiliation to the Army alone. A group who considered the Army as their church, but had kept their membership of the Norwegian Church or other churches because there were no other alternatives to choose. A group who, for faith reasons, considered it problematic to continue to belong to the church to which they formally belonged.[9]

The main reasons were internal and based on the needs of different groups of soldiers and officers. Because of the appeal from a group of officers during the congress of 1992 the Leadership Conference in September 1992 decided on the basis of the meeting that "the question concerning registration of Frelsesarmeen as an independent faith community should be examined and a status report for the Leadership conference in 1993 be presented. A final processing ought to happen in 1994 at the latest."[10] The letters to the members asking them to be part of the commission were sent out

---

8. From 1 January 1996 all international Salvation Army press releases would be published via the Internet. IHQ was preparing to help Salvation Army territories around the world to be present on the net. An international coordinator was being employed. *Krigsråbet* no. 2 1996, 10.

9. *FA-Kirkeutvalget 1993–96 Rapport*, 5 (The report from Frelsesarmeen's Church Commission).

10. Minutes from the Leadership Conference 8–10 September 1992, 5.

five months later on 16 February 1993, with the date of the first meetings stated. The comparative late start of the commission and the many concrete details needed for this work meant that the results did not come as quickly as the Leadership Conference of 1992 had wanted or anticipated. The mandate given to the commission was to report on the possible registration of Frelsesarmeen as an independent faith community on the basis of which a decision could be made. The work had to build on the 1978 report from Frelsesarmeen's Commission. The research had to be undertaken in such a way that it uncovered as many different views as possible. It was not the task of the committee to take decisions concerning the future status of Frelsesarmeen. Salvation Army doctrines and O&Rs (Orders and Regulations) were not considered part of the work of the commission.

The members of Frelsesarmeen's Church Commission 1993–96 consisted of seven officers and three soldiers/local officers. The secretary, a soldier, together with the chairman brought the number to twelve. The members came from different parts of the country and were a mixture of young and old. The officers represented both corps, social, and administrative work. Even so, Frelsesarmeen's Church Commission signaled a commission closely linked to the administration, especially the fact that only three out of eleven were soldiers/local officers and that the chairman was the appointed CS. It is striking that only three out of ten were women, two officers and one soldier/local officer as the gender balance in leadership positions was improving in these years compared to the situation in 1975. Bernhard Slettholm had been the chairman of Frelsesarmeen's Commission 1975–78. By his membership the link was secured to the former commission. As the mandate included the expectation that the work had to build on the Commission of 1975–78 the choice of Slettholm strengthened this. Frelsesarmeen's Church Commission 1993–96 arranged sixteen meetings. They were spread over a period of three and a half years. During the whole process only one person outside the commission was invited to present a paper, Engulf Diesen from Misjonsforbundet (The Non-Conformist church). He gave an account of the process of registration his church had been through as well as the model for registration the church had chosen. His paper and presentation became influential for the work as well as for the final registration in 2005, because the registration of Misjonsforbundet became the model for the Army's own registration. The greater openness the Army had adopted during the interim years in order to give soldiers and officers a voice in decisions and planning was not emphasized during the process of appointing the members of the commission, but became visible in the way information was given and shared concerning the work of Frelsesarmeen's Church Commission 1993–96. During the three years information was shared through *Krigsropet,* at the yearly congress, and at Leaders Conferences. Added to this was a letter sent to all soldiers with a summary of the work.

The material from Frelsesarmeen's Church Commission 1993–96 consists of minutes from meetings, letters/correspondence, and the final report. From the minutes of the meetings some of the presentations from the members of the commission could look as if they had been mainly verbal. During the first meeting, 17 April 1993, the group went through the report from 1978 and decided which themes it wanted to concentrate on: 1) Frelsesarmeen's relationship to the Norwegian Church and other churches as it was presently and earlier and its participation in inter church councils, 2) A comparison between the faith of the Army and of the Norwegian Church plus an evaluation of the consequences of registering as an independent faith community, 3) Frelsesarmeen's identity and ecclesiology, 4) Preparation of a questionnaire among soldiers and officers with the main question: Do you regard the Army as your church? The themes were taken from the report of 1978, but most of the time was used on the themes of identity and ecclesiology. A central question was whether the situation had changed since 1978. The conclusion to this question was that there had been a development toward a greater sense of independence with less affiliation to the Norwegian Church, especially among the younger generation during these fifteen years. The word church was still difficult because for most Salvationists it was identical with the Norwegian Church. An interesting development was that this group found it foreign to consider the Army a religious order in contrast to Frelsesarmeen's Commission 1975–78, who found that concept relevant for Frelsesarmeen.

The third meeting, 28 of August 1993, was centered upon the presentation of a paper from Engulf Diesen from Misjonsforbundet (The Non-Conformist Church). The impact of this meeting with Ingulf Diesen could be seen in the following meetings as they were now concentrated upon the possible model of registration. Misjonsforbundet's model was evaluated and altered so it later became Frelsesarmeen's model. It was basically a model where the Army continued as an organization, but registered a faith community within its structure. Soldiers and adherents could choose to be members of this faith community and would have to resign their membership of the Norwegian Church or other churches. To be enrolled as a soldier would not automatically mean membership of Frelsesarmeen as a registered faith community. It meant membership of Frelsesarmeen as it had been traditionally. Others could be members of the faith community without being soldiers. The rough draft of what later became the pattern of registration was already present at this third meeting based on the paper from Ingulf Diesen from Misjonsforbundet.

At the very first meeting it had been decided to make a questionnaire for soldiers and officers, but the process of sending out a questionnaire never materialized. The minutes did not reveal why this process never continued, but the final report did. In the final report three reasons for dropping the questionnaire were given: 1) Problems were more complicated in this phase than at the time of Frelsesarmeen's Commission 1975–78, because the choice then was between two simple models. Very early the committee saw the possibility for a third model. It made it difficult to pose clear questions that would not be misunderstood. 2) There was a great confusion among officers and soldiers concerning the question of a faith community. A questionnaire would perhaps give opportunity for more confusion and it would hardly give a statistically valid expression of opinion. 3) When the decision was taken to abolish a questionnaire several people had already given comments to the commission. These reasons given seemed most of all to be rather vague excuses for not pursuing the promised questionnaire and could be interpreted as mistrust in ordinary soldiers' and officers' ability to judge, think, and evaluate the situation. By this decision the commission missed out proper figures and facts. Because it had originally been announced that a questionnaire would come out, Frelsesarmeen's Church Commission 1993–96 had to give reasons for this not happening and it was faced with the problem of giving reason for a decision that was not really based on solid reflection. According to the minutes the focus was centered on investigating the model from Misjonsforbundet, because that would give room for all opinions—people could continue as they had done for years without making any changes, those wanting a membership of a registered faith community could make this choice. The third choice of the Army registering as an independent faith community as such would mean that all soldiers and officers would have to sever their membership of the Norwegian Church and other churches. At least that was how it was perceived and presented.[11] From the minutes it is clear that nobody really believed in this model unless the church and state separated.[12] From the third meeting onwards the focus was on the process of registration as well as the production of a brochure describing three options-Frelsesarmeen remains a Christian organization/movement, Frelsesarmeen becomes a registered faith community—the radical model, the model of Misjonsforbundet.

11. In 2005 Frelsesarmeen registered a faith community. As the Non-Conformist Act of 13 June 1969 did not demand a certain number of members in order to register a faith community it did not matter if a number of soldiers did not pursue a membership with the consequence of severing their bonds to DNK.

12. Minutes from the meeting 21 and 22 January 1994. This argument had been a constant one since Frelsesarmeen's Commission 1975–78 started its work.

Responses from selected officer representatives

The reason for dealing with letters from selected officer representatives was that they represented the input Frelsesarmeen's Church Commission asked for and received. The choice of these particular letters cannot be regarded as representative either for the Army as such or for the officers alone. The focus was on the hierarchy—past and future. All five were officers, two active Major Erling Mæland, corps officer, later CS in Norway and TC in Denmark, and Major Odd Berg, corps officer, later CS in Denmark and Germany, and three retired officers, Commissioner Karsten A. Solhaug, who as TC took the initiative to the Commission in 1975, and also made the final decision not to register, but strengthen Salvation Army identity, Commissioner Haakon Dahlstrøm, who had strong opinions against the Army's membership of the Free Church Council, and Colonel Arne Ødegaard, who had been CS in Finland and Norway. It was a very small group. The majority, the three retired, were long into their retirement. All five chosen were men. Two of the retired officers were Commissioners. There was a lack of women, a lack of young officers and a lack of soldiers and local officers.

In their replies the five not only gave answers to the concrete questions posed, but also made comments on the whole issue of raising the question of registration again and revealed their own attitude to this new process. The questions from Frelsesarmeen's Church Commission[13] were:

1. In your opinion, how is Frelsesarmeen's relationship to the Norwegian Church today and how was it before?

2. How do you consider Frelsesarmeen's relationship to other faith communities?

3. Do you have any idea why Frelsesarmeen did not register as a faith community when it began in Norway?

As an introduction to Solhaug's four-page long letter[14] he expressed that he considered the three questions irrelevant, but gave short answers to each. In the main part of the letter he posed five other questions which he considered relevant for the process. His answer to the first and second questions were the same:

> "Varied after many years of talks in Forum for Theological Dialogue". The answer to the third question was: "It was based on two conditions—the ecclesial structure in Norway—The

---

13. Letter to five selected officers 15 July 1993 from Tone Gjeruldsen.
14. Letter from Solhaug 14 August 1993.

founder's and first Salvationists' self-understanding concerning their own mission and that of the Army."

These answers didn't provide much input to the working group's research, but the questions he phrased and answered were of interest. They expressed his personal views. Solhaug's viewpoint concerning the right time for registration have been expressed throughout the process by different people showing that his influence was still present. His questions were:

1. Do we have a problem of identity (that could be solved by a registration)?
2. Do we have a problem of authority (that could be solved by a registration)?
3. Do we have a problem with recruiting (that could be solved by a registration)?
4. Do we have a theological problem (that could be solved by a registration)?
5. Do we have a financial problem (that could be solved by a registration)?

His answer to the first was that Frelsesarmeen had become a church whether it had wanted it or not, and it functioned in that way for its members. Solhaug commented that registration neither created a church nor gave it theological substance. The other point he made was that the Army had a strong identity in its doctrines and structures. His conclusion was that Frelsesarmeen's identity and characteristics would not be strengthened by registration, rather the reverse. The Army had no need for it. To his second question he answered, that if any officer or soldier thought that registration would give greater authority they were mistaken. The authority of officers was based on personal qualities and education, plus the position and authority Frelsesarmeen gave to the officer. He neglected the importance of legal matters in both answers. The position and authority Frelsesarmeen gave its officers was important within the Army, but outside the Army legal registration could very well strengthen the officers' authority as ministers. The answer to the third question would be based on belief, therefore he would not give any judgment on the recruitment of new people. What he would make a judgment on was the size of Frelsesarmeen as a registered faith community. It would be small as only those who resigned their membership of the Norwegian Church could be members. The Army would lose a lot of its influence. When the questionnaire was sent out concerning registration, the assumption was that the Norwegian Church would become a free folk church in a near future. From the outside it seemed as if at the moment this was laid on ice. But as he repeatedly had said, the right timing for Frelsesarmeen to register as a faith community would be when great and radical changes happened with the Norwegian Church. At such a stage

Frelsesarmeen had to consider how Salvationists should resign their membership of the Norwegian Church, because it would not be self-evident for Salvationists to stay as members of a free folk church. A sort of collective resignation ought to be possible at the point of a change in the status of the church. He knew that the present law demanded individual resignation, but foresaw this would lack general support. Solhaug had kept his conviction that the Army's registration was connected to the possible separation between state and church all through the years. The idea that Frelsesarmeen had to register in connection with a separation between church and state could be seen as an expression of Solhaug's image of the Norwegian Church as a civil religion. This was a focal point in his letter. He considered Frelsesarmeen as a church and registration as such of no importance for its identity, theology, and organization as long as the State Church existed. He did not take into account the wish of those with no affiliation to the Norwegian Church to belong to a registered faith community. His idea of a collective resignation of Frelsesarmeen from the Norwegian Church was surprisingly naïve for a man of his experience. He had an idea of the Army as an organization that would be favored with special arrangements. His reply to the fourth question was short. If anyone thought that we had one or more theological problems they would not be diminished by registration, but rather get more complicated. Personally he could not see that the Army had such problems, but it was a field that had to be given great interest at any time. That had been the case with the Army internationally as could be seen in the continuing work with doctrine books.[15] He did not specify which theological problems he had in mind that could be more complicated by registration, but it might have been in the area of the sacraments. The last reply concerned finance. He didn't consider the financial subsidies from state and borough to be enough to solve possible economic problems. The sums would not be great.[16] It would be fairly easy to make the calculation. The consequence could also be a diminishing interest from the public to support Frelsesarmeen. In the conclusion he underlined the need for a constant focus on Frelsesarmeen's status, looking from time to time into the question of registration, but as the situation was at the moment it would be the wrong timing. The challenges for the Army were in other areas. The timing for registration would be crucial and had to be chosen with greatest care. It would be better if at the moment Frelsesarmeen maintained its

15. The International Doctrine Council who wrote *Salvation Story* had been established in 1992. *Salvation Story* was published in 1998.

16. This calculation must be based on his anticipation that only few would register and not his idea of collective resignation of the Norwegian Church in order for all to be registered.

role as bridge builder and ecumenical pioneer movement. Solhaug gave the Church Commission substantial input, but the minutes did not reveal a proper discussion. At the second meeting the report from these letters of reply was verbal, at the third meeting a written report and the letters of reply were given to the other members, at the fourth meeting the letters were discussed, but from the minutes none of Solhaug's points were mentioned or the fact that he had phrased alternative questions.

The letter of reply[17] from Haakon Dahlstrøm was four pages long as well, but the actual arguments were covered by three pages. He did not answer any of the questions, but expressed his strong resistance against any changes in registration. His language was very picturesque and emotional. He believed in one church—those who confess Christ as Lord, Savior, and Son of God. His belief in the one church in accordance with the Apostles Creed was his main argument in 1988, when he opposed Frelsesarmeen's membership of the Free Church Council. Here he stressed that the State Church had a thousand-year-old history, and that it had been the backbone and strength of the people through difficult times. He didn't agree with all it postulated, but wanted to remain in the State Church because of its historic character and its significance for the people and country through countless generations, because he confessed himself as Christian, and because he wanted Norway to remain a Christian nation. He considered the Army as God's Army, not a church. Apparently in his thinking this was the only Army God had, while he had many faith communities. He kept warning against driving the Army in reverse gear. He even called the ones working on the issue iconoclasts. He had no sympathy whatsoever for a registration of Frelsesarmeen as an independent faith community. He had his firm conviction of the status and importance of the Norwegian Church as well as that of the Army. Dahlstrøm's attitude was different from Solhaug's. His resistance was based on his belief in the unity of the universal church and in the Norwegian Church as an expression of the holy catholic church, in Norway the true one. Its historic position was of importance to him as well as the influence on the people it had, and the fact that it stood as a symbol of Norway as a Christian nation. His attitude can be seen as a different expression of civil religion than Solhaug's. It posed no problem for him that he didn't agree in the theology of the State Church. His appreciation of its historic role might very well have been shared with a number of other Salvationists. The fact that he did not agree with all its "claims," which could be interpreted as doctrines/theology, might not be very much different from the attitudes of other Salvationists. In these areas mentioned he might have represented a larger group of Salvationists.

17. Letter from Haakon Dahlstrøm 27 July 1993.

The reason for this special focus on Solhaug and Dahlstrøm is that both of them still had influence. They were considered the grand old men of Frelsesarmeen, Dahlstrøm was eight-seven at the time and Solhaug seventy-nine. Their arguments and attitudes were different. Solhaug was concerned about the *Kairos* of the whole process, but convinced that the Army should register if a separation between state and church became a reality. For him the Army was a church and functioned as such while the Norwegian Church was the general religious institution of the state, perhaps an expression of civil religion. Dahlstrøm had a national, romantic attitude to the church. For him it was the Church for Norway, even though he did not agree in all its beliefs. Both of them were concerned that a situation that functioned in the country should not be disrupted. Neither of them wanted the Army to cause any harm to the Norwegian Church or to take any steps that would weaken the Army. They represented two different attitudes which might have been representative for the Norwegian Salvationists. One attitude was to consider separation between church and state determinative for Frelsesarmeen to register. Because of this a question could be if the concept of civil religion in relation to the Norwegian Church was implicitly present. The other was based on a belief that the Norwegian Church as a state church was the only one expression of the Church according to the Apostles Creed. To support the unity of the universal church was a Christian duty. A concept of civil religion could also be implicitly present in this attitude.

The three remaining letters of reply actually answered the questions posed by the Church Commission. Ødegaard[18] looked at the changes from the time of pioneering to the present day concerning the relationship between the Army and the Norwegian Church from opposition to co-operation and goodwill. He mentioned personal experiences of co-operation. He recalled the fact that the pioneering officers did not baptize their children, but that it was never demanded that soldiers should sever their bonds to the Norwegian Church. He underlined that most Salvationists only had a nominal membership of the church with no real connection to the church. His arguments could be seen as a support to Solhaug. Odd Berg[19] also recalled history, but settled with what he considered the one key question—the sacraments. He stated that Salvationists agreed with the Army's teaching on the sacraments in spite of a tradition of having the children baptized. He referred to that tradition and especially the intention not to break a family tradition. Concerning the Lord's Supper, he saw a change from older times, where Salvationists would attend services in the Norwe-

---

18. Letter of reply Oslo 22 July 1993.
19. Letter of reply 25 August 1993.

gian Church for communion on special occasions to the present where this would seldom happen. Salvationists considered communion a place where to receive blessing and strength to their service, but as they considered the mercy seat to have the same function the use of communion was rare. The Army's introduction of confirmation had weakened the bonds to the Norwegian Church. The wedding ceremony was still a bond to the church, as Frelsesarmeen did not have the right to perform legal weddings. As committal services were now conducted by the Army, another bond to the church had been weakened. From his letter he seemingly had no personal bonds to the Norwegian Church. Mæland[20] underlined that there had never been any organizational relationship between the Norwegian Church and Frelsesarmeen, but referred to the church's central and dominant role for the Norwegian people. As the Norwegian Church was losing its dominant place among people, it seemed even stranger for Salvationists who in reality considered the Army as their church to seek another church for the great celebrations of life. The Army had started to move in the direction of celebrating the great ceremonies, such as confirmation, weddings, and funerals within its own corps. The natural and traditional bonds to the Norwegian Church were getting weaker, apart from the more nostalgic feelings for the old historic buildings, the sound of the organ as a special frame round family celebrations. Both Berg and Mæland mentioned the fine relationship to other churches. Mæland concluded his letter with his personal views even though they had not been part of the questions. He hoped that the Army had the courage to move to registration as an independent faith community for those who wanted that. The other point was, that he found it difficult to comprehend that the commission should not be allowed to look into the sacraments, because the real issue was hidden there. Even though Salvationists accepted that the spiritual blessing the sacraments represented could be received without visible ceremonies and acts, the Army also taught that outward signs could facilitate an inward spiritual experience. With his knowledge of the grass roots he claimed that many Salvationists in the country would have great difficulties in belonging to a faith community without the sacraments. To refer the question of the sacraments to international decisions, Norwegian Salvationists had no say in what would not satisfy people. By this he took up the subtle conflict between the international and the national attitude towards an observance of the sacraments that had never been expressed. The decisions concerning translations of the 1901 and 1930 Doctrine books revealed that there were conflicting views in this area. Both Berg and Mæland referred to the sacraments.

20. Letter of reply, Stavanger 6 August 1993.

The minutes of the October meetings of the Church Commission[21] revealed that the commission mentioned the sacraments in connection with these letters, but not what they discussed. At the following January meeting[22] the minutes mentioned that different views on the sacraments could be seen among the soldiers, but that the Army's stance towards the sacraments did not pose any difficulties. Later the minutes[23] stated that the commission anticipated a discussion concerning the sacraments at gatherings in different corps in connection with the questions of the brochure. Even though these sentences looked like disconnected opinions it was obvious that a discussion concerning the sacraments took place. In the October meetings of the following year,[24] when the replies from the corps had been received, it was clear that the question of the sacraments in connection with a formation of Frelsesarmeen's faith community was a key issue. Even though this question was outside the mandate given, the commission considered it necessary to work with it because of the answers from different corps. Mæland had been proved right when he pinpointed the question of the sacraments as the real issue at stake.

The letter from Frelsesarmeen's Church Commission did not ask for an opinion on the matter of registration, but nevertheless some of the replies included that. Solhaug and Dahlstrøm disagreed with the matter being dealt with, but for different reasons. Ødegaard answered the questions, but did not give an opinion concerning registration as such, though he underlined that Salvationists' membership of the Norwegian Church was nominal without any real connection to the church. Berg did not express his own view concerning registration, while Mæland welcomed such a step. These letters gave answers to more than had been asked for, and by this gave an idea of the opinion among officers. As nothing seemingly was submitted from younger people,[25] the input was very restricted. However, some letters had been received by the leadership after the announcement of Frelsesarmeen's Church Commission in *Krigsropet*.[26]

---

21. Minutes of 29 and 30 October 1993.

22. Minutes of 21 and 22 January 1994.

23. The minutes from all the meetings were points made during the meeting. In between they looked like a kaleidoscope of opinions. A conclusion was not always drawn.

24. Minutes of 28 and 29 October 1994.

25. In the minutes of 29 and 30 October 1993 it was stated that questions and replies from younger people would be presented. I have not found any indication of such material in the following minutes or in the files.

26. *Krigsropet* no. 24 1993.

Letters to the leadership concerning registration

The announcement in *Krigsropet* provided an impetus for some to express their personal opinion on the matter of registration. The first letter[27] was from a lady in the Norwegian Mission Society who was a reader of *Krigsropet* and who supported the Army with donations and old clothes as often as possible. Her point was that Frelsesarmeen was considered to belong to everybody and many members of the Norwegian Church were used to supporting the work financially. She was worried that the donations for the Army would stop if it registered as an independent faith community, and wanted to share that worry. The worry about diminishing financial support was the same as Solhaug had. Hers was a voice from the general public and important in that capacity, but the only one found in the archives. This issue never came on the agenda. The second letter[28] was from Tor Martin Ødegaard, a soldier and bandsman from the Temple corps in Oslo. He had been a member of Frelsesarmeen's Commission 1975-78. He protested against taking the issue of registration up again as there were no valid reasons for this. At the time of Frelsesarmeen's Commission 1975-78 the situation of a possible separation between state and church was central, but that was not the case at the moment. The reasons for considering the issue again were too thin. The fact that some officers, who had no other affiliation than the Army, wanted this looked into was not a valid reason. The Army should use its time in working on future strategy and corps development. It should put the other issue aside. His main point followed the theme of timing which Solhaug had also underlined. The attitude towards the officers who wanted registration was similar to Solhaug's. Their reasons were dismissed as not valid. The third letter[29] was from a young soldier. He welcomed the initiative of looking into the matter of registration. He looked forward to the possibility of the soldiers having a say in the decision.[30] The main part of his letter concerned baptism both infant and believers' baptism. He saw it as a key issue that the Army would start baptizing as an independent faith community.[31] He also mentioned communion, but only as a detail that could be taken up as well. He personally wanted to belong to a Frelsesarmeen that

---

27. Oslo 9 June 1993.
28. Jessheim 11 June 1993.
29. Kritiansand 19 June 1993.

30. In the notice in *Krigsropet* no 24 1993 concerning the start of Frelsesarmeen's Church Commission 1993-96 it was mentioned that a questionnaire would be sent out.

31. It is uncertain if he meant infant or believers' baptism. Apparently he had no problem with soldiers who had been baptized as infants, but had a believers' baptism as well. He stated such a situation as an example of the necessity of baptism.

was registered as an independent faith community. The fourth letter[32] was from a young couple who were soldiers. They were happy that the issue was being discussed and strongly supported Frelsesarmeen registering as an independent faith community. They themselves belonged to the Norwegian Church, but their two children were not baptized. They had considered resigning their membership of the church, because they strongly believed that one should only belong to the community that was one's spiritual home. For them this was the Army. They suggested that new soldiers should resign their membership of the Norwegian Church, but the ones who had been soldiers for years should have a choice.

Two of the four letters welcomed both the work of the commission and a registration of Frelsesarmeen as a registered faith community, meaning half of the replies stemming from the information in *Krigsropet*. The input to the work of the commission referred to in the final report had most probably been based on these four letters and the five letters answering the questions of the commission, at least these are the ones found in the archives. They were an important input to the process, but hardly representative for all soldiers and officers. The input was used to give reason for not having a research based on a questionnaire, and in light of that the letters were not representative enough. The brochure, aimed at corps gatherings for discussion and sharing of attitudes towards the mode of registration, was the tool used for giving soldiers and officers a voice in this process.

The process of giving a voice to soldiers and officers

Well over a year after Frelsesarmeen's Church Commission had started its work the brochure was ready to be distributed to all corps. The material was sent to all corps on 15 June 1994. It included a letter of explanation, the brochure, a print of the Non-Conformist Act of 13 June 1969, circular No 686/76 from the Legal Department of Stortinget concerning the Non-Conformist Act, a brochure from Misjonsforbundet concerning their registration. Replies to the questions in the brochure were expected to be returned to the commission before 23 September 94. The letter suggested the process at each corps: 1) The corps officer and all local officers should gather and make themselves familiar with the brochure, the Non-Conformist Act, Frelsesarmeen's Doctrine Book as well as Orders and Regulations for soldiers, *Chosen to be a soldier*.[33] 2) The corps council should discuss the whole issue in August/September. 3) The corps councils should arrange soldiers'

---

32. Tønsberg June 1993.
33. *Chosen to be a soldier* 1977. Norwegian translation *Kalt til soldat* 1992.

meetings where information would be shared. 4) A written response from the corps based on the soldiers' meeting should be returned as well as the minutes from the corps council. The use of soldiers' meetings had the advantage of the matter being debated, a debate that might very well continue in the corps. The disadvantage of such a procedure would be the pressure a few people of strong opinion could put on the group. A combination of a soldiers' meeting and a chance for giving a personal answer would have given more secure feedback.

The brochure itself gave information about the mandate of Frelsesarmeen's Church Commission 1993–96 and the reason for forming the commission. Three options were given and explained:

> Frelsesarmeen remains a Christian organization/movement. Frelsesarmeen becomes a registered faith community—the radical model. The model of Misjonsforbundet.

The brochure explained under 1) that the Army in Norway and Finland was in a special situation because it was an organization and not a registered faith community. William Booth's original idea was not to create a new church, but in most countries the Army had become an independent church. The consequences of this first option would be that Frelsesarmeen continued to function as a spiritual home for all Salvationists independent of their formal church adherence. Frelsesarmeen continued to function as an inclusive organization and a bridge builder between many faith communities. A number of Salvationists would still regret that Frelsesarmeen did not offer a formal church adherence. Under 2) it explained that this model was examined by Frelsesarmeen's Commission 1975–78, because at that time it looked as if a separation between church and state would become a reality. Such a model would mean that from a certain date Frelsesarmeen would be an independent faith community. The consequences would be that Frelsesarmeen could offer church membership to those who wanted this. Salvationists would have to resign their membership of the church they formally belonged to. Such a situation could create unrest among some Salvationists, and some could feel forced to make a choice they did not want to make. Salvationists would be more conscious about the Army's faith. Frelsesarmeen could choose another variation of this model which would mean, that all new officers and soldiers from a certain date would be registered in the faith community, Frelsesarmeen. An offer of registration would be given to all other Salvationists. The explanation under 3) was that this model was used by Det Norske Misjonsforbundet. The situation in Misjonsforbundet was that about half the members were registered in the faith community and the other half in other churches. By choosing such a model

Frelsesarmeen would register a faith community within its organization, which would give legal church membership to those who wanted this. Others could continue with the formal church membership, they already had to other churches. This would rest on a voluntary basis and Frelsesarmeen would still function as an organization for all its members. Salvationists would be more conscious about the Army's faith. For some this would be perceived as a halfhearted solution. The task was to make a choice between these three options. 45 out of 120 corps answered the questions of which model they would choose. 24 corps wanted model 1: that things stayed as they were now. Only a couple of corps could support model 2: the radical model. 21 corps supported model 3, and 33 of the 45 could accept model 3.

After the responses from the different corps had been received, Frelsesarmeen's Church Commission 1993–96 published findings that included the choice of each corps, the number of soldiers who expressed that they would register in a Frelsesarmeen faith community, general comments, plus comments on the sacraments. There had not been any questions concerning the sacraments, but 24 corps had brought that question up. The general comments concentrated on too little information given, the short time limit for giving response, the fear of division within the Army and of soldiers being divided into A and B groups according to who registered and who didn't, and a fear that the prospect of financial support from registration would add pressure on soldiers to register in the faith community. 24 corps wanted the question of the sacraments to be dealt with, including the need of more teaching, for some corps that included the possibility of observing the sacraments within the Army. Not even half of the corps gave answers to the brochure. It could mean that the interest in the whole process was not overwhelming, at least not among the officers. In a process such as this the corps officer was the one to take the initiative. Some corps had distributed the brochure by post, at least there is one letter of response directed to the TC from a soldier living in the country side who had received it by post. The corps he belonged to explained in its letter that all soldiers had received the brochure by post. In the material from Frelsesarmeen's Church Commission, only seven letters of reply from corps have been kept.[34] According to these letters the place for discussion was in the corps councils and at soldiers' meetings.[35] The letter of reply mentioned from the soldier who had

---

34. It is clear from the material in the files of Frelsesarmeen's Church Commission that proper filing was not attended to, therefore only random letters have survived.

35. The corps which had posted the brochures did not reply until the end of November. They wanted more time and used the time for two separate soldiers' meetings during two months' time so people had time for debate and reflection. They also had invited two of the members from the commission to the last meeting to get more

received it by post is of interest. Apparently he had been in the Army since childhood and during the years had been a local officer in different positions. He had also been active in politics for fifty years and been elected to different honorary offices. His conclusion was to keep number 1. He had the impression that it was pressure from abroad that had started the process, and such should not be the case. The comment on a possible pressure from abroad is interesting. It is the only such comment, but the feeling of international pressure might have been more widespread, as Mæland suggested in connection with the sacraments. If that had been the case it would support the majority's choice of model 1 signaling that no interference into the Norwegian situation was welcome. The last letter in the archive to the TC was from a soldier in an Oslo corps complaining about the short time limit for this process, and that the case of registration had never been an issue among the soldiers. One of the responses in his corps had been: "Haven't we been a faith community all along?" He called for more and better information. He also commented the way Misjonsforbund's model was used, stating that this model included much more; for example on administration of the sacraments—infant, believer's baptism, as well as communion. If the model was used, all it included had to be stated. The comments from different corps and these individual responses were important. The one concerning the short time limit was an issue that might have had great influence. Both the short time span and the timing at all, being during the holiday months, might have influenced the number of corps that responded, and perhaps also the number of soldiers present at the soldiers' meetings. The result with the majority being able to support model 3 would most probably not have been different, but it could have raised the consciousness among the soldiers to a greater extent. The limited information could have connection to the time limit, as time did not allow for the possibility of seeking more information or posing questions to the commission. The fears expressed were basically fears of destabilization. Most corps wanted things to continue as they were, and so such fears would be natural. Changes could alter a situation that the majority was content with. The comment "haven't we always been a faith community" could indicate that, for ordinary soldiers, there weren't any problems, as the Army was their church—their faith community and why question that. The issue of registration as an independent faith community seemed not to be of importance to the majority of soldiers. The fear of a general division within the corps, or that the soldiers would be divided into an A and B class were issues the later process of registration took

---

informed input to the debate. The majority vote was model no. 3.

into account.[36] This with the fear of financial pressure was also addressed at the registration.[37]

All corps received a letter of response late January 1995 with an overview of the results from the questions in the brochure, including some of the matters different corps had raised. This gave all corps an insight into the problem areas being raised and also a clear indication of which model would be pursued.

Comments from corps concerning the sacraments

It can appear surprising that the question of the sacraments came up so strongly from over half of the corps responding. The Salvation Army in England had practiced the sacraments—infant baptism and communion—during its first years, and until 1883, without any strong conviction. When the Army began in Norway the sacraments had not been observed for five years, meaning that there had never been an observance of the sacraments in Frelsesarmeen's history. The unique choices of Frelsesarmeen in contrast to the other Nordic countries concerning translations of different doctrine books have been mentioned. In the 1975 translation of the 1969 Doctrine Book, the appendix on the non-observance of sacraments was included. The question of the sacraments was now coming up eighteen years after this doctrine book had been published, still the need for teaching concerning this issue was evident from the comments. As the doctrine book was mainly used for teaching the cadets preparing to become officers and recruits preparing to become soldiers, this would mean that the older and middle generations had been taught according to previous doctrine books, and might not have had proper teaching concerning non-observance if any at all. The younger generation, the officers who had been ordained since the late seventies and soldiers who had been enrolled after the publication of the new book should have had some insight into the question. It might have taken time before officers started to use the new doctrine book and some might have ignored the appendix when they were teaching recruits, as they had not usually been teaching this part. The effect of the choices made in 1930 was still seen, as this translation was in use until 1975 and perhaps even further. This could explain this focus. The teaching on the basis of the doctrine book was one

36. The members of the faith community were registered in a central register and not in the corps. The corps had the register over soldiers and adherents and members of different groups within the corps as had always been the case.

37. All funding from government and borough went to the central office for the faith community. The finance of the local corps was not affected by the funding.

issue; another was the possibility of administering the sacraments in the corps, if Frelsesarmeen registered as an independent faith community. The two were connected as the last one might rest on ignorance of the Army's position. The wish for such an administration could also be an expression of influence from Lutheran ecclesiology—the church as the place where the gospel is purely preached and the sacraments rightly administered. At least some soldiers/corps considered a registered faith community without the sacraments inconceivable. There might have been a mixture of these two issues. One corps commented on why they chose model 1. They did not want to leave the Norwegian Church, not because they ever attended a service or made use of the sacraments, but because of tradition it was unthinkable to be members of a free church. This statement did not explicitly concern the sacraments, but it could illustrate that it might not so much have been the observance of the sacraments that mattered, but that sacraments had to be administered to be a proper church. That group did not want to leave the Norwegian Church anyhow because of tradition.[38] These attitudes could be similar to Dahlstrøm's, at least the focus on tradition and that it was unthinkable to be members of a free church. They did not state why this was the case, but implicitly some of Dahlstrøm's arguments might have been present.

In the final report, extracts from the answers of nineteen corps were printed. Some of these commented on the sacraments. One corps stated that several people had said, that the sacraments were so important that they took priority over membership of a Frelsesarmeen faith community. Another remarked that the question of the sacraments had to be clarified if Frelsesarmeen was to register as an independent faith community. The importance of teaching the Army's position was underlined by yet another corps, because it was disheartening that people should experience themselves as inferior in this matter. The last comment was that a number of soldiers could not conceive that the Army should remain without the sacraments and that they wanted baptism and communion in a registered faith community. As mentioned earlier, Erling Mæland in his letter of response to the questions given mentioned the sacraments as a key question. With his knowledge of the grass roots he had claimed that many Salvationists in the country would have great difficulties in belonging to a faith community without the sacraments. By the comments coming in from the corps he was proved right. Odd Berg also took up what he considered the one key question—the sacraments. He stated that Salvationists agreed with the Army's teaching on the sacraments in spite of the tradition

38. The findings from the questionnaire of Frelsesarmeen's Commission 1975–78 showed the percentage of attendance in the Norwegian Church and participation in communion. The practice was there, but seldom.

of having their children baptized. The comments on not observing the sacraments in the Norwegian Church in the letter supports his claim that attending communion would be seldom. He implied that people had actually received teaching concerning the sacraments, which of course must have been the case for many Salvationists, but from the comments, teaching had been lacking in several places for a number of Salvationists. Frelsesarmeen's Church Commission commented on the responses concerning the sacraments and pointed to this as a key question in connection with registration as a faith community. This question was outside the mandate given to the commission, but because of the response it had to be addressed.[39] The commission concluded the meeting by asking the leadership to bring this to the International Doctrine Council at IHQ.[40] The minutes did not state exactly what they wanted to bring up internationally. As there were a number of books published concerning the Army's position and at least two of these[41] translated into Norwegian they could hardly get more information from the council. If the request was that Frelsesarmeen would like the sacraments to be reintroduced in Frelsesarmeen, the question would have to be dealt with internally in Norway before such a request was sent to the General. The decision in the minutes to ask for this to be brought to the International Doctrine Council could reflect an uncertainty about what to do. What they did was to include a smaller paragraph on the reasons for the Army's non-observance in the final report.

From January 1995, after having evaluated all responses from the questions in the brochure, the focus was on the model from Misjonsforbundet. Ingulf Diesen from Misjonsforbundet was consulted and material such as schemes and correspondence covering legal procedures were given to the commission. During all four sessions in 1995, discussion and clarification was sought concerning different issues such as structures, rules of membership, boards, etc. Different legal matters were clarified as well. In 1996 the five meetings concentrated on the task of finalizing the commission's report. All members were writing and summarizing previous material or results from the research done. At the final meeting of the Church Commission on 26 August 1996 the draft was ready to be handed over for printing.

---

39. Minutes from 28–29 October 1994.

40. I was a member of the International Doctrine Council from 1992–2004 and cannot recall any letters from Norway concerning this. The minutes from the Doctrine Council's meetings in 1995:6–8 March, 26–28 June, 16–18 October do not have this on the agenda. It might not have been passed on to the Doctrine Council from the General's office had it been there. It has not been possible to trace such a letter from the TC in Norway to IHQ in the Leadership files nor a reply. Most probably it was never sent.

41. The General, *The Sacraments*, and Metcalf, *The Salvationist and the Sacraments*.

Frelsesarmeen's Church Commission's final report

The final report was published and distributed to soldiers all over the country as a little booklet of sixty-eight pages. It gave a wide scope of information as can be illustrated by the following: twelve pages concerned the background for the commission, the mandate, the chosen method of work, the way of giving information to the Army at large during these three years, the reasons for canceling the promised questionnaire, and the results of the questions from the brochure. Fifteen pages explained Salvation Army doctrines including the sacraments, ecclesiology, identity, and relationship to the Norwegian Church and other faith communities. Six pages explained the suggested model of registration and its implications, plus a short exposition of the legal base for registration. The last five pages contained Frelsesarmeen's Church Commission's conclusion and recommendations. At the end of the report twenty-five pages of appendices[42] were enclosed. By covering these issues, Salvationists had an opportunity to take informed decisions whenever registration would take place. It also gave a background for further reflection and debate. All practical and legal matters were informative and to the point. In light of some of the responses received, that had revealed a lack of knowledge of Army doctrines, it was appropriate to include a chapter on the doctrines. The report printed each doctrine supported by different Bible quotations. It was a traditional simple way of explaining doctrines. As there were no comments there would be no interpretation either. Half a page on the sacraments was to the point in light of the limited space. The Norwegian situation was mentioned and it was underlined that the Army did not reject the sacraments, but believed that Christ bestowed upon his people all sorts of spiritual blessings also without use of visible means. No sacraments could lead people into the kingdom of God, but faith alone. Neither doctrines nor sacraments were included in the mandate of the Church Commission, but this was important to mention in light of the comments they had received. The chapter on Frelsesarmeen's identity and ecclesiology exhibited some of the confusion already implied in the report from Frelsesarmeen's Commission 1975–78. A number of the small paragraphs had disconnected statements, as the writers of the church com-

42. 1) A summary of the paper from Ingulf Diesen, *"Frelsesarmeen as a registered faith community,"* 2) Summary of letters from officers, soldiers, and others, 3) A print of the brochure, 4) The letter sent with the brochure and a print of a status report from Frelsesarmeen's Church Commission, 5) Facsimiles of the feedback from 19 corps, 6) Prints of information given in *Krigsropet*, 7) A summary of the paragraphs of the Non-Conformist Act of 13 June 1969 no. 25, 8) An overview of all liaison committees the Army was represented in, 9) Suggestions for revised instructions concerning adherents in Frelsesarmeen.

mission's report took different statements from the 1978 report and added them together with no regard for the explanations given. This ended up in paragraphs making no sense. It appeared as if the commission took words and concepts as mantras without knowing the meaning of them. All this illustrated that teaching on Army theology and history had not been at the top of Frelsesarmeen's agenda for some time. The mistakes from the report of Frelsesarmeen's Commission 1975–78 were highlighted as they stood as statements disconnected to each other. Part II of the article concerning identity and ecclesiology was a review of changes that had happened since 1978. Of interest was the claim that Frelsesarmeen had moved towards greater independence as a church. The introduction of confirmation, the Army having its own funerals as well as initiating a membership of adherence, and Frelsesarmeen gaining full membership of the Free Church Council and the Christian Council of Norway; all these new initiatives were reasons for the change. It stated that Frelsesarmeen was now considered church to a greater degree for a number of families and individuals. The dedication ceremony was also used by people who were not soldiers. It mentioned that a statement such as "Frelsesarmeen—my church" was unproblematic, in contrast to 1978 where such a statement was unthinkable. The development of the years in between the two commissions was recognized, and by this the implementations of the recommendations from Frelsesarmeen's Commission 1975–78. The weakness of this paragraph was that no statistics supported the claims. The article also included a part III which had short paragraphs evaluating Frelsesarmeen's present identity and ecclesiology by looking at three different designations, such as an interchurch salvation movement, a church, or an organization. When dealing with the first one, the report repeated the claim that William Booth envisioned the Army as a salvation movement for many churches. Recruitment for the movement was unimportant, only that people got saved. This was against historical evidence as recruitment had been very important, as can be seen in the Army's great interest and use of statistics. The report used this as a contrast to the present time where the Army wanted to recruit and teach new Christians. Concerning church it was mentioned that many had difficulties with this designation as it was identical with the Norwegian Church for them. The comment for organization was that by using this designation Frelsesarmeen had avoided taking the consequences of its own theology. It had weakened the development of its own identity. It concluded this small chapter with evaluating the question whether Frelsesarmeen as a revival movement would be weakened by being registered as an independent faith community. The answer was that they did not exclude each other as examples from the Army abroad would illustrate. This short chapter showed a critical distance developing from seeing the Army as an organization, a designation that was commonly used and accepted as the right description of the Army.

The chapter on Salvationist's relationship to Frelsesarmeen and the Norwegian Church was of interest. Even though it did not build on a questionnaire, but on what the commission assumed was the case, the claims in the small paragraphs at least gave an indication of the diversity of the situation. The first statement was that a number of soldiers had theological reasons for not belonging to the Norwegian Church because of profound differences between the teaching of the Army and the church. They wanted to belong to a faith community based on Salvation Army teaching. The second claim was that the majority of active soldiers lived their worship life within Frelsesarmeen. They would only attend the church on special occasions and seldom or never participate in communion. For these Frelsesarmeen was their church. The impression was that a growing number of families abstained from having their children baptized. Others had come from new faith communities and wanted to belong to an established faith community like the Army. They had already severed their bonds to the Norwegian Church or other churches. At vacant corps and outposts, a number of soldiers had strong affiliation to the Norwegian Church, for others the affiliation to the Army was as important and strong in spite of difficulties of practicing active soldiership, because of the sparse program available; for these membership of a Frelsesarmeen registered faith community would strengthen their affiliation to the Army. There were soldiers who found it of great importance to belong to the Norwegian Church, as they felt secure in having a membership there and could not imagine it otherwise. Soldiers in the countryside generally had a stronger connection to the church than in the bigger cities. Some regarded Frelsesarmeen as an organization within the Norwegian Church like other Lutheran organizations. There were soldiers for whom the sacraments were important and who were conscious in their choice. Others were bound to the traditions of the church for family reasons and customs. In many cases the Norwegian Church wanted Salvationists in vestries and church positions. Finally, there were soldiers belonging to other churches than the Norwegian Church and who wanted to keep their membership. The last segment mentioned was those who were ignorant about the teaching of the Army as well as of the church. They adhered to the Army because of the fellowship, while questions of doctrines and faith were of less importance. The report stated that lack of proper teaching in preparation for soldiership for some could result in a weaker Army identity. This was quite a variety of attitudes. The first three to four would most probably support registration, while the next ones were bound to the Norwegian Church for different reasons. One group was bound to other churches, while the last group would be able to adhere anywhere depending on the quality of the fellowship. The fact that some have regarded Frelsesarmeen as an organization within the Norwegian Church has seldom been spoken of. It has been a somewhat common attitude within the Norwegian Church to regard Frelsesarmeen in this way, but seldom from within the Army itself. As there were no percentages indicating what could be majority, minority, or tiny minority, it did not clarify the situation apart from expressing the diversity.

In the same chapter two more questions were dealt with: "Does Frelsesarmeen have what is needed to be a church?" and "Does Frelsesarmeen function as a church already?" The answer to the first was a list of seven statements where the verbs were of importance. The verbs used were in the first person plural "we are" (used only once) the other six were "we have." This was a natural outcome of questions that focused on what the Army had, but still function was more important than being. By using first person plural the fellowship aspect came to the forefront. This "we" coming up was the strongest evidence of a church identity. The statements were: "We are a part of Christendom. We have a theology and a creed. We have a purpose. We have a worshipping fellowship. We have a priesthood. We have an organization that functions."[43] This reflected a visible church and not the invisible one the report had earlier claimed that the Army only related to. The answer to the second question continued with first person plural that "we are" church, mostly for the active. The challenge of the elderly, those passive and those at the outposts was not always met. The responsibility of these groups had to be a more conscious effort on the side of Frelsesarmeen. These answers expressed a church identity that at least the members of the commission gave voice to. The last paragraph in the chapter did not have a question as a heading just "The officers as ministers." It stated that both officers and soldiers experienced the officer role in different ways, but did not explain how. It also stated that many officers gave conflicting signals concerning their own identity. When they compared themselves to officers in other countries, as for instance England, they felt inferior to them. The conclusion was to work towards raising the status of officers. If Frelsesarmeen registered as an independent faith community, this would strengthen the officers' status and identity as ministers. This must have been an important issue in informal debates as Solhaug took this issue up in his answers to his own questions. His attitude was that the authority of officers was based on personal qualities and education, plus the position and authority Frelsesarmeen gave to the officer. From his viewpoint the hope of change in status by registration was not liable to be fulfilled. In a way he dismissed the sugges-

---

43. FA-Kirkeutvalget (*Frelsesarmeen's Church Commmission*) 1993–96 Rapport, 27.

tion that the problem of identity as well as inferiority could be linked to the lack of clear registration as a denomination. On the other side a number of officers in the commission must have considered this as the main reason for lack of clear identity.

The issues of attitudes, identity, and debate in the report have been in focus because these partly could provide an answer to the question of why Frelsesarmeen registered as a faith community. The details the report described concerning a possible model of registration will be dealt with in the chapter on the actual model of registration Frelsesarmeen chosen in 2005. It was the model described in this report. These chapters were most helpful in giving Salvationists proper information of the legal as well as the practical aspects of registration. The conclusion of the report stated that Frelsesarmeen could begin the process towards registration as an independent faith community as a unit within the organization. It would be registered centrally in Oslo as one congregation for the whole country. The congregation would have a number of ministers with license to conduct marriages. All business would be administered centrally. Frelsesarmeen's Church Commission 1993-96 unanimously agreed that the model from Misjonsforbundet was the best, as it opened up membership for soldiers, officers, adherents, members of Army groups and others who wanted Frelsesarmeen as their church. Long term it would strengthen Frelsesarmeen, because those who needed a church membership would be offered this within Frelsesarmeen, Salvationist identity could be strengthened, more people would get a greater insight into Army doctrines, and the status of Frelsesarmeen would be consolidated by gaining new rights as for instance the right to perform marriages. The commission believed that Frelsesarmeen would get a better future by registering a Frelsesarmeen's Faith Community. On the basis of this conclusion the church commission gave the following recommendation and presented it at the Leaders conference at Jeløy, Frelsesarmeen's Conference Center:[44]

> "Frelsesarmeen should remain a Christian organization. It should safeguard and further the heritage of Salvationism that was rooted in William Booth's call to serve his age. It should turn towards the 21st Century by listening to the needs of the present age and arrange its organization and structure, its work methods and its congregation building in such a way, that people could get their spiritual and religious needs covered within Frelsesarmeen. In a secularized and rootless society Frelsesarmeen should help create stability and belonging. Nobody that had or wanted Frelsesarmeen as their spiritual home should

44. Minutes from the Leaders' Conference 10-12 September 1996 item 6.

need to turn to other faith communities in order to get a legal church membership. Frelsesarmeen's Church Commission recommended unanimously that Frelsesarmeen's leadership register a Frelsesarmeen's faith community after the described model."[45]

It was signed by all the members at Jeløy 11 September 1996. It looked like a mixture of a vision and a recommendation. The recommendation from the 1978 report was more concrete. It did not recommend any registration but recommended an active effort in strengthening Frelsesarmeen identity by a wider scope of teaching and by introducing confirmation. There were no concrete suggestions in this 1996 report, but a clear aim of accommodating so nobody needed to seek other church affiliations than the Army's, plus a recommendation of registering a faith community within the Army. The following day the Leaders' Conference signed a statement also unanimous:

> "The Leaders' Conference is positive towards the recommendation of Frelsesarmeen's Church Commission and recommends further work towards establishing Frelsesarmeen's Faith Community according to the Frelsesarmeen Model.
> We assume that Frelsesarmeen continues with the present form of organization under one leadership and that the faith community will be established with the purpose of complying with those who need such a legal church adherence."

This statement was not as clear as it might look. It did not state an agreement with the recommendation of Frelsesarmeen's Church Commission, only that the leaders were positive towards it and would recommend further work. A statement of agreement that defined a time schedule for the process of registration to begin was lacking. Much legal work had already been done as for instance meeting[46] with the County Governor for Oslo and Akershus in order to clarify different questions, such as the possibility of registering one congregation covering all of Norway, the number of ministers that could be accepted, the procedures in order to gain the right to perform weddings, administration, economy, registration of members, etc. Legal advice had been sought and the model from Misjonsforbundet had been scrutinized. The commission had even made an organizational chart of Frelsesarmeen's Faith Community as well as an organizational chart of THQ illustrating how the faith community would fit into this. There would naturally be more work to be done both internally in Norway as well as in

---

45. *FA-Kirkeutvalget Rapport*, 41–42.
46. Minutes from meeting with the County Governor, 15 March 1996.

co-operation with the legal office at IHQ in London and the General. The recommendation of further work was followed so the process continued with another little committee, seeking legal advice and working with a constitution the following years, but it was a slow process that didn't appear high on the agenda of the leadership. The second part of the statement seemingly lacked enthusiasm for the prospect of registration as a faith community. The Army was staying as it was for now and the reason for a faith community was to accommodate a specific group. From the response to the brochure and from the letters coming in this group could look like a minority. Seemingly it was not a central issue for the Army at large, but a willingness to accommodate a minority wish. The TC, Commissioner Edward Hannevik, stayed until January 2000, so it was surprising that the registration did not happen within these well over three years under the same leadership.

The recommendation from Frelsesarmeen's Church Commission and the statement from the Leaders' conference came out as a press release 2 October 1996. The outcome was small articles in papers all over the country. They were factual and showed quite an interest in the Army's process in these matters. The first article in the Christian daily paper, *Vårt Land* was published 8 October 1996 and was an interview with Commissioner Edward Hannevik with the headline: "Nobody to be commanded into a new faith community," where he gave the reasons for a possible registration of an independent faith community within the organization, Frelsesarmeen, and underlined that it most probably would be a minority who would make use of this offer. It could look as if he wanted to avoid any debate on the issue by these apologetic statements, but if this had been his intention, he did not succeed. This spurred on a debate in *Vårt Land* especially between Tor Martin Ødegaard[47] and Nils Petter Enstad.[48] Ødegaard opened the debate by a feature article[49] protesting against any decision to follow the recommendation of establishing a Frelsesarmeen Trossamfunn. He was answered[50] by Enstad who supported the registration of a faith community. It is clear from the articles that there were two fundamentally different issues at stake in the debate. The first one, expressed by Ødegaard, mainly saw the Army as an organization and therefore structures, hierarchy, and the question of democracy were central. The other, which Enstad gave voice to, saw the Army as a church, registered or not, therefore theology and doctrines were

---

47. Soldier in the Temple corps, Oslo, and member of Frelsesarmeen's Commission 1975–78.
48. A former officer and editor of Army papers, at this time soldier in Askim corps.
49. *Vårt Land* 28 October 1996, 16.
50. Ibid. 4 November 1996, 26.

all important. It gave voice to different attitudes within the Army. The focus on structures did of course not rule out a profession of faith also including Army characteristics, but the Army was seen as an organization and the group Ødegaard represented did not want any changes. For those whom Enstad represented with a stronger interest in theology the structures were important as well, but not a focal point. They wanted registration to support the Army's church identity. The debate lasted more than two months with a smaller number of soldiers and officers joining apart from the two mentioned, but did not have the wished impact on the leadership as the process towards registration continued. Even so it made the leadership careful not to go too fast and alert to the tensions.

Work towards registration 1996–1998

Following the report from Frelsesarmeen's Church Commission a process of clarification took place that lasted two years. Just after the Leaders conference in September 1996 while the debate in the press was going on, a small working group was formed to work on statutes of Frelsesarmeen's Trossamfunn (Salvation Army Faith Community) as well as application-and resignation forms, new rules for adherents and revising the marriage ritual. It was a group of six (the secretary included), of whom two had been members of Frelsesarmeen's Church Commission. The working group had four meetings from November 1996 to March 1997 where they gave the results of the work asked for. The group wrote the drafts of the statutes, the revision of the instruction for adherents, and the marriage ritual ready to be discussed at the DC's conference in January. All this indicated an intention of pursuing registration in the near future. According to the final report from the working group this was planned to be decided at the Leaders' Conference in September 1997.

All matters of registration, including the statutes, would have to go to the General at IHQ for approval. This process of approval was started by the TC, Commissioner Edward Hannevik, with a letter of explanation concerning the Norwegian situation to the General[51] 7 November 1996. In the letter he gave a historical view of the beginning in Norway with a strong Lutheran tradition and a dominant state church. He underlined that the Army never requested that the soldiers should relinquish their membership of the state church. The practice of soldiers having their children christened and confirmed in the church was established, and Salvationists retained a nominal

---

51. General Paul Rader (1994–99) was American, had served in Korea for over twenty years and another ten years in leadership positions in USA.

membership. The two commissions' work was referred to, also the importance of the introduction of confirmation in raising Salvationists' awareness. The present situation with the choice of model 3 "The SA registers a church where those who so desire can apply for membership"[52] indicated a continued strong tradition of belonging to the Norwegian Church. The 1996 Leaders conference decided to follow the recommendation of Frelsesarmeen's Church Commission to register a Salvation Army Church in Norway. The conclusion of the letter signaled that this was just a matter of convenience, but not of importance. There was nothing mentioned about legal matters and the demands of the Non-Conformist Act of 1969 in relation to such a registration:

> "As this is really only a provision for legal membership in a registered church, it is most practical to have membership protocol at territorial headquarters and not in every corps. Soldiership is still the most important Salvation Army affiliation and belongs to the local situation. The other is only a formal registration at national level. 'Church' membership has no practical significance than the payment to the Army of the personal 'church tax' paid by each member. There will also be a possibility for an officer to apply for permission to conduct weddings if he/she is registered in the 'church'[53]".

In view of the details he described concerning the process and history these comments lacked the most obvious legal details which IHQ most probably would need. The Salvation Army's legal and parliamentary secretary, Major Peter Smith, asked for more details on behalf of the General. His letter was faxed 28 November to Hannevik. The letter recalled the previous correspondence of 1978 informing IHQ about the process there had been and the decision not to register at that time. In that correspondence there was an issue that needed to be explained: "If we apply at a certain time for registration according to this law we will have to adhere to the letter of this law". Peter Smith wanted to know the exact legal implications of registering as a church. The sentence from the correspondence of 1978 did not fit into Hannevik explanation that it "has no practical significance than the payment . . . etc." Peter Smith wanted comments from the Army's legal adviser concerning the consequences of registration, as for instance if the property held by the Property Company needed to be transferred to "the church", tax implications and if there could be legal restrictions placed upon officers. A

52. Appendix to Hannevik' s letter, *Salvation Army in Norway—Registration as a Church*, 2.
53. Ibid., 2.

draft constitution of the official "church" would be needed as well. Frelsesarmeen's legal adviser, Knut Johan Onarheim, a soldier of Bergen I must have been consulted as there was a note and a draft constitution from him three months after the letter from Peter Smith, IHQ. Consulting him would most probably have been the result of the letter from Peter Smith. Onarheim's note revealed his views as a soldier and might have had a resemblance to general views among soldiers. He produced a note of 8 pages plus a draft for the constitution on the basis of the draft from the working committee. Even though as a lawyer he gave advice in light of the Non-Conformist Act of 1969, his own opinion as a soldier was dominant throughout the document[54]. He stated that the decision to establish Frelsesarmeen's Trossamfunn was not final and questioned if this was the right time to make such a decision. Perhaps the question should rest until the Norwegian Church had made its decisions concerning the relation between state and church. It was interesting that the argument Solhaug used for establishing Frelsesarmeen's Commission in 1975 was still around and repeated here. The new situation would appear as and when a separation between state and church happened. Onarheim's other hesitation was the danger of confusion or mixture of two legal entities, if Frelsesarmeen's Faith Community became a legal entity within the organization, Frelsesarmeen. These two legal entities would interfere with each other. It would divide the members of Frelsesarmeen into two main groups, those who registered as members of the faith community and those who did not. It would bring Frelsesarmeen into a new situation. Onarheim envisioned that the group of registered members would be a very active group forming its own unity while the others would retain their legal registration in other churches, but still be soldiers, local officers, officers and adherents. In the conclusion he changed from a "might be" to a "would be" where he foresaw that the registered members of the faith community would be a very strong and pronounced group, that would demand to be heard and hold the truth in matters of faith and in the administration of these. The risk would be polarization and a monopoly of attitudes and power. The main question would be the influence or role the organization Frelsesarmeen would have within Frelsesarmeen's Faith Community as this community would be "owned" by its members. In principle the members controlled the faith community. In a situation of conflict between the two legal entities a consequence could be that the members of Frelsesarmeen's Trossamfunn would leave the organization Frelsesarmeen. He could not

54. *Notat vedrørende opprettelse av Frelsesarmeens trossamfunn* of 28 february 1997, 3 sec. III, 1 "Oprettlese/stiftelse av Frelsesarmeens trossamfunn?" (Note concerning establishment of Frelsesarmeens Faith Community of 28 February 1997 p. 3 sec. III, 1 "Establishment/founding of Frelsesarmeen's Faith Community?").

see that the leadership had the same authority over the faith community as over the organization, because the faith community was built on individual membership based on rights and principles laid out according to legislation. Lately, he had experienced currents concerning doctrines and faith that could cause great problems within the faith community. He did not specify which currents, but as he took up the sacraments in the following paragraphs it could be these currents. He called it a central point that had not been dealt with in the commission, but which according to his knowledge was being looked into at IHQ[55]. Onarheim thought that teaching and observance of the sacraments could be a flammable theme in the faith community and could cause division, a result that was the opposite of the intention with the registration. This eight-page long note was supposed to be legal considerations or advice, but most of it was a mixture of legal consideration and his opinions. The last point he took up was that according to the draft constitution Frelsesarmeen's leadership would appoint the board of the faith community. This would hinder the important grass root influence. Onarheim suggested that it would be wise to start a democratization process with direct election to the board and with a "church meeting" with appointed and elected members of Frelsesarmeen's Trossamfunn, who could meet and discuss different matters together with the leadership of Frelsesarmeen. Onarheim's note did not answer the main questions from IHQ especially those concerning the placement of the Property Company, tax implications, or legal restrictions upon officers. Onarheim's note could be seen as an expression of a Salvationist's concern at least as much as legal considerations. The issue of conflict between Salvationists was shared by other Salvationists, not so much about competition between two legal entities, rather a fear that there would be A and B soldiers. There was one point in the draft constitution that lingered on for a while and which was the basis for some of Onarheim's worries concerning the outcome of the registration. It was the role of the TC. Paragraph 6 of the draft constitution concerning the board said: "The Territorial Leader in Norway or the one he appoints has the right to appear and speak in the board, but not to vote."[56] With the Salvation Army constitution in mind, where all powers are in the hands of

---

55. It could be the International Spiritual Life commission he was referring to. It was formed in 1996. The focus of their work was Salvation Army worship. They wrote a small pamphlet, *Move forward in freedom*. It was distributed to all territories for translation and it was translated into Norwegian. The sacraments were on the agenda for discussion, but no changes were made to the practice of the Army. A substantial part of pamphlet was used on the sacraments. The relationship between the soldier enrollment and water baptism was explained in ten points.

56. Draft (28 February 1997) to Statues for Frelsesarmeens Faith Community §6, 3.

the General who delegates power to the TC, such a paragraph would not be possible to enable any Salvation Army registration. The final decision would always rest with the TC. The questions from IHQ must have been the background for Onarheim's note. As the correspondence with IHQ stopped in the files at this point there is no further information of how these matters were presented to IHQ,[57] if presented at all. Onarheim's note was presenting his personal views so clearly, that it could hardly be representative of neutral legal advice which IHQ needed for the final approval. It raised more questions than it answered and would add to the uncertainty concerning Norwegian law. Such confusion could be seen in Peter Smith's letter from IHQ where he asked the question:

> "It is not clear to me whether or not Norwegians must belong to a church and be formerly registered as a member of a registered church. Perhaps it is not so much by law but by tradition that Salvationists wish to retain their membership of the Lutheran (state) church."[58]

As no further correspondence with IHQ on this matter can be found until 2003/2004 when the actual registration as a faith community began, it is clear that a number of issues were not clarified in the presentation of the matter to IHQ. The TC might have decided to postpone further correspondence until the situation was clearer.

From March 1997 the new CS, Colonel Thorleif Gulliksen followed up on legal matters together with Onarheim. The minutes from an informal meeting 3 June 1997 with the Governor's representatives were presented to the Leaders Conference 9–11 September 1997 as well as Onarheim's note. The minutes made clear the statements from Frelsesarmeen's Church Commission concerning registration were legally correct, but that the Governor as well as Onarheim had expressed doubt about how it would work out in practice. The uncertainty was also if Frelsesarmeen's leadership could have the full control over the church. The debate revealed opposing views from deciding not to register to a wish of registration straight away. It was decided to postpone the issue and to continue to work with the issues referred to. The

---

57. The confidential files from the Leadership office at THQ in Oslo have been searched. The questions Peter Smith asked were not answered. It looks as if the process stopped. As Onarheim's note was predominantly personal views the note could not have been sent to the legal department at IHQ for clarifying the questions. Search have been done at IHQ as well, but with no result. It supports the theory that matters simply stopped and were not pursued further.

58. Peter Smith's letter of 26 November 1996.

Leaders' Conference 8–10 September 1998[59] looked into the process so far and discussed the way ahead. The debate centered round the situation in the other Nordic countries where only the Army in Denmark was registered as a faith community, while the Army in Sweden was in the process of change. State and church would separate in the year 2000. It was decided to use the time needed to reach a responsible decision. The Leaders' Conference concluded that the CS should continue the process both with the model and with improving the democratic process. This was the last paper concerning the issue of registration as an outcome of the recommendation of Frelsesarmeen's Church Commission to register Frelsesarmeen's Trossamfunn. Then it seems as if the work towards registration was put on hold for a couple of years. Some of the reasons for this hold in the work could be found in the fear of tensions within the Army as well as the influence of rather subjective legal advice concerning registration from Frelsesarmeen's legal adviser.

Conclusion

The work and process towards producing the final report in Frelsesarmeen's Church Commission 1993–96 differed from Frelsesarmeen's Commission 1975–78. The mandate was to build upon the report from 1978 meaning that all theological and theoretical questions would be based on this, and not a new process. That gave a different approach, but the greatest difference was that the planned questionnaire did not materialize, so discussions were based on presumptions more than facts. It was claimed that there had been great changes in Salvationists' understanding of Frelsesarmeen as a faith community, but they were not substantiated. The results from the process with the brochure showed that a small majority[60] wanted things to stay as they were, while a majority could live with a possible registration as long as this did not influence the present status, but was an extra possibility for those who wanted it. However, the replies uncovered a different ecclesiology than the Army's. Half the responding corps took up the question of the sacraments even though there were no questions about this. A number could not imagine Frelsesarmeen being a faith community without observing the sacraments, because the image of a church as an independent faith community was that the sacraments had to be observed. One of the results of the questionnaire from Frelsesarmeen's Commission 1975–78 showed that 7 percent would participate in Communion regularly either in the

59. Minutes from the Leaders' conference, 10–11.
60. 24 corps out of 45 wanted things to stay as they were, 21 supported the proposed registration (model 3) and 33 could accept model 3.

Norwegian Church or in other churches, so the wish for the sacraments seemed not to be based on a tradition for attending Communion. One corps from Frelsesarmeen's Church Commission's research expressed that explicitly. Infant baptism had been observed by the vast majority. The individual letters that came as a response to questions or as a result of the information in *Krigsropet* had uncovered different attitudes. They expressed both resistance and support to registration as an independent faith community. The resistance had two main reasons, one concerned Kairos, determining the right moment for action. Registration would come, but it should be at the right time, when the state and church separated. This could support seeing the Norwegian Church as an expression of civil religion. The other reason was concern about the unity of the church. The Norwegian Church was looked upon as the true expressions of the apostolic church in Norway as well as state churches in other countries. Seemingly personal belief and doctrines needed not to be in accordance with the Lutheran belief, but it was paramount to adhere to the Norwegian Church as Norwegian citizens. The reason for this was based both on nationality and Christian unity. Some of those who supported registration took up the question of the sacraments because Frelsesarmeen as a registered faith community would in their view have to introduce and observe them. Among the supporters were also those who agreed with the Army's present view of a non-observance, but the other attitude seemed to be dominant. Because this question was taken up, subtle attitudes came to the forefront this time in comparison to the results from Frelsesarmeen's Commission 1975–78.

The final report presented a wide scope of information that gave Salvationists and the leadership opportunity to take informed decisions and as background for further reflection and debate. However, the chapter concerning Frelsesarmeen's identity and ecclesiology exhibited some of the confusion already present in the report of Frelsesarmeen's Commission 1975–78. The report from the church commission made the confusion even greater by misunderstanding some of the issues and by disregard for correct quotation. The chapter exhibited a lack of interest or knowledge in Salvation Army history and theology while the other chapters of the report gave valid information.

Frelsesarmeen's Church Commission 1993–96 unanimously recommended registration as a faith community after the model of Misjonsforbundet, meaning that the main registration would stay with the organization, but also includes registration with the independent faith community as an option for Salvationists and others. The Leaders' Conference unanimously signed a statement that the leaders were positive of the recommendations and supported the decision that further work towards establishing

Frelsesarmeen's faith community should be done. It was clear that this would be done in order to accommodate a minority, not because of great enthusiasm of any changes. It was nine years before registration became a reality, but the work continued as if registration was expected to be pursued within a short horizon. Press releases were sent out from THQ and a debate in the press took place. It revealed a difference of opinion among soldiers. In spite of the debate the process did not stop which seemed to have been the aim of those protesting against registration. The main reason for the pause in the process was the fear of division among Salvationists and also the written statement of the Army's legal adviser. It should have been legal advice given in order to answer concrete questions from IHQ, but instead it gave voice to the adviser's personal resistance towards registration at the present time by presenting a mixture of legal and possible organizational difficulties. The process with IHQ concerning registration seemingly was stopped as well. The note from Onarheim would hardly have been shared with London, because it did not answer the legal questions asked and it raised questions of division, sacraments, and the possibility of TC's authority being eroded in the board of the congregation. This made the leadership uncertain of the whole issue. Looking into *Frelsesoffiseren* and *Krigsropet* the question of registration did not resurface in any debate or article during the following years.

Chapter 8

Frelsesarmeen's Registration as a Faith Community in 2005

THE PROCESS TOWARDS REGISTRATION as a faith community lasted thirty years. The work and recommendations of two commissions had been evaluated and published so that all Salvationists had been given the opportunity to be well informed. In spite of that situation the general interest from ordinary Salvationists had not been intense, but for a minority of officers and soldiers the issue of having their membership in Frelsesarmeen as a registered faith community was central.

Information technology influenced Salvationists' lives as it did for everybody else with the wider and more general use of the internet as well as the advantages and disadvantages of the mobile phones and its wide distribution. Communications intensified both via the internet and the mobile phone. It gave new impulses from society at large as well as from abroad. Communication between Frelsesarmeen and the general population reached a stage that had not been seen since the years just after the war because of the special National TV fund raising in 1995,[1] where Frelsesarmeen had been chosen as the recipient. In the months ahead of the day of fundraising, TV presented the projects that were to be supported. 40 percent of the funding that had to be used in the country reflected some of the challenges that society at large was facing. In politics the issue of a growing number of elderly people was in focus at the elections in the 1990s, especially at the election in 1997. One of the worries was how the welfare state would manage the increasing expenses associated with the needs of such a large percentage of elderly people. Life expectancy grew dramatically. From the TV fund raising a project for elderly people was further developed

---

1. Ellis, "Omsorg for hele mennesket," 97–99.

at Ensjø in Oslo. Another challenge was drug abuse that had become more widespread since the 70s. Frelsesarmeen used money from the funds to create a project for drug addicts in Heskestad in Rogaland. The funds also gave the Army the possibility of employing youth workers in many places in the country to meet the challenges of vulnerable children and youth who were facing upheavals in their families. This work had previously rested on volunteers alone. The majority of the funds were used abroad, especially in projects where Frelsesarmeen already had Norwegian officers, such as in Haiti and India, or had been involved in the work, such as in St. Petersburg where a center for homeless people including street children was opened in August 1997 as well as an HIV project.

The TV fund raising and the number of programs shown prior to the actual fundraising day gave the public a unique insight into Frelsesarmeen's work, not only social work, but also the Army's musical resources. The day of fundraising started with a worship service from Frelsesarmeen. In the following years Frelsesarmeen's PR work was extended and renewed in order to communicate in more contemporary language than had been the case. The dust seemed to be removed and a modern Frelsesarmee appeared in the mind of the public.[2] According to Størksen the younger generation especially within the Army had been embarrassed by belonging to Frelsesarmeen because of its image of being old fashioned and closed. Being involved in the TV fund raising and seeing the Army being presented so broadly in the media helped remove the embarrassment and made room for a greater pride in the Army. It seemed as if all Salvationists shared the pride in the Army's work, but there was also a fear that treasured values should be lost. Frelsesarmeen's leadership was deeply involved in the follow up work on TV-aksjonen while the process towards registration was kept low key, but not forgotten.

It would have been natural to look into the development within the Norwegian Church during this period, as the question of separation between state and church had played such an important role in the arguments during the years. Even so there are no documents that revealed any special interest in developments within the Norwegian Church during the years around the millennium that had influence on the process within the Army. The Norwegian Church was facing upheavals and changes. With Frelsesarmeen's membership of ecumenical bodies its leaders must have been aware of the situation, but they seemed not to feel a need for hurrying the process of registration within the Army. On the contrary they gave time for things to adjust, waiting for the right time. The social-democratic party pointed

---

2. Størksen, "Vaske grunnmuren," 105–107.

to the values the Norwegian Church represented and wanted an open and inclusive folk church.[3] In 1996 Stortinget (the Parliament) passed a bill concerning the Norwegian Church as a replacement for the bill of 1953. A main point was to develop self-government within the church further.[4] The contrast between different traditions and theological movements was evident during the 1990s. The celebration of a millennium of the church in Norway in 1995 had shown that the Norwegian Church held a strong position in the population, but there were different opinions concerning the identity of the church. Was it a folk church of all the baptized or a church for those who were actively engaged?[5] Bishops and deans were still appointed by the minister for church affairs, while ordinary ministers were appointed by the Church Assembly. The State had tried to balance the different traditions through the appointment system, but could only do this now when it concerned bishops and deans. At least the conservative part of the Norwegian Church wanted the authority of appointing bishops and deans to be under church control. In 1998 the Church Assembly formed a commission to look into the relationship between state and church called Bakkevik-utvalget after the chairman Trond Bakkevik. The report came in 2002 with the title "Same church—new settlement." The majority in the commission wanted the relationship between the state and the Norwegian Church to be altered. The principal discussion concerned equality between faith and humanist communities and wanted the policy from the state to be supportive toward all religions. This would demand an alteration of the paragraphs in the Constitution that concerned relationships between the state and the Norwegian Church. The Church Council supported the recommendation while only half of the local church councils gave such support when the answers to the hearing came. In March 2003 a public commission was appointed to look into the future of the State Church. The Commission had members both from the Norwegian Church and faith and humanist communities. The report came in 2006 and had three different models: a Folk Church based on the Constitution, a Folk Church based on a separate church law, and a Free Folk Church. The majority wanted to dissolve the State Church and have a Folk Church based on a separate law, passed through Stortinget, and recommended that the paragraphs in the Constitution concerning the Norwegian Church should be altered. Bishops and deans should be appointed by the church itself, but the church should still be financed by the state. In the process of hearing the majority of local councils were against dis-

---

3. Furre, *Norsk historie 1914–2000*, 342.
4. Elstad, "Hundre års debat om stat og kyrkje i Noreg."
5. Furre, *Norsk historie 1914–2000*, 343.

solving the State Church. 10 April 2008 the political parties came to terms with a bill that would transfer the right to appoint bishops and deans to the church in 2011 when the process of democratization within the church was fulfilled. Ministers, bishops, and deans would remain public servants. The Constitution's §2 and 16 would be altered. The change of the Constitution happened 21 May 2012. The new §2 was: "The value foundation will remain our Christian and humanistic heritage. This constitution will secure democracy, constitutional state and human rights." The new §16 was: "All citizens of the country will have freedom of religion. The Norwegian church, an evangelical Lutheran church, will remain the Folk Church of Norway and as such will be supported by the state. Decisions concerning its regime will be stipulated by law. All faith-and humanistic communities shall be supported equally."[6] These commissions concerning the Norwegian Church were happening parallel with Frelsesarmeen's work on registration as a faith community.

During this same period new theological impulses came from the international Salvation Army.

International influences

One of the theological impulses that had come to Frelsesarmeen from the international Salvation Army was the response to the BEM document. This process signaled a new emphasis on theological reflection and a wish to communicate this to ordinary Salvationists. The doctrine book had been revised and rewritten in 1969. In light of the theological reflection it was considered time for a new doctrine book to be written. A real change came in 1998 with the publication of *Salvation Story Salvationist Handbook of Doctrine*, followed in 1999 by *Salvation Story Study Guide*. The propositional nature of the doctrine books was exchanged for a narrative approach in communicating doctrine. This new style of a doctrine book was written by an international doctrine council as a joint venture. In 1992 the International Doctrine Council[7] was appointed by The Salvation Army's world leader General Eva Burrows to write a new doctrine book. The council was encouraged to make a fresh approach to SA doctrines, to think and discuss

6. Elstad, "Hundre års debat om stat og kyrkja," 9. *Kristeligt Dagblad* 4 July 2012, 4–5

7. The members were David Guy from UK, Earl Robinson from Canada, John Amoah from Ghana, Phil Needham from USA, Ray Caddy from UK, Christine Parkin from UK and Gudrun Lydholm from Denmark. Apart from the actual council there were corresponding members from Australia (Douglas Davies, Graham Durston), Brazil (John Jones), Korea (Kim Joon-Chul) and Switzerland (Geroge Mailler). David Guy: "The International Doctrine Council". *The Officer* 1993, 195.

freely without restrictions and not to be bound by previous doctrine books. The mandate given was to debate, evaluate and rewrite a doctrine book, a solid theological book written in a way that communicated to ordinary Salvationists. There were different reasons for making the change from a British Doctrine Council to an international one. A letter from General Eva Burrows explained her reasons for the change. The decision was made in 1992 and the letter was from 2013 so present day agenda and the distance of well over twenty years have to be taken into account,[8] but this was how she considered her decision at this time:

> "Being an internationalist, and having served in so many parts of the world including Africa and Asia, I was surprised that the Doctrine Council was entirely British.... I felt I needed a world view in discussion on our Articles of Faith... I wished the book to be more user friendly for ordinary Salvationists who could read it and enjoy it, in more contemporary, fresh language. I also have seen the struggles of translators in Sri Lanka and Zimbabwe to get to grips with the last Doctrine Book, where there was so much repetition in the language, that they seemed to translating the same thing over and over again."[9]

In my letter, written in May 2013 to Eva Burrows, I had suggested that the process round the BEM document prepared the way for having a different approach to the writing of a doctrine book. Her answer was that it was not the BEM document that inspired her to form the International Doctrine Council, but the other reasons already mentioned. However, looking into this whole process of responding to the document it at least gave the members of the Doctrine Council inspiration to work as a committee also in their task of writing the new doctrine book.

The BEM document came up as a question at the High Council[10] of 1986. Eva Burrows was one of the nominees and the one who was elected. One of the questions to the nominees was: "What is your view of The Salvation Army's recent response to the Baptist/Eucharist/Ministry Lima Document?"[11] The response from Eva Burrows was two paragraphs ending with this statement: "The other helpful effect of our response to the BEM

---

8. Concerning validity of memory, see Thompson, *The Voice of the Past*, 100–103.

9. Letter from Eva Burrows 29 May 2013.

10. The High Council elects the General. Membership of the High Council includes all Commissioners and all other Territorial Leaders. In the eighties it was all Commissioners and Territorial Commanders with the rank of Colonel if they had been in this position for two years.

11. Minutes of The High Council 1986, 136.

document is that it proved enriching and challenging to us, as we prepare more adequately to train our own people in the understanding of our position."[12] Even though the BEM document was not at the forefront of Eva Burrow's decision to form an International Doctrine Council, the issue of publishing a new doctrine book that in a more contemporary form aimed at ordinary Salvationists all over the world certainly fulfilled her response "as we prepare more adequately to train our own people in the understanding of our position." The BEM document was not explicitly the reason for this new doctrine council, but implicitly it was there at least as an inspiration that gave an atmosphere of thinking and discussing theology to a greater and much broader extent than had previously been the case.

The International Doctrine Council met in London for the first meeting in July 1992. After four years, in September 1996, when the first draft was ready, it was sent out to all Salvation Army territories in the world. A number of territories made working groups to read and comment the draft. In the territories that did not send the draft to be examined and commented by working groups the Territorial Commander responded after having consulted a few other persons. The responses coming in at the end of 1996 and the beginning of 1997 were absolutely overwhelming. Many of the working groups had prepared thick documents filled with suggestions for a different approach, another style, different language, and complaints about the theology coming through the first draft. Others agreed with both style and theology. A retired officer (Lt. Colonel Robert Waddams) was asked to read through the enormous amount of paper, to sort according to themes, and then to write an agenda of problem areas, questions, and suggestions for change that had been received. Even with all this done the amount the council had to consider was considerable. The revision based on all the input from the Army world was ready by December 1997. The many voices from around the world were listened to and reacted upon in one way or another. Because of this lengthy process a world view came into the discussion not only through the members of the council, but through all the comments on the first draft. The narrative style was kept and so was the arrangement of the chapters based on themes and not on individual doctrines. The Doctrine Book was authorized by the General and finally published in 1998. In the introduction to *Salvation Story* the narrative form is explained:

> "It is narrative in form, so that teaching is presented in short paragraphs, rather than point by point. This should enable the progression of thought to be clearly seen and allow for flexible use in both study groups and the classroom. The narrative style

12. Ibid., 139.

means that we examine the truths of our faith on two levels, both as the work of God in history which accomplished our salvation, and as the record of our own journey of faith, from sin through to salvation and holiness. The narrative approach is reflected, too in the Handbook's title: *Salvation Story*. Salvationists base their understanding of doctrine on the witness of the Bible, the living word of God. Our Articles of faith make that clear, and therefore this book *seeks* to be faithful to Scripture."[13]

Salvation Story was formed in a more systematic way than its predecessors as the title of the chapters illustrates: 1) Word of the living God, 2) The God who is never alone, 3) Creator of heaven and earth, 4) God's eternal son, 5) The Holy Spirit, Lord, and giver of life, 6) Distorted image, 7) Salvation story, 8) Salvation experience, 9) Full salvation, 10) People of God, 11) Kingdom of the risen Lord. Theologically it covered more ground, as there was a chapter on ecclesiology, but even so it was not a full academic systematic theology. There were no chapters on methodological or hermeneutical considerations or sources of theology and the like. *Salvation Story* was more to be seen as a kind of catechism that could be used for teaching purposes, or just read and studied by Salvationists and others who wanted to know what the Army believed. In order to substantiate *Salvation Story* and put doctrine and theology even more on the agenda of local corps communities both in teaching and worship *Salvation Story Study Guide* was produced.

> "Perhaps the purpose of the Guide can best be summed up by describing it as a link between the doctrinal teaching of the Handbook and the thinking and living of the individual Salvationist as well as the Salvationist community in particular settings. It is not enough to assent to the truths of Scripture and to the Army's doctrinal positions. Our faith must penetrate, transform, and enliven both the mind and the life of us all. It must be a living faith. It must be our own faith. The purpose of the Guide is to stimulate our ownership of a faith that is alive and thought out."[14]

As can be seen from the introduction to the *Study Guide*, it was vital for the Army "to stimulate an ownership" of the faith so it could be transformed from an intellectual doctrinal exercise to a living faith. To help this process, all the chapters in the Study Guide included four sections: 1) Belief 2) Life 3) Worship 4) Bible studies. It was at the top of the agenda of the Doctrine Council that both books should be readable to ordinary Salvationists at the

---

13. Introduction to *Salvation Story*, xiv.
14. Introduction to *Salvation Story Study Guide*, vi.

same time as more scholarly minded Salvationists would be able to recognize a more profound theological base of both *Salvation Story* and *Salvation Story Study Guide*.

Frelsesarmeen translated *Salvation Story* the year after its publication. The translation was close to the original manuscript, but one paragraph was taken out. It was from the appendix on the sacraments, a very central one which concluded the appendix:

> "We observe the sacraments, not by limiting them to two or three or seven, but by inviting Christ to suppers, love feasts, birth celebrations, parties, dedications, sick beds, weddings, anniversaries, commissioning, ordinations, retirements—and a host of other significant events—and, where he is truly received, watching him give a grace beyond our understanding. We can see, smell, hear, and taste it. We joyfully affirm that in our presence is the one, true, original Sacrament. And we know that what we have experienced is reality."[15]

This claim of observing the sacraments by interpreting them as part of Salvationist practice and experience was new in comparison to the Army's traditional apologetic dealing with the issue. It connected to the interpretation of the sacrament that was in the previous paragraphs, but took the interpretation a step further by claiming that the Salvationist understanding was an observance of the sacraments. For Frelsesarmeen this claim apparently took the interpretation too far for a Norwegian setting. The exclusion of the paragraph followed the line of free translations in the Army in Norway and it uncovered the possible tension there might have been between Frelsesarmeen and the international Army since 1900, concerning the question of the sacraments. Every doctrine book was altered in the Norwegian translations apart from the 1975 translation.

The International Spiritual Life Commission[16] published its report concerning Salvation Army worship, *Move forward in Freedom,* in 1998, the same year that *Salvation Story* was published. This report was also distributed to all territories for translation and it was translated into Norwegian. It was not only translated and printed as a separate document, but *Krigsropet*[17] also published General Paul Rader's message concerning the document,

---

15. *Salvation Story,* 114.

16. It was formed in 1996 to work with the theme of Salvation Army worship and met for five separate weeks. Two of the members, Phil Needham and Earl Robinson, were also in the Doctrine Council in order to be a link between the two. The committee had 17 members from around the world, one from Sweden, Lt. Colonel David Löfgren became CS in Norway in 1999.There were eight corresponding members.

17. *Krigsropet* nr. 48 1998, 16–17.

explaining the process and the recommendations from the commission. In the following number *Krigsropet*[18] published the twelve challenges from the document. The wide circulation of *Krigsropet* made this come out not only to Salvationists, but to the public.

The two main influences from the international Salvation Army on Frelsesarmeen during the years around 2000 were *Salvation Story* and *Move Forward in Freedom*, both of them interpreting the sacraments differently from what had previously been the case. From *Salvation Story's* presentation the sacraments might even be interpreted as embedded in Army practice. It is difficult to know how much the ecclesiology coming forth from *Salvation Story* might have influenced Frelsesarmeen's identity as a faith community during these last few years before registration, but the theme came up in *Frelsesoffiseren* in the beginning of 2001.[19] Mæland wrote about identity as a faith community and quoted from the ecclesiology chapter in *Salvation Story*. His main point was that the Army was a church, whatever it called itself, and the importance of knowing one's own identity. He did not take up the issue of registration, but focused on identity as a church. His viewpoints were taken up four issues later[20] where Henrik Bååth agreed with his statements, in contrast to a description of Frelsesarmeen by Per Fugelli as "Norway's most acknowledged Christian Humanitarian Organization." The center of Bååth's article was also identity as a church. It seems as if the focus had changed from the need of registration in order to be an independent faith community to having a stronger identity as a faith community, as a Frelsesarmeen. These two articles might illustrate a wider debate among Salvationists where the narrow focus on registration had widened to the question of identity and acceptance of Frelsesarmeen as a faith community independent of registration. This debate might very well have been influenced by *Salvation Story*. These two articles concerning ecclesiology and an article on the Atonement also quoting *Salvation Story*[21] is the written evidence of its influence. The book was translated within a year, distributed and from then on taught at the training college. Looking at the history of reception of doctrine books both from 1930 and 1975 it took some years before the influence really could be charted. The influence of the inclusion of the Army's non-sacramental position in the 1975 translation became clear

18. *Krigsropet* nr. 47 1998, 6–7.

19. *Frelsesoffiseren* had been out of production for a couple of years, but was published again from October 2000. As *Frelsesoffiseren* had been out of production there had not been any possibility of written debate in a year or two after the translation of *Salvation Story*.

20. *Frelsesoffiseren* no. 1 2002, 8–10.

21. *Frelsesoffiseren* no. 2 2001, 10–12.

twenty years later in the fact that a number of corps took this up in their responses to the different models of registration, even though there were no questions concerning the sacraments. In these few years from the Norwegian publication in 1999 to the actual registration in 2005 the influence had shown up in writing in *Frelsesoffiseren*. The number of officers who would have been taught according to *Salvation Story* during their training between 2000 and 2005 was thirty-three. It would take a bit longer before the preparation classes for soldiers would have an impact as the officers might not use the latest doctrine book, but the one they were familiar with. Even though there are only these few articles it can be seen as evidence of the reception of the book. The group of soldiers and officers most interested in the question of registration and Frelsesarmeen's church identity were generally the ones most alert to new publications such as *Salvation Story*. This would concern both those who opposed the changes as well as those in favor of them.

Frelsesarmeen's registration as a faith community in 2005

After thirty years and the work and reports of two commissions Frelsesarmeen registered a faith community 22 June 2005. The time seemed to have been ripe as the protests had calmed down or been silenced. There was seemingly no division or the question was not as urgent any longer as it had been during the 1990s, but there was confidence in the compromise that had been achieved and which all seemed to accept.[22] The nine years since the report from Frelsesarmeen's Church Commission had been used for looking into legal matters with a question of whether there were other ways of registering than the one chosen. The process resurfaced in 2000 on the agenda of the Leaders' Conference 22–23 September 2000.[23] The matter of registration was now kept on the agenda on the Executive Board as well as the yearly Leaders' conference during the next couple of years.[24] It is striking that the minutes only have small paragraphs concerning registration giving brief information, that work had been done on the drafts of the constitution or a visit to the County Governor, but nothing that indicated a longer debate. The small paragraph from the Leaders' Conference 9–11 September 2003 reflected a consensus that the whole situation had been eased because

---

22. There are no letters of protest in the confidential files. This is how the situation was described by the CS of the time Lt. Colonel Miriam Frederiksen in a mail of 23 November 2013.

23. Minutes from the Leaders' Conference 22–23 September 2000.

24. Minutes from the Leaders' Conference 9–11 September 2003 paragraph 08/03 and 7–9 September 2004 paragraph 11/04.

there were no great problems left, as no changes needed to happen for officers and soldiers. One issue that seemed to be of concern was who could be members. It was clear from the minutes that the leaders wanted membership to be open for others than soldiers and adherents. This came up again in the Leaders' conference of 2004[25] where the majority wanted membership to be open for all who wished to be members. This was repeated in the minutes of the Executive' Board[26] as a principle, but "desirable, if possible, to have some rules for some sort of connection to Frelsesarmeen for those who would be members." It was surprising that criteria for membership should be different in the registered congregation than in a Salvation Army corps. The enrollment ceremony for soldiership was quite demanding.[27] It was less demanding to become an adherent, but at least an adherent was expected to know Salvation Army doctrines, to join in Salvation Army worship and to support the Army financially. In the discussion the registered congregation appeared to be considered as of another kind, with membership open and free for whatever belief or engagement they might have, even though there was a wish for some connection to the Army. This could indicate that registration as a faith community was considered a strictly legal matter, not something that concerned Army belief or practice. It could also indicate that the way Frelsesarmeen portrayed itself to the public as an inclusive organization with a low threshold was reflected in this registration. In a way it opened up for a sort of nominal membership—at least a low commitment membership. The communication strategy not only influenced the general public, but also Frelsesarmeen's internal matters, such as registration and membership. By such a choice there would be coherence between the portrayed Frelsesarmeen and this new congregation to be. Another issue that came at the 2004 Leaders' conference was that no pressure should be put on any soldier or officer to register in the faith community.

In August 2004 a letter[28] of information concerning the planned registration of a congregation with a draft constitution was sent to IHQ. The letter mentioned that in the previous attempts to register, the subject had become divisive and emotive, but that the approach now was different as the leadership had stressed for more than a year that it was a purely legal step that would not "change anything, nor will any demands be made on Salvationists." Another point made was that the only membership that would be mandatory would be that of the TC, in order to ensure that the TC could

---

25. Minutes from the Leaders' Conference 7–9 September 2004 paragraph 11/04.
26. Minutes Thursday 26 October 2004 paragraph 45/04.
27. See appendix II.
28. Letter of 19 August 2008 sent Europe Department, IHQ by the CS.

be head of both the organization as well as of the congregation. The answer from the Legal and Parliamentary Secretary at IHQ, Major Peter Smith was that he would be happy to recommend the Constitution to the General for his approval, but he needed some clarification on four different paragraphs. In essence the questions were to ensure that control stayed with the TC and the General. The final constitution did not open up democratic processes as for instance a general assembly for the members or an elected board, instead the main board was appointed by the TC. Two months later 29 November 2004 Peter Smith in a letter to the Chief of Staff, Israel L. Gaither, recommended the proposed constitution for approval. The constitution was approved by the General, John Larsson, 16 December 2004. The application for registration was sent on 27 April 2005 to the County Governor in Oslo and Akershus. The document of registration was issued by the County Governor on 22 June 2005.

The Constitution had ten paragraphs: 1) It included the date of the beginning in Norway, its relation to the International Salvation Army, the overall leadership of the General based at the International Headquarters in London, the foundation in International Orders and Regulations adapted to Frelsesarmeen as well as the Salvation Army Doctrines 2) Name/Headquarters 3) Aim divided into two parts: the organization and the congregation 4) Organization and meetings underlining that meetings were part of the activity of both the organization and the congregation 5) Faith and teaching with the eleven doctrines quoted 6) Membership which was divided between the organization and the congregation. 7) Executive Council (or Main Board) 8) Finance/accounts / administration 9) Changes to the constitution 10) Dissolution of Frelsesarmeen. Paragraph 2 of the Constitution stated that the name of the organization and congregation was Frelsesarmeen. Paragraph 3 first dealt with the organization, then the congregation:

"The organization

>is a part of the universal church, preaching the gospel of Jesus Christ through corps (congregations), social centers and community outreach, meeting human need for all ages without ethnic, cultural or religious discrimination?
>
>Is part of and an alternative to the public welfare system by operating different forms of social centers for people with various needs.
>
>Will together with the international organization seek to alleviate need and conduct mission.

The Congregation

is established to provide membership status to those who wish to be legally registered as members of Frelsesarmeen."

Paragraph 3 illustrates the tension within Frelsesarmeen through the way the organization and congregation each were described. The most striking was that the organization was described as part of the universal church, preaching, and being engaged in mission, rather than the congregation. The congregation was downgraded to a legal provision for those who might wish so. Even though Frelsesarmeen had this dual registration, it did not as such register as a faith community or congregation. It registered a congregation without a mission or any notae ecclesiae. This poses the question of how the image of a registered church or congregation was understood by a great number of Norwegian Salvationists. How did they consider the Norwegian Church, which they had a nominal membership of in order not to be churchless? Because of their nominal membership, the concept of church became identical with a legal institution where only nominal membership was required, with no faith commitment and without any specific mission? Was church identical with civil religion as it might have been for Solhaug? Was the Norwegian Church identical with the church as unam, sanctam, catholicam, and apostolicam, as for Dahlstrøm as in his mind there could only be one of that kind in a country? Did the reasons for Frelsesarmeen continuing to identify itself as an organization in a legal sense lie in these questions? Why this reluctance to identify the Army's mission and ministry as a congregation? It was important for the present leadership to keep the organization as the main registration describing the Army's identity in order not to change the situation. The language of organization corresponded to the tradition Frelsesarmeen had developed in the country, therefore it was not threatening if it stayed that way. Also it prevented the congregation being given too much value for those who opposed any such registration. As organization was the preferred and well accepted designation of Frelsesarmeen it could continue to develop its identity within this frame. The debate in *Frelsesofficeren* concerned identity on the basis of *Salvation Story*, not registration. The doctrine[29] of the church from *Salvation Story* could be pursued also within this designation: "We believe in the Church, the body of Christ, justified and sanctified by grace, called to continue the mission and ministry by Christ."[30]

29. It was actually the summary of chapter 10, "The People of God." Each chapter ended with a summary. The summaries were originally revised doctrines written by the Doctrine Council in response to the task given. After they had been submitted to the General it was decided not to revise the doctrines. They were then used as summaries in *Salvation Story*.

30. *Salvation Story*, 110.

The first section of paragraph 3 concerning organization, highlighted membership in the universal church and described its mission and ministry. The Army's sacramental understanding, as explained in *Salvation Story*, interpreted the Army's traditions in sacramental language and as sacraments so that the Army's way of expressing itself as faith community would be as always. There were no changes, but a different interpretation. The decision to keep the designation of organization as the primary part of the constitution can be seen as a pragmatic solution that would not lose the ultimate goal of continuing the Army's mission and ministry.

The way congregation was described as a purely legal matter could be an attempt to open Frelsesarmeen up for nominal or low commitment membership. In communication to the public it portrayed itself as an inclusive movement with a low threshold welcoming all. That had always been true when it came to attendance in Army activities and meetings or making use of social outreach, but for church membership such as soldiership the threshold had been pretty high with demanding commitment. This was still the case. By registering a congregation without any specific expectation of commitment or lifestyle the open door or inclusive fellowship was extended to a church membership. That could be one interpretation. The registration might also signal that the designation church or congregation had become identical with legal registration, rather than faith commitment. This could be the case because of the nominal membership most Salvationists had to the Norwegian Church. For Salvationists who actually registered in the congregation this change did not seem to be a purely legal matter, rather a matter of belief.

It was paramount for the leadership to keep things calm and avoid any division, and to emphasize that Frelsesarmeen would not be changed, but stay as it had always been. The reason why it was so important to avoid any conflict could be that Frelsesarmeen, in its culture, was not accustomed to embrace contrasting opinions. The Salvation Army published statements on different ethical issues and Frelsesarmeen published similar statements, not translations but statements that would fit into a Norwegian reality. The culture was that such statements as well as the doctrines were not disputed, but accepted by most Salvationists. To have the military metaphor as the leading one did not give room for deeper conflicts, at least it gave the urgency to settle conflicts and seek harmony. The TC, Commissioner Donald Ødegaard, was Norwegian, even though he had wide international experience, and so were the members of the Executive Council apart from the CS, Lt. Colonel Miriam Frederiksen, who was Danish. This meant that they knew the different parties and fractions thoroughly and in a way were part of it. They might have considered it difficult to distance themselves from a possible conflict. This could be one reason. Another could be that registration by the leadership was considered to be of minor importance and therefore not worth creating a conflict over. The first option was the most likely reason, as it would be difficult to comprehend, that registration was of minor importance as so much work and energy had been vested into this process. The outcome was this division of the registration and the unusual description of the congregation in comparison to the organization.

Paragraph 5 stated that The Salvation Army was building its faith and teaching on the Salvation Army's articles of faith and stated the eleven doctrines. As both organization and congregation shared the name, Frelsesarmeen, the doctrines would be foundational for both. This made the empty congregation stand out even more. It was built on a creed, but it was only there to provide legal membership status for those who might wish so. Paragraph 4 mentioned that meetings were part of the activity of both organization and congregation. All sorts of gatherings within the Army had traditionally been called meetings regardless of their kind. At the time of the registration gudstjeneste (worship service) seemed to be the preferred designation at least for Sunday worship. By using the traditional name of meeting the Army avoided making any distinctions. Reading paragraph 3 it would be natural to imagine that the meetings in the congregation would be a General Assembly.

In paragraph 6 the same division as in paragraph 3 is seen:

> "Members of the organization are officers, soldiers, adherent and junior soldiers who are enrolled according to orders and regulations of the Salvation Army. In addition, officers, soldiers, adherents and junior soldiers and others can be legally registered as members of the congregation should they so wish."

Then it quoted the conditions according to the Non-Conformist Act of 1969 of not being members of another registered church, the demand of Norwegian citizenship or residence, and the age of fifteen as the youngest. It was mentioned that children of parents who registered would automatically become members of the congregation. It was the "and others" that made the difference between the two and then the automatic membership of the children. The discussion in the executive board had concerned the opportunity for anybody who wished so to be members of the congregation. This could very well relate to members of Frelsesarmeen's women's organization or youth organizations such as scouts, but the minutes only mentioned this as an open door with no specifications. The application form on the other hand stated "Present affiliation to Frelsesarmeen" and then the four categories plus "the other" had boxes just to cross. The application form connected "others" to an affiliation to the Army. The automatic membership of children was part of the Non-Conformist Act, but it was far from Salvationist practice. Infants could be dedicated by the ceremony of dedication or children from the age of seven could be enrolled as junior soldiers, but all of this required promises given. The parents in a dedication ceremony accepted that the child belonged to God and promised to bring it up in the Christian faith. Junior soldiers confirmed a belief in salvation through Jesus Christ and promised to live as his child. Automatic membership was foreign to Army tradition.[31]

Paragraph 7 concerning the Executive Council stated: "The Organization and the congregation are under the leadership of a territorial commander (TC) appointed by the General of the Salvation Army." It made clear that all was under the control of the TC and implicitly of the General. This paragraph safeguarded the interest of IHQ. The TC appointed the executive council with 7–9 members, and the TC and CS were ex officio members. Paragraph 9 stated that changes to the constitution could be made by majority in the executive council. This was the only place a majority could decide matters. The executive council functioned as other Army councils with members appointed by the TC and the TC having the final word. There was no provision for voting reaching majority decisions apart from paragraph 9. The clarifications Peter Smith from IHQ needed in 2004, that the control was secured in the hands of the TC and the General was made clear in the constitution.

Frelsesarmeen had registered a faith community, but in a low key manner to avoid any division, or A and B soldiers, as had been feared from those protesting against registration in connection with Frelsesarmeen's Church Commission 1993–96. At the soldiers' meeting during the congress 1–3 July the registration was explained. The speeches from the Territorial leaders, Commissioners Donald and Berit Ødegaard[32] underlined that the registration was a purely legal and not a theological issue. It had no consequence for those who chose not to be legally registered members of Frelsesarmeen. "Everything will remain as always and Frelsesarmeen will not be changed."[33] This sentence expressed the wish to calm down the fear that registration could be divisive. At least some Salvationists were forcefully against any

---

31. It was usual with membership of children-and youth clubs as well as Women's fellowships just to be registered, but membership to the Army itself was based on commitment.

32. They were Norwegians having served for a number of years in Africa, he in the Army's educational work and she in the medical. Before coming to Norway as Territorial Leaders, they had been Territorial leaders in Kenya.

33. *Krigsropet* no. 37 2005, 8–9.

changes, the leadership felt the need to assure people that, "everything will remain as always." Donald Ødegaard underlined the choice of keeping a low profile because it only was a legal matter, a formality. The registration was done for the sake of those who wanted it, and who might not have a legally registered membership of any church. The decision not to advocate for membership was kept. Application forms were present at the congress and would be available in all corps. The need to cancel membership of other churches was explained as well as the procedure for this.

Considering thirty years of work in commissions and endless discussions, the traditional pragmatism[34] of the Army won the day. Pragmatism within the Army had historically expressed itself by making use of anything that worked, and kept the focus on the ultimate goal of its mission. Ideas were tested by the practical consequences. It seems as if these criteria might have been in use. The situation with registration as an organization as the all-important one did not excluded the traditional adherence to the Norwegian Church as Norwegian citizens. Registration as an independent faith community had been tested through the work of two commissions. There had at no time been a clear majority for such a step. Considering this, it looks as if pragmatism won the day. Another reason could be that registration as such had never been a key issue in Army history, as it apparently had never really influenced the Army's mission, at least not negatively. It might rather have been positive in the Norwegian setting to be registered as an organization, because it might have opened doors for mission, which might otherwise have been closed. Registration as an independent faith community appeared as a reluctant step taken—kept in low key in order not to offend anybody. It became a compromise that could include all. The leadership decided that registration had to be done, but the main focus was to avoid division, as division would harm the mission of the Army. The chosen form of registration can be seen as a method to calm those who opposed any changes. In a farewell interview in *Frelsesoffiseren*,[35] Donald Ødegaard stated that he wanted to mention that it was good to have the debate concerning the faith community behind him. It did not reveal enthusiasm over the whole issue, rather that it had to be done in order to get the debate over with. As a Norwegian he would have been aware of the thirty-year long debate, even though he served in other countries. The debate was not intense in his five years as TC, at least there were no articles concerning registration in *Frelsesoffiseren* from 2000 to 2005.

34. William Booth's general measure for decisions was: "Does it work?" In Norway things had worked with having registrations for business matters and later as an organization.

35. *Frelsesoffiseren* 2005 no. 4, 2–5.

From the outside it could look like an anti-climax, but there were no comments of disappointment in the decision to keep the matter low-key. In whatever form the matter had been presented or whatever compromises had been reached, Frelsesarmeen had registered a congregation, and those who had been working for it had reached their goal. For them it was important that Frelsesarmeen had registered a congregation, as they no longer would be regarded as churchless in a legal sense now that their membership of Frelsesarmeen's congregation was a legal reality. Looking at the register of the congregation, the names of those who years earlier wrote articles in *Frelsesoffiseren* concerning the Army as a church, people such as Nils Petter Enstad and Roger Rasmussen, can be seen. For these people the registration of a congregation was not just a legal matter, but also a matter of theological substance, even though that was not present in the constitution. "Everything did not remain as always" for this group.

The immediate impact of registration

A couple of examples might illustrate the immediate impact of registration. The first example was an officer couple who differed from each other in their attitude and choice. Their answers were given eight and half years later, but this was how they consider their different choices these years later. The other example was from the little corps in Røros. I visited the corps 17 October 2005 according to my calendar from 2005. The group mentioned made an impact on me, but with a distance of more than eight years, there were details I had to check with the records of the corps.[36] The two officers were Knud and Lisberth Welander. The first member of the congregation, Frelsesarmeen, was Colonel Knud David Welander, a Danish/Norwegian officer, who has lived in both countries with his officer parents. Most of his service has been in Norway, but since 2010 the Welander couple served in the Philippines and from March 2013 to September 2014 as Territorial Leaders in Denmark, since then at IHQ in London. The reasons for him registering as fast as possible can be seen from his answers in the following.[37] In his letter he recalled his affiliation to the Army alone in his childhood and

---

36. Concerning the validity of memory, see Thompson, *The Voice of the Past*, 100–103. This concerns both the records of Lisbeth and Knud David Welander as well as my own.

37. I wrote Knud Welander an e-mail 9 January 2014: "Would you write me a mail that states the reasons why it was important for you to register in the faith community. As you were the first to register it could look as if this was important." "Did you have a double membership or was the Army your only affiliation?" The answer came in an e-mail of 27 January 2014.

youth both in Denmark as well as in Norway. He was not baptized. When he came to the training college in Oslo in 1982 for his officers' training, it surprised him that most of his fellow cadets had an unreflective attitude to the question of membership of the Norwegian Church. They belonged to Frelsesarmeen, but still remained members of a sacramental church. "I regarded this as if they downgraded Frelsesarmeen and our theological viewpoint. In a way they said that Frelsesarmeen was not sufficient as a church—not for their own part nor for those they were going to serve as officers." He recalled the influence the Army's response to the Lima text had on him. He scrutinized the text of the original English response in order to find his own understanding of the Army's non-sacramental foundation. Another important issue was his understanding of his call. "I have a very clear experience of being called to serve God in Frelsesarmeen, and believing that in his eyes we are equal to any church in spite of us being a minority church and our attitude to the sacraments." When the debate started in Norway he advocated that the Army should register as an independent faith community. He did not want to be counted as churchless in a legal sense. "At the same time I hoped that this would strengthen Norwegian Salvationists' self-knowledge and by this strengthen our identity and pride." When Frelsesarmeen registered a congregation in 2005 he had no reason to wait, so he joined straight away.

On the other hand, his Norwegian wife Lisbeth Welander did not register. Their different stories can be seen as an illustration of two main attitudes to the issue. Lisbeth Welander answered[38] by telling her background. She came from a little town in the west coast of Norway where the Norwegian Church represented formal Christianity. The minister was the one preparing the pupils in the school for confirmation and everybody joined, apart from a few. Her family used to live on one of the small islands as fishers/farmers, but moved to this little town when her grandmother was in her mid-40s. They were members of the Norwegian Church and made use of the church

38. I sent Lisbeth Welander an e-mail of 9 January 2014 where I asked: "Would you tell me why you did not become a member of Frelsesarmeen's congregation? Not so much your attitude today, but your reasons in 2005 when it became possible. Did you feel that membership of the Norwegian Church was important for you as Norwegian, that it was part of being a Norwegian citizen? Did you feel that you would desert something important by resigning the membership of the Norwegian Church? How was your relationship to the church as a child, in your youth and further on? Did your family attend services in the church? Have you made use of the church in connection with communion at special occasions or as a regular custom? Did you feel a security by keeping your membership of the church? Or was it just something you didn't really consider? Did you regard the Norwegian Church as the unifying expression of Christianity in Norway or as a symbol for the history of Christianity in Norway?" The answer came 10 January 2014.

for baptisms, confirmations, weddings, and funerals. She described the relation to the church as mainly a cultural one. Her grandmother was saved and became a soldier in Frelsesarmeen in this little town. The grandmother's Christian life and service centered round Frelsesarmeen, but she remained respectful of the church as the great overall symbol of Christianity. That was the tradition she was brought up in. As a child, Lisbeth was introduced to the corps by her grandmother, and she actively joined the different groups and became a soldier when she was old enough. She left to be trained as an officer in Oslo at the age of nineteen in 1982. At the training college she met a different attitude towards membership or affiliation to the Norwegian Church than she had been used to, because there were four Danish cadets in training with the Norwegians. Her Norwegian attitude was challenged. She married one of the Danes and later their two sons were not baptized. She never really engaged in the discussion concerning Frelsesarmeen's registration as an independent faith community. She experienced the issue as a question for each individual officer to decide upon, and nobody talked about their personal choice. She didn't remember that anything was done to motivate people to register as members in the faith community. As there never was a debate after registration, she just left things as they were. Her attitude was different after having served in the Philippines and Denmark. Her story illustrated that the issue was not a major one, at least not for her. It might have been the case for a number of other Salvationists, but there is no material to substantiate if Lisbeth Welander's attitude could be representative of a silent majority. The consequence of the decision to keep the question of registration at low key, with no appeal to soldiers and officers to make up their minds concerning this, was that it became privatized. It was an offer each individual could decide upon, but not a natural outcome of the Army's registration. The story did not describe the Norwegian Church as civil religion, rather as a cultural institution that embraced everybody and also as a central symbol for Christianity in the country. She never considered her membership of the Norwegian Church as connected to her nationality, but "rather in the town of my childhood being socialized into an understanding of being Christian in contrast to Communists, Humanists and Jehovah's Witnesses." The double membership had not been considered a problem and was hardly seen as a double membership, rather two different ones. In her letter she mentioned that her grandmother got saved and became a soldier. Apparently her grandmother had not considered her membership of the church as an expression of faith, rather a bond of tradition and culture. Her soldiership was centered round her personal faith, and the Army was her worshipping community as well as her place of service. Knud's story on the other hand could express a minority attitude, perhaps shared by a number of other Salvationists, but there is no data to substantiate how widespread his attitude was. His partly Danish background played a role, as he was unfamiliar with the general attitude of the other cadets at the college towards their membership of the Norwegian Church. The influence of the Army's response to the Lima text in strengthening his conviction concerning Army ecclesiology was interesting, an influence he might have shared with other officers. He also brought up the question of identity and self-understanding and even pride or self-respect. In his reference to the attitude among his fellow cadets he had seen an attitude of inferiority of being a Salvationist, as the Army was not considered equal to any other faith community. The expectation that registration would strengthen identity and be a reason for self-respect that Knud hoped for must have been more widespread as an argument, as Solhaug in his letter to Frelsesarmeen's Church Commission also took up the question of identity. Solhaug denied that registration would make any difference as the Army had a strong identity in its doctrines and structures. He also denied that authority and position would be different with registration. As these matters were central in his letter they must have appeared in discussions. These two are examples of attitudes present among officers as Frelsesarmeen registered as a faith community. The Welander couple were at the time in their early 40s and had been officers around twenty years serving only in Norway. They illustrate two different positions and two different choices, the one advocating that registration should take place and therefore membership was pursued straight away, the other expressing an indifference to the matter. There was neither urgency nor motivation and therefore membership was not pursued.

An example of how some soldiers apparently had been waiting for the situation of registration to appear came from the little corps in Røros, where during September 2005, 30 percent[39] of the soldiers resigned their membership of the Norwegian Church and became members of Frelsesarmeen's congregation. The surprise was the age of the soldiers: two men age 91 and 82, and four women age 82, 80, 75 and 42. Some of the arguments from the opponents to the issue of registration had been that it was only a few officers who supported this. The soldiers in Røros refuted this argument. Even with a lifelong membership of the Norwegian Church and many years as soldiers with the traditional double affiliation, this was what these soldiers had been waiting for. They not only went along to the minister to resign their membership; they also took the trouble to travel to another town to have new uniforms made by a tailor in order to celebrate this registration as something significant.

39. The percentage was made up by six soldiers. Letter of 19 August 2013 from the corps leader Astrid Hansen as a reply to my question of the number of soldiers who registered, the percentage of the soldiers in the corps they made and the age of these.

On 31 December 2005 after half a year the membership of the congregation counted 343, of these 84 officers (8 retired officers), 141 soldiers, 4 junior soldiers, 42 adherents, 13 others, and 60 were children under 15 years old.[40] The 2005 statistics for the Army as such showed: 199 active officers, 247 retired officers, 6.075 soldiers, 124 junior soldiers, and 124 adherents.[41] Two and a half months later by the 20 March 2006 the congregation had 408 members—108 officers (13 retired), 157 soldiers, 6 junior soldiers, 53 adherents, and 13 others, and 71 children under 15. The percentage of officers was the biggest as by March close to 50 percent of the active officers were registered in the congregation while it was only just over 5 percent of the retired officers, well over 3 percent of the soldiers, nearly 5 percent of junior soldiers and adherents. The number of children under 15 signaled that among the adults who registered, a substantial percentage must have been younger parents, or families with children. The figures show that the active officers were the ones that wanted to take hold of this opportunity of church membership as well as younger families. It could be officer families or soldier families. Ordinary soldiers had not yet started to change their legal church membership. That 30 percent of the soldiers in Røros registered as members was an exception. Growth was slow, but steady. The application for the right to perform legally valid weddings was sent 14 October 2005 and was given 14 December 2005.[42] A brochure was printed with all information needed. It was a folder of four pages with the last page as a registration form. It stated that Frelsesarmeen had in reality functioned as a congregation even though the legal registration had not included this. It gave information of the different kinds of membership: soldier, adherent, junior soldier, or member of one of the groups in the corps. It underlined that membership of the registered congregation was open for all and no other affiliation to Frelsesarmeen was needed. It gave information on the status of the congregation that members were centrally registered at THQ, that Frelsesarmeen had the right to perform weddings, and that the congregation received public financial support for each member. It also gave short information on how to resign membership of the Norwegian Church. All information needed was available at the local level, but no pressure or no drive to undertake new members happened in accordance with the decision made before registration. For the vast majority—according to the figures of those who registered—it was probably not an important issue. Some might,

40. Årsmelding 2005 for trossamfunnet Frelsesarmeen. (Annual Report 2005 for the Congregation Frelsesarmeen).
41. The Salvation Army Year Book 2006, 193.
42. Årsmelding2005 for trossamfunnet Frelsesarmeen.

like Lisbeth Welander, have been indifferent to the whole issue, as nothing was done actively to call attention to the matter. The minority of Salvationists, those who registered within the first months, had most probably been waiting for this with expectation as the soldiers in Røros, or with impatience as Knud Welander who had been advocating this for a long time. Active officers and younger families made up the body of the congregation. The voice of those who opposed the situation seemed to have been silenced by the assurance that "everything would remain as always." It did for the vast majority, but for the minority who registered a significant change had happened.

Frelsesarmeen's new book of ceremonies

The sentence "everything would remain as always" did not quite ring true when a new book of ceremonies, *Seremonier i Frelsesarmeen*, was published in 2005. The difference between this new one and the previous Norwegian edition from 1981 was remarkable. The 1981 edition was fairly close to *Salvation Army Ceremonies*, an edition revised in 1989 and had kept the spirit of the ceremonies, while the 2005 book differed on central issues such as promises and commitment given. It was ready in time for the congress where Frelsesarmeen's registration as a congregation was announced.

The changes were present in the Dedication Ceremony, the Marriage Ceremony, and the Junior Soldier's Enrollment. The dedication ceremony is aimed at Salvationist parents making promises concerning the upbringing of their child. However, in the *Salvation Army Ceremonies*, there is also a ceremony called "Thanksgiving or presentation ceremony" aimed at non-Salvationists wanting to present their child to God for a blessing. It might be parents who are reluctant to make the promises required by the dedication ceremony. The dedication ceremony is as follows:

> "In the dedication of this child you desire to give him/her fully to God. You wish to thank God for entrusting this precious life into your hands, and you want him/her to be nurtured in all that is pure, lovely and honest. To this end you promise that you will keep from him/her, so far as you are able, everything which is likely to harm him/her in body, mind or spirit.
>
> You also promise that, as he/she grows in wisdom and stature, you will teach him/her the truths of the gospel, encourage him/her to seek Christ as Savior and support him/her in the commitment of his/her life to the service of God. You must be to him/her an example of a true Christian.

> If you are willing to make these promises, I will receive the child in the name of God, and on behalf of The Salvation Army."[43]

The officer will receive the child in recognition of the promises given, offer a prayer, and give the child back to the parents with the charge of caring for the child in the name of the Lord and to keep the promises given.

In *Seremonier i Frelsesarmeen* of 2005, there was only one ceremony which was more like the thanksgiving ceremony than the dedication ceremony. Extra sentences were inserted into the thanksgiving ceremony, which are in italics:

> "By presenting (name of the child) to God *in his house* you wish to give thanks to him for his great gift. As parents you want the best for your child. *You wish that he/she shall grow up under the blessing of God, learn to know Jesus Christ and be taught in the Christian faith.* You will keep from him/her, as far as you are able, everything which is likely to harm him/her in body, mind and soul, *and teach him/her the road to goodness.*"

The parents are asked if this is what they want, followed by a prayer and the benediction. In the thanksgiving ceremony there is no promise at any stage and no charge to the parents after the prayer of dedication. In the Norwegian there are these comments, not a charge:

> "God's blessing is a great gift to bring with us. You can therefore look back on this day with joy and confidence. May God strengthen and help you in your responsibility as Christian parents."[44]

The most striking differences between the Salvationist dedication ceremony and the Norwegian edition are the downscaling of promises requested from the parents. The commitment to nurture the child in all that is pure, lovely, and honest, and not only to keep away harmful things is different. The promise actively to teach, to encourage and support, and to be an example are lacking in the new book. The charge to keep the promises is also absent. The comments that stand instead of the charge could imply recognition of what the ceremony itself could do independent of any promise. It seems as if the focus on the parents' promises has changed over to confidence in the actual ceremony. In a tradition where the focus is on inward conviction and personal faith while ceremonies are symbolic and not in

43. The General, *Salvation Army Ceremonies* 2004.
44. The General, *Seremonier i Frelsesarmeen* 2005.

themselves instrumental for divine grace, this is a profound departure from traditional Army faith. The dedication ceremony was not seen as conveying grace, rather pointing to salvation conditioned by repentance and faith. The underlying faith, that the child belongs to God from its first beginning and therefore is not in need of a ritual to become the child of God, is implicit in both the new and the old ceremony, but the difference is this new confidence in the ceremony itself. A new addition is also a sort of godparents for prayer. At the conclusion of the ceremony it has been tradition to turn to the congregation gathered and ask them to remember the child in prayer. This is still part of this ceremony, but then in addition the godparents are mentioned by name and charged to bring the child to God in prayer and teach it about Jesus. This does not depart from Army teaching, as intercession and responsibility for others are deeply rooted within Salvationism, but the way it is incorporated into the ceremony here makes it different. The bible text from Mark 10:13–16 with the well know words: "Let the little children come to me, and do not hinder them, for the kingdom of God belongs to such as these" is also incorporated into the ceremony. This bible text would often be used anyhow, but it supports the act of blessing in contrast to dedication. The alteration in the ceremony is already signaled in the change of name for the ceremony. The Norwegian translation of dedication used to be Barneinnvielse (dedication of the child), but that was changed to Barnevelsignelse (blessing of the child). This ceremony has a different focus, it is a blessing and not a dedication. The commitment and promises of the parents are no longer a strong issue. A possible influence from the Lutheran Church is reflected, also theologically. In Salvationist tradition the commitment and the promises are central in all ceremonies, therefore departure from these two was a real change.

When it comes to the ceremony of marriage there was a change in the 2004 *Salvation Army Ceremonies* concerning the articles of marriage:

> "We do solemnly declare that, although we enter into this marriage for reasons of personal happiness and fulfillment, we will do our utmost to ensure that our married status and relationship will deepen our commitment to God and enhance the effectiveness of our service as soldiers of Jesus Christ in The Salvation Army. We promise to make our home a place where all shall be aware of the abiding presence of God, and where those under our influence shall be taught the truths of the gospel, encouraged to seek Christ as Savior, and supported in the commitment of their lives to the service of God. We declare our intention to be to each other, by the help of God, true Christian examples and, through times of joy, difficulty or loss, to encourage each

other to grow in grace, and in the knowledge of our Lord and Savior Jesus Christ."[45]

This used to be the opening part of the ceremony, but was made optional instead of mandatory. In the Norwegian book they were excluded and by this the Salvationist characteristics of the ceremony was no longer an option.

Concerning the Junior Soldier's enrollment both the name as well as the ceremony was changed. It was a Junior Blessing as junior soldiers had been changed to juniors. The Junior Soldier's Promise as follows was no longer used:

> "I know that Jesus is my savior from sin. I have asked him to forgive my sins, and I will trust him to keep me good. By his help, I will be his loving and obedient child, and will help others to follow him. I promise to pray, to read my Bible, and to lead a life that is clean in thought, word and deed. I will not use anything that will injure my body or my mind, including harmful drugs, alcohol and tobacco."

The card used to be signed by the Junior Soldier and the Corps Officer. The new ceremony was simply a prayer ending with a laying on of hands and the benediction. After this the child would get a junior certificate. The certificate has a heading, Junior Blessing, the benediction is printed and the aim of the Juniors, to be better acquainted with Jesus, learning to take care of oneself and others and getting better acquainted with Frelsesarmeen. It is signed by the corps officer alone.

The juniors had been through a time of preparation, but it is quite different from the Junior Soldier Promise that had previously been the focus for the time of preparation together with Bible studies, Salvation Army history, and ethical issues. These three areas were still part of the present Norwegian preparation, but not the promise. The three profound characteristics of Salvation Army membership such as witness to salvation, focus on mission, and Salvationist lifestyle which are present in the Junior Soldier Promise had been eliminated.[46] Traditionally a junior soldier would be considered a Salvationist, but that would hardly be the case with a junior as no promise or pledge was given.

Seemingly it was the registration of Frelsesarmeen as an independent faith community that provided the reason for this change. It was published

---

45. The General, *Salvation Army Ceremonies*, 18–19.

46. In 2013 the Junior Soldier enrollment and the junior soldier's promise was reintroduced.

at the time of registration and prepared while the registration was prepared. The way the constitution described the congregation could look as if Frelsesarmeen wanted to open up for nominal membership, and the alteration of the dedication ceremony would support this. It does not require the parents to be members. Perhaps there had been a determination that the ceremonies had to be more broadly religious to seek acceptance within a wider community, as membership to the faith community was open for all. By taking away the Army characteristics from the three ceremonies and aiming at the minimum common denominator, they could be used more widely. A feature that could have supported such a decision, especially for the dedication ceremony, was the widespread contact Frelsesarmeen had with young families through baby song.[47] It had an appeal to ordinary families in communities all over Norway and in smaller towns a high percentage of parents would join the Army's baby song with their young ones.[48] The more general ceremony with its inclusive language could make this a possible choice for parents.

The updated communication strategy from Frelsesarmeen promoted an image of Frelsesarmeen as an organization with a low threshold where everybody could join in different activities. This was done by communicating in contemporary language and images an open and inclusive Frelsesarmeen. The book of ceremonies could also support such a communication in the ceremonies for children. This 2005 Norwegian book was more independent and less a translation than the previous books of ceremonies. With such significant changes in the ceremonies everything did not "remain as always."

---

47. The concept started in Sweden and was taken up in Norway. In the yearly report for Frelsesarmeen 1996: "New popular activities in 1996: Baby song is an offer to mothers and fathers with children under one year." This was the first report of this activity. There is nothing in 1995. The statistics concerning membership of baby song from 2000—2005 show the influence: 1084 in year 2000, 1100 in 2001, 1208 in 2002, 2140 in 2003, 1864 in 2004, 1602 in 2005. The numbers were highest in 2003 and 2004 during the time where the new book of ceremonies was prepared and finalized.

48. A reference to Røros again where the corps leader at the time, Major Astrid Hansen, in a mail of 25 July 2014 informed that one of the years in question (2000–2005) the number of children born in Røros was thirty-one, of these, twenty-five were brought to Frelsesarmeen's baby song. The outcome was that the schedule for the public baby examination had to be coordinated with the Army's baby song. The children from baby song continued to be connected to the corps through toddlers' song. Here the effect was that the meetings of the local government had to change to another weekday in order for a political active mother to attend. In my mail of 17 July 2014 I asked if any of the children from baby song had been dedicated in the corps. There was one child that had been dedicated. One couple with a child in toddlers' song had been married.

Conclusion

In this chapter the influence from society, and especially the experience in connection with the TV-fundraising, was helped by new communication technology spurred on a newfound pride in the Army's national as well as international work. This process led to a modernization of communication and PR within the Army so it changed Frelsesarmeen's own image as well as the image in the public mind from a bit dusty, old fashioned Army to a more modern Army. This change had an influence on the prizes the Army won because the Army's traditional values and work became more visible and up to date. In 2003 Frelsesarmeen won two prizes, in April the prize of the Association of Communication for "effective demonstration of communication of a very high standard" and in November the Reputation prize from Norwegian Information Advisers because of "its strong brand which everybody associates with something important and very positive, being creative in its communication and making use of new and exciting means in order to communicate its message. Over a long time it has built up its fantastic reputation in a low-voiced, consistent and clear manner in spite of attitudes that the majority of the population do not agree with."[49]

The PR work was one factor that influenced Salvationist self-esteem. Another influence on Salvationists identity was theological reflection coming from the international Salvation Army. The new focus on ecclesiology, especially the reinterpretation concerning the sacraments as part of Salvationists practice, could have given a new impetus for wanting Frelsesarmeen's registration to mirror that. In a way it did, because it described the Army's ecclesiology independent of any registration. The Army had never combined its mission and ministry to any particular form of registration, as registrations that worked had been used. What mattered was what kind of identity Salvationists had as could be seen in the two articles in *Frelsesoffiseren*. The chapter on ecclesiology interpreted Salvation Army practices differently from what had previously been the case, especially the sacraments. It did not add new practices, but gave ecclesiological interpretation to practices already there. This showed that the Army was a church with its own notae ecclesiae. This interpretation would also be valid for Frelsesarmeen's corps in Norway as they had always functioned. Because of this the church identity was not dependent upon a registration as a congregation, it could carry the marks of a church as an organization. Still it seemed surprising that the designation congregation was emptied of any substance, while organization carried it all. The registration as a faith community was achieved at long last,

---

49. http.//www.na24.no/propaganda/arkiv/article 2012700.ece.

but it was marked by the strong parties within Frelsesarmeen that wanted the Army's status as an organization to stay in focus. The registration was therefore twofold, as organization and congregation, with the notae ecclesiae placed under the organization and the congregation as a purely legal accommodation. The modernized PR strategy was not activated for the sake of church registration. The new registration was kept low key all through. Considering how much time and discussion the issue had taken, more focus on the subject could have been expected. By this it showed a deep seated fear of division or tension surfacing. It also signaled that the parties who wanted things to stay as they used to legally be stronger or more vocal than the ones for whom registration was the step that had been missing. The number that registered straight away was not large, but they were there. As the decision was not to propagate anything apart from an article in *Krigsropet* and a press release the silent majority might not have bothered to make any changes. The soldiers from Røros might be examples of this silent majority. Their corps officer had registered herself, and even though she said, that it came as a surprise when the vicar phoned to say that this group of soldiers were at his office to resign their membership of the Norwegian Church, her example most probably had an effect. The wish to be registered as members in a legal sense must have been there, but needed to be activated as it was. The example of the Welander couple exemplifies two different positions, those for whom this was important and those who were not really concerned, but felt things were ok as they had always been.

Even though it was claimed at the announcement of the registration during the congress that, "everything would remain as always," the new book of ceremonies pointed in another direction. The registered faith community that would offer these ceremonies seemed to be a community that welcomed everybody without having any expectation of a declaration of faith or commitment. Even though a confession of faith was not called for, the Salvation Army doctrines were printed at the beginning of the document of constitution. In a way it promoted nominal membership because it was a legal construction and seemingly value free. Promises and commitment were reserved for the soldier's enrollment, but not ceremonies connected to family life or the children's own ceremony of membership. The outcome of the wish that everybody should be equal in the three ceremonies mentioned was that the minimum common denominator was sought.

How much had the influence from the Norwegian Church colored the concept of being a congregation? Was the membership of the church an adherence to civil religion? This will be the focus of the next chapter.

Chapter 9

The Theory of Civil Religion in Relation to Salvationists' View of the Norwegian Church

THE CONCEPT OF CIVIL religion has been mentioned several times during the book in connection with Salvationists' nominal membership of the Norwegian Church, starting at the time of nation building and formation of an independent state in 1905. The early Frelsesarmeen's officers had by and large resigned their membership of the State Church and abstained from having their children baptized. A change towards a practice of double membership happened around 1905 for both officers and soldiers. This became a general practice for the rest of the century. This most probably happened because Salvationists wanted to show that they were proper Norwegians and not dissenting from this central religious institution of the state. Frelsesarmeen never registered as a dissenter community. When the different commissions within the Norwegian Church worked on the church's identity and structure in the 1960s and 1970s, and especially when the State/Church commission published its report in 1975 with a majority recommendation of a separation between state and church, the argument came up within Frelsesarmeen that, in case of such a separation, it had to register as a faith community. The TC, Commissioner Solhaug and other Salvationists found it inconceivable to remain as members of a Lutheran Church, when it was no longer a State Church. The change from being the religious institution of the state to becoming an independent Lutheran Church would cause difficulties, mainly because of the difference between Salvationist ecclesiology with non-observance of the sacraments and Lutheran ecclesiology, where the sacraments were foundational. Salvationists had a Salvationist faith, but adhered to Lutheran praxis concerning the sacraments, especially infant baptism. It was considered a rite marking connection to the Church, the religious institution of the State, adhering to a thousand-year culture and tradition, as well as receiving God's blessing on the child. By this practice they stated that they were proper Norwegians keeping a family tradition which had been celebrated through many generations. It was common practice from which they did not want to dissent. I have connected the change in adherence to the church between 1900 and 1910 and the urgency of starting a process for registration as an independent faith community in 1975, when it looked as if church and state would separate, as they could illustrate Salvationists' perception of the Norwegian Church as an expression of civil religion.

Historical analysis and interpretation have revealed that folk churches in the Nordic countries have had a civil religious function for the Nordic people and were centers in a civil religious culture, even though the situation of the Norwegian Church was more complicated. Norwegian research has shown that civil religion in low key could be seen within the Norwegian Church as there were elements of civil religion present, but empirical research could not substantiate a greater merging between civil religion and the Norwegian Church. From the research concerning Frelsesarmeen a question has arisen as to whether a concept of civil religion has been implicitly present in Salvationists' view of the Norwegian Church and their own adherence to the church.

Civil Religion

The term civil religion has a history of its own originating with the French/Swiss philosopher Jean-Jacques Rousseau who was of the opinion that any society needed a civil religion in order to integrate its population. Christianity had a spirituality that was vital for individuals as Rousseau considered it a religion of inward devotion, therefore it had no obvious political role, except for the possible contribution it could have on what he phrased as "civil religion":

> "The dogmas of civil religion ought to be few, simple and exactly worded, without explanation or commentary. The existence of a mighty, intelligent and beneficent Divinity, possessed of foresight and providence, the life to come, the happiness of the just, the punishment of the wicked, the sanctity of the social contract and the laws: these are the positive dogmas. Its negative dogmas I confine to one, intolerance."[1]

---

1. Rousseau, *The Social Contract and Discourses*, 307–8.

The roots of the civil religion Rousseau advocated were Christian and so was the influence of the concept on American society for many years. As pluralism in both religion and culture increasingly marked American society, the term was reintroduced in more recent times by the American sociologist Robert Bella in 1967.[2] According to Bellah there existed a civil religion in America alongside official religious bodies and churches. He used the Declaration of Independence of 1776 and the inaugural address of President John F. Kennedy from January 1961, as well as George Washington's first inaugural address and his farewell address, to substantiate his idea. Bellah's definition was:

> "This public religious dimension is expressed in a set of beliefs, symbols, and rituals that I am calling American civil religion. The inauguration of the president is an important ceremonial event in this religion."[3]

The oath the President swears before the people and God was another expression of civil religion. An important issue was that sovereignty belongs to God, meaning that, "the will of the people is not itself the criterion for right and wrong. There is a higher criterion in terms of which this will can be judged."[4] Thanksgiving Day[5] became a holy day within the civil religion. After the Civil War the theme of death, sacrifice, and rebirth became part of civil religion and Memorial Day gave ritual expression to this theme. Bellah claimed in 1967 that this religion was still very much alive. He also suggested that American civil religion could become part of a new civil religion of the world. In his conclusion he underlined that behind the civil religion, even though it was a religion alongside the religions in the country, were biblical archetypes such as:

> "Exodus, Chosen People, Promised Land, New Jerusalem, Sacrificial Death and Rebirth. But it is also genuinely American and genuinely new. It has its own prophets and its own martyrs, its own sacred places, its own solemn rituals and symbols."[6]

It functioned as a uniting factor that could integrate the population as was the original meaning behind the term coming from Rousseau and now two hundred years later reinterpreted by Bellah. He also considered civil

---

2. Bellah, "Civil Religion in America," 40–55.
3. Ibid., 42.
4. Ibid., 43.
5. It was proclaimed by George Washington at the request of both houses of Congress 3 October 1789 to be celebrated November 26 of that same year.
6. Ibid., 54.

religion to possess a critical, prophetic dimension, because there was an awareness that the nation stood under higher judgment. His article gave rise to an intense debate in different parts of the world with many opponents and supporters, often with different definitions of what civil religion was. His article remained influential in years ahead, even into the 21 century.

Gerald Parsons took up the theme from Bellah some thirty-five years later in research on a national level in UK and USA concerning the remembrance of those killed in war and the local traditions, culture, and rituals of the Italian city of Siena. In the case studies he used a five-point definition of civil religion by Richard Petard and Robert Linder. They had these characteristics:

> "First, it will refer to the widespread acceptance by a people of a shared sense of their nation's history and destiny. Second, it will relate their society to a realm of absolute meanings. Third, it will enable them to look at their society and community as in some sense special. Fourth, it will provide a vision which ties the nation together as an integrated whole. And fifth, it will provide a collection of beliefs, values, rites, ceremonies and symbols which, taken together, give sacred meaning to the life of the community and thus provide an overarching sense of unity that transcends internal conflicts and differences."[7]

Pierard and Linder's definition has been used as a general definition by scholars working in very different national and local contexts[8] and used by Parsons in researching civil religion in USA, the United Kingdom, and Siena.

The previous definitions of civil religion were the historical, as well as contemporary international definitions, but the influence also came to the Nordic countries as the Lutheran World Federation (LWF) in a process studying civil religion arranged an international consultation in Finland with the theme, "The Church and Civil Religion in the Nordic Countries of Europe," in 1984 with representatives from Denmark, Finland, Iceland, Norway, and Sweden under the chairmanship of Béla Harmati from Geneva. The working definition of civil religion put forward for the consultation was as follows:

> "Civil religion consists of a pattern of symbols, ideas and practices that legitimate the authority of civil institutions in a society. It provides a fundamental value orientation that binds a people together in common action within the public realm. It is religious

---

7. Parsons, *Perspectives on Civil Religion*, 5–6.
8. Ibid., 6.

in so far as it evokes commitment and, within an overall world view, expresses a people's ultimate sense of worth, identity and destiny. It is civil in so far as it deals with the basic institutions exercising power in a society, nation or other political unit. A civil religion can be known through its ritual observances, holidays, sacred places, documents, stories, heroes and other behavior in or analogous to recognized historical religions. Civil religion may also contain a theory which may emerge as an ideology. Individual members of a society may have varying degrees of awareness of their civil religion. It may have an extensive or limited acceptance by the population as long as it serves its central function of legitimating the civil institutions."[9]

It was a very broad definition that could give rise to studying different elements of the Nordic societies. However, the focus was the role of the Lutheran Folk/State Churches within a possible civil religion. Susan Sundback[10] from Finland could not see civil religion, according to the definition, different from existing dominant religious institutions. She found that in Finland a civil religion would build on the religious foundation of the church, and therefore argued that there was a symbiosis between the folk church and civil religion.

In later research concerning the four Nordic countries of Denmark, Finland, Norway, and Sweden, Susan Sundback[11] looked at the paradox of the fairly strong adherence to the state churches in view of the rather weak religious engagement and found that the folk churches had a civil religious function for the Nordic people and that they were centers in a civil religious culture. She did not find civil religion outside the national churches. She suggested that the clearest expression of civil religion was found in the political parties' programs marked by loyalty towards the church and in the speeches held by church officials on all occasions that underlined the churches' general social significance. The cooperation between the church and the public sector concerning conscripts, prisoners, patients, and socially exposed people could be seen as examples of civil religious functions. In spite of these theories of civil religion in the Nordic countries, the situation of the Norwegian Church was more complicated. She referred to the split from the end of 1800 with a strong and growing Norwegian and popular pietistic Christianity as an opposition to the State Church that hindered the development towards a civil religious consensus more than in the other

9. Harmati, *The Church and Civil Religion in the Nordic Countries of Europe*, 5.
10. Sundback, "Folk church religion-A kind of Civil Religion?"
11. Sundback, "Medlemskapet i de lutherska kyrkorna i Norden" (Membership of the Lutheran churches in the North), 34–73.

Nordic countries, but found that the situation within the church in Norway in the last decades expressed a more general Nordic situation. The overall view of the Nordic folk churches was that they expressed pragmatism toward different issues in society showing a great deal of adaptation to the new developments as well as being theologically liberal. By this they kept the support in membership by the majority of the population. By including the adaptation of the church to society she gave reason for civil religion still to be an issue within the Nordic countries including Norway.

At the consultation in Finland in 1984 one of the Norwegian participants, Even Fougner,[12] wrote concerning the Norwegian Church as civil religion:

> "From the perspective of civil religion, it is possible to assert that the Evangelical Lutheran religion has been the civil religion of Norway. The clergy are civil servants who, together with other civic officials, have contributed toward giving legitimacy to the Norwegian state and its institutions. There are very strong bonds between monarch and church. The king participates in all important ecclesiastical events as, for example, the ordination of bishops."[13]

The way he connected the Norwegian Church with civil religion was by a purely functional definition. There could have been other functions to be mentioned such as the central role of the church in a national tragedy. This central role appeared as late as in 2012, when a memorial service was arranged in the Cathedral of Oslo after the Utøya massacre of Social Democratic youth in July 2012. The Government, the King and Queen, bishops and ministers, as well as representatives from different spheres of society and from different religions, were gathered to commemorate and share the grief. A massive crowd of ordinary people gathered outside the church. The church was the natural choice for this memorial, and it symbolized a civil religion of the country.

The researcher Inger Furseth referred to Fougner's article when she took up the question of civil religion in Norway in an empirical sociological study to ascertain if civil religion was a present or past phenomenon.[14] Her conclusion was that civil religion was not an equivalent to the Norwegian State Church, because it was still a confessional church, but that on the whole religious leaders were expressing civil religious views. Also the lay

---

12. Even Fougner was at the time Dean in Frederiksstad, later he became Bishop in Borg in 1990.

13. Fougner, "Church and State," 130.

14. Furseth, "Civil Religion in Low Key," 39–54.

movements within the church could be seen as "organizational vehicles that carry the belief system that civil religion is." Pål Repstad, another researcher, referred to later empirical surveys from 1992 and 1994 that supported Furseth's hypothesis "that civil religious perspectives are mainly reserved for the religiously active."[15] The political elite had changed from hostility, or indifference, towards religion, to a wish that the inclusive folk church would move in the direction of civil religion, because that was seen as liberal and tolerant and could serve as a barrier against more sectarian religious movements. For the Social Democrats the welfare state also needed to provide religious welfare at critical stages in people's lives. The folk church seemed to meet these needs. Civil religion was manifested through different events involving the monarchy, at the opening of the national assembly, on national days and at celebrations at the end of school and kindergarten years. By the method and definition used, Furseth concluded that civil religion was low key in Norway and that the data did not support civil religion as equivalent to the Norwegian State Church. Neither Furseth nor Repstad found any symbiosis between civil religion and the Norwegian Church, as Susan Sundblad argued concerning Finland.

The definitions presented by different researches pointed to a wide scope of civil religion within a given society. Common for Bellah, Pierard, and Linder, as well as Furseth, were a transcendence, or absolute meaning, as a higher criterion for right and wrong, or direction and meaning. The definition from LWF is not so clear in connection with transcendence, but still there was something religious in an overall world-view that provoked commitment. Bellah's focus on beliefs, symbols, rituals, and sacred places were shared by the definitions by LWF, Pierard, and Linder, while Furseth narrowed this down to national rituals. Only Bellah had the focus on prophets and martyrs, while focus on identity, worth, and destiny was in the LWF definition, and Pierard and Linder mentioned sacred meaning to life, unity, and the history and destiny of the nation. Furseth had none of these, but stressed the public speeches at national events that had to have some religious statements, which made the criteria for civil religion rather limited. Fougner looked at the function of the clergy as civil servants giving legitimacy to the state and state institutions, plus the close bonds between monarch and church. Sundback underlined the loyalty of the political parties towards the church, speeches by church officials underlining the church's social significance, and the cooperation between the public sector and the church concerning people in connection with the penal system, hospitals, and social challenges. Both Fougner and Sundback focused on

---

15. Repstad, "Civil Religion in Modern Society," 168.

the functions to support a claim that the state churches were expressions of civil religion.

In my interpretation of Salvationists' implicit perception of the State Church as the expression of civil religion, the functions were in focus with a single exception finding a resonance with Pierard and Linder's definition.

Discussion

One issue is the role of the Norwegian Church in the Norwegian society as a vehicle of civil religion from an overall view, another is if this could have been the case in the minds of Salvationists. They are a tiny minority in Norway, but still play a significant role in society and are generally known, recognized, and appreciated by the Norwegian public, both by institutions and people. I have connected the early practice to the Salvationists' wish to be identified as proper Norwegian citizens and the urgency in 1975 of starting work towards registration as a reaction towards separation between state and church, because I see membership of the State Church being implicitly considered as membership of a civil religion. I see it as a religion that was considered a uniting or integrating factor in Norwegian society, and therefore closely linked to its members being considered proper Norwegian citizens. Multiculturalism and pluralism have been marking Norway for a number of years, but still during the period of this book the Norwegian Church as a state church seemed to be considered an important national and cultural symbol by Salvationists. They seemingly considered membership as a natural part of being Norwegians, even though it would be of nominal character. The reason for connecting their choices and attitudes to the concept of civil religion, is first and foremost the combination of state and church which they adhere to as a civil religion. A separation between the two would alter the whole concept and membership would no longer be natural. To this could be added the long history of the Norwegian Church uniting the Norwegian people. Membership meant staying within family and national tradition and being part of the dominant culture. It also guaranteed a central place for Christianity in the country.

Fougner's definition that supported the idea of the Norwegian Church as an expression of civil religion might very well be similar to how Norwegian Salvationists comprehended the church as the important institution to belong to as Norwegian citizens. The concept of civil religion has not been mentioned or argued for by any Salvationists during this time and the arguments why it was so important to adhere to the Norwegian Church are few, but their continued and strong adherence to the church, as well as the few arguments present that reveal a special bond to this institution. So do their choices of nominal membership of the Norwegian Church without commitment to a Lutheran faith in order to be identified as proper Norwegians. This they shared with many other Norwegians, but Salvationists generally had a strong faith commitment that otherwise would exclude nominal membership. It could work because their Christian faith was lived out in Frelsesarmeen's congregations and expressed through Salvationist faith, mostly in accordance with Army doctrines. Their membership of the Norwegian Church expressed their decision to be identified as proper Norwegians. This was first and foremost seen in the adherence to the ritual of infant baptism. Very important is the argument that registration would be necessary if and when state and church separated.

In looking into Furseth's research and her conclusion, I find that the ones she identified as vehicles of civil religion could support the interpretation of Salvationists, considering the Norwegian Church as an expression of civil religion. She did not suggest that civil religion was equivalent to the Norwegian State Church, as Fougner did, or as Susan Sundblad suggested, not only for Finland, but for the for all the Nordic countries. Furseth described civil religion as low key in Norway and primarily carried by religious groups, the church itself, and religious leaders. Salvationists were a religious group and a minority group. There is no evidence that Frelsesarmeen, as an organization or faith community, considered the Norwegian Church an expression of civil religion, but Solhaug as a religious leader within Frelsesarmeen strongly and persistently upheld the argument that a separation between state and church would create a new situation of affiliation to the church, as if the unity of state and church was of utmost importance for adherence. Dahlstrøm, also a religious leader within Frelsesarmeen, argued differently. He saw the State Church as a guarantee for Christian unity, for Norwegian culture and history, and for Norwegian identity. He referred to other European countries with state churches and also saw them as guarantees for Christian unity. For him, registration would be splitting this unity, and unity had to be preserved.

The definition Parsons made use of included an *ethnos* identity as constitutive for attitudes, being expressions for civil religion. He stressed the shared sense of the nation's history and destiny, society related to a realm of absolute meanings, the society as in some sense special, the vision of the nation as an integrated whole, the collection of beliefs, values, rites, symbols, and ceremonies that gave meaning to life and created a sense of unity. In this substantive definition above I can recognize a Salvationist attitude, such as an explicit ethnos national identity as expressed by Dahlstrøm and his view of the state church (he always used this term and never The

Norwegian Church) and its historic position as a symbol of Norway. The views which Dahlstrøm represented could cover a view of the State Church as an expression of civil religion as a thousand year-long religious tradition of the Norwegian people and as part of Norwegian cultural identity. It was as if he considered the combination of state and church as guarantee for Christian unity. According to Parsons' definition, Dahlstrøm's view could fit into the theme of civil religion, even though it was very different from the way Solhaug considered the situation. Dahlstrøm's bond to the Norwegian Church was based on his Norwegian nationality and the Norwegian culture that united people. He connected membership of the Norwegian Church to the faith of the Apostles' Creed concerning the unity of the Church. The Norwegian Church expressed this true unity in Norway, therefore membership of the church was crucial for being a Norwegian Christian. Even though the attitudes to registration as an independent faith community differed profoundly between Solhaug and Dahlstrøm, the bonds to the Norwegian Church seemingly were not based on a Lutheran confession for either of them. Solhaug argued that it was difficult or even unthinkable that Salvationists belonged to an independent confessional Lutheran church. Dahlstrøm seemingly did not have problems with such a scenario, as he saw the Norwegian Church as the uniting factor of the Norwegian people expressing the Apostles' Creed concerning unity, but by his use of language to describe Lutheran belief and practice as "hobby horses" he did not agree with, he did not signal strong connection to Lutheran confession. I consider Solhaug's attitude to the Norwegian Church as a definite functional expression of civil religion while Dahlstrøm's attitude to the church could be seen as a cultural, historical, or substantial expression of civil religion in the meaning of civil religion as used by Parsons. The relevance of the concept of civil religion was not exhausted when Frelsesarmeen registered as a faith community in 2005. There was a new relevance of the concept redefined in the challenge of the years of the new millennium.

Civil Religion in connection to pluralism

The concept of civil religion has been revisited and redefined in a new setting by Martyn Percy[16] in 2012. He focused on the British scene while also embracing Western Europe, stating the difference to USA and the development there concerning the place of religion in the public square. He was using the term in order to make a bridge between religion and human rights and between religion and the state. Percy referred to the first Hindu

16. Percy, *The Ecclesial Canopy*, 109–126.

peer in the House of Lords, Bhabhi Parehk's new paradigm for relationship between religion and state, where Parekh argues that religion's distinct contribution to public life should be recognized, and faith given a stake in the maintenance of an open and free society, instead of marginalizing faith. Religion on the one hand plays an important role in moral life therefore the community should have a collective interest in the well-being of churches and their beliefs. On the other hand, society can civilize the church that would have to accept the constraints of public life when entering politics. Examples of these constraints were "speaking in a 'public' language that is intelligible to all citizens, and accepting 'the burden of public judgment' which sometimes requires people to live with deep disagreement." Inspired by the thoughts of Parekh on politics and religion Percy argued:

> "Being a Christian in the twenty-first century cannot simply be about belonging to a church, but should rather be seen as equally consisting of being a certain type of citizen within society. 'Civil religion', therefore, becomes something significantly more than 'social glue' or 'the spiritual dimension' to society. Rather, it also becomes bound up in the actual aspirations of society which are themselves related to the common good."[17]

Percy takes the concept of civil religion into a contemporary situation mainly as a challenge to the churches to be present and participate in the public arena. He is clearly rejecting the idea of religion remaining in the private sphere as a private faith. He sees the concept of public space as a challenging frontier the churches find themselves engaging with at the beginning of the twenty-first century and states that "the problem of how religion takes its place in society and shapes public space is an issue now faced by many of the world's major faiths." Percy posed different questions which he found crucial in a situation such as this and which called the church to "a more intentional public theology". The two main questions concerned the interaction with economy and the welfare state, and how to articulate "a genuinely confident and rich theological leadership, that shapes national public life and social values?"

Questions like these as well as the challenge of participating in the public sphere seemed important for Frelsesarmeen as the publication *Til hvilken pris—takseres et menneske?* (At which price is a human being valued?) sent to all politicians on local and national level before the election in 2009 could illustrate. The six feature articles were written by Salvationists who were well known in the public debate in their different fields, as for instance economics, penal system, human rights. Focus was on the economic situation and

17. Ibid., 118.

consumerism, freedom (of speech, thought, and belief), the penal system, the culture of alcohol in society, the care of vulnerable children. During the spring of 2009 the leaders or deputy leaders from all the political parties met individually with representatives from Frelsesarmeen's Social Services at different social outreach centers. Quotations from these meetings were part of the publication as well. During the electoral campaign a public debate was arranged in Oslo by Frelsesarmeen between politicians from all political parties and the writers of the featured articles. Participation in the public sphere has been part of Army history all through its existence, but mostly through deeds rather than words. One of the challenges for Frelsesarmeen was to take part in the public debate, to be vocal and visible. The paper from 2009 took up such a challenge.

The reason for referring to Martyn Percy was to give an example of how the term civil religion seemingly is not outdated, but still being revisited and reformulated. For Percy the reformulation had a focus or a mission of getting the churches involved in society and refusing to be placed within the private sphere. The reason was also that a definition such as his would be in accordance with how Frelsesarmeen seemingly is defining its role in contemporary Norway at the present time. The redefinition should be seen against the background of the outcome of religious pluralism in the form of the privatization of religion.

The reformulation of civil religion made by Percy is important in view of the development of religious pluralism during the last decades. Civil religion in Norway had expressed itself in close bonds between the state and the church connecting Norwegian religious culture with national identity and belonging. This situation is changing as religious pluralism is growing stronger.

During the years which were in focus for this book, pluralism in Norway had grown covering cultural, ethnic, and religious differences. Religious pluralism had changed from a pluralism of minority, mainly Christian denominations, to a pluralism of different religions. Figures from 1980 concerning religious pluralism implied that changes were already emerging. 1000 Muslims were registered in 1980, a figure that grew to 80,000 in the next twenty four years.[18] The secular organization concerned with humanist philosophies, Human-Etisk Forbund founded in 1956, increased its membership drastically from its 8,300 members in 1980 to 69,610 members in 2004.[19] Immigration into Norway also had a great effect on the growth of the

---

18. Schmidt, ed., *Endring og Tilhørighet*, 20.
19. Ibid., 19.

Catholic Church that grew from 26,580 in 1990 to 46,308 in 2004.[20] Even though religious pluralism was evident within Norwegian society during these years towards the end of the millennium and the beginning of the new, the vast majority of the Norwegian population 85.7 percent were still members of the Norwegian Church in 2004.[21]

Some of the key elements of religious pluralism are that religion is being privatized—that it is influenced by market mechanism. Charles Taylor[22] commented that in a pluralistic world, with the many forms of belief and unbelief, these depreciate each other. Therefore "the outcome of pluralism and mutual fragilization will often be a retreat of religion from the public square." In spite of differences, the agreement has been that religion has been transferred to the private sphere. José Casanova challenged the situation that religion necessarily would stay in the private sphere or automatically belonged there by stating that the "privatization of religion is a historical option, a "preferred option" to be sure, but an option nonetheless."[23] He gave examples of the "deprivatization" of religion in the modern world, in the 1980s Islamic revolution in Iran, the rise of the Solidarity movement in Poland, as well as the public reemergence of Protestant fundamentalism as a force in American politics. He explained what he meant with "deprivatization":

> "By deprivatization I mean the fact that religious traditions throughout the world are refusing to accept the marginal and privatized role which theories of modernity as well as theories of secularization has reserved for them."[24] "What I call the "deprivatization" of modern religion is the process whereby religion abandons its assigned place in the private sphere and enters the undifferentiated public sphere of civil society to take part in the ongoing process of contestation, discursive legitimation, and redrawing of boundaries."[25]

Casanova also stated that "deprivatization" of religion presupposed the privacy of religion and could only be justified if the right to privacy and freedom of conscience were legally protected. He assumed the privatization of religion as a condition for religion being "deprivatized." The example Martyn Percy used these eighteen years later could be seen as a sort of

20. Ibid., 20.
21. Ibid., 16.
22. Taylor, *A Secular Age*.
23. Casanova, *Public Religions in the Modern World*, 39.
24. Ibid., 5.
25. Ibid., 66.

"deprivatization" that the Hindu peer in the House of Lords, Bhikhu Parekh, wanted. He voiced the wish to reclaim religion for the public square and get it out of the private sphere by a new paradigm for the relationship between religion and the State, so its distinct contribution to public life could be recognized. The dominant attitude of religion as belonging to the private sphere has influenced the expectations of religious minorities for assimilation to take place within the spheres of politics, economy, and work, while religion would remain within the private sphere. Part of this expectation has also been that the religious minorities to a certain extent would be marked by secularization.[26] The development during the last years has shown that this has not been the case, rather have religious minorities claimed to be heard and seen in the public room.

The Norwegian Church has accepted the premises of pluralism over the years and been aware of other religions. It has been engaged in dialogues and involved in ecumenical fellowship. It has been able to afford this openness towards pluralism, because of its very strong position in the country as the religion of the state, a situation that was clear according to §2 of the constitution. The State Church's response to the situation of pluralism has historically been an acceptance of the different laws on religion, as they developed from religious tolerance to religious freedom—laws that made room for dissenter communities to be registered and openly live out their faith to a later economic equality, by faith communities receiving support from the state and borough, even though the Evangelical-Lutheran religion was the religion of the state. The laws of religion were dissenter laws and the Norwegian Church was not included in these laws. That was also the case with the Non-Conformist Act of 1969, even though the definition of other religious bodies had changed from dissenters to faith communities. The Norwegian Church was regulated by its own law. The norm was to be members of the church, dissenters were exceptions to the norm, therefore religious pluralism was growing and flourishing within a minority of the population, while the majority belonged to the Norwegian Church, even though it seemed to be a nominal membership for a large part of the population. Within its own borders it made room for different interpretations of faith with a clear intention of keeping a living contact with society. Neither orthodoxy nor fundamentalism became strong or majority reactions to pluralism within the church, as has been the case around the world for some religious groups. As religious pluralism within Norwegian society changed from a pluralism of minority Christian denominations to a pluralism marked by multi religious groups, the influence of other religions and

---

26. Furseth and Repstad, *Inføring i religionssociologi*, 211–15.

attitudes to this situation might mean a change in loyalty to the Norwegian Church as religious pluralism grows even stronger. The percentage of members out of the total population has fallen from 85.7 percent in 2004 to 75.2 percent in 2013.[27] There has been a decline in membership over the years, but it could look as if this decline is growing stronger.

It seems as if Frelsesarmeen has followed a similar path as the Norwegian Church by underlining a living relationship with society around it and avoiding being pushed into a private sphere as well. The constitution of the denomination from 2005, as well as the introduction of adherents opened up for plurality rather than uniformity in interpretation of faith and practice. The reaction towards pluralism from Frelsesarmeen was not orthodoxy or fundamentalism, rather lowering the threshold between society and the Army. Frelsesarmeen has a mission of serving the present age and for this still to be true it has to keep a place in the public arena and avoided being confined within the private sphere.

Conclusion

As an overwhelming majority of Salvationists kept their membership of the Norwegian Church, in spite of being enrolled as soldiers in Frelsesarmeen, an implicit attitude towards the Norwegian Church as an expression of civil religion might have been more general than the limited accessible material could substantiate. The outcome of Furseth's research was to see The Norwegian Church as civil religion in low key, which might correspond to the attitude of Salvationists. She found that the notion of civil religion was especially present among church leaders and the religious lay organization. This would correspond to the examples given, both by leaders and members. Gerald Parsons' definition of civil religion was defined in a way which included Dahlstrøm's attitude to the church and could contain his continued resistance to registration as an independent faith community. Perceiving the Norwegian Church as a national, historic symbol of unity and belonging, as Dahlstrøm did, could also be accepting it as civil religion.

The research from the British scene concerning a redefinition of civil religion was mainly seen as a challenge to the churches for involvement in the public square, a challenge Frelsesarmeen has responded to in various ways within the last years. This concept of civil religion could show that the term was not outdated, and for Salvationists no longer connected to membership of the Norwegian Church, but by redefinition might play a role in the future. As a consequence of this redefinition, a section on religious pluralism, as

27. www.ssb.no/kultur-ogfritid/statistikker/kirke-k.

it has developed in Norway, has been included. One of the characteristics of pluralism has been that religion was expected to be confined within the private sphere. Percy's contribution was a protest against this confinement of religion as well as a challenge to the churches to be present in the public room. The Norwegian Church has been visible in the public square in its role as the majority religion and as a vehicle of civil religion, even if it was in low key. The reaction from Frelsesarmeen has been taking up the challenge for sustaining and keeping a place in the public square by being more vocal and entering into dialogue with the political system.

In the process of finding its voice in the public square, Frelsesarmeen also had the challenge of its own registration and the question of what it meant to be church in this situation and how that challenge had been met during its history in Norway.

Chapter 10

Which ecclesiology?

SALVATIONISTS' MEMBERSHIP OF THE Norwegian Church has been interpreted in this book as an adherence to the culture and customs of the country, to a civil religion in order to be proper Norwegians. However, the Norwegian Church is more than culture, customs, and civil religion. It is a church and has an ecclesiology that has implicitly influenced Salvationists and their understanding of church. The reports of the two commissions, Frelsesarmeen's Commission 1975–78 and Frelsesarmeen's Church Commission 1993–96, revealed such an influence as they described Frelsesarmeen's ecclesiology. The issues were spiritualistic Christianity and the invisible church. In the minds of the two committees these two issues became connected.

During the work of Frelsesarmeen's Commission 1975–78, Professor Block-Hoell was invited to present a paper. The impact of Bloch-Hoell's paper, given at their second meeting, was long lasting. It concerned his label of the Army as an expression of spiritualistic Christianity, which he considered dangerous and indicated by The Salvation Army's non-observance of the sacraments. He explained what he meant by spiritualistic, a presumption that material things and physical phenomena in themselves had no real spiritual significance. He did not expand his definition further. Presumably it was just to place the Army in the ecumenical landscape and call attention to his understanding of the dangers of Christianity without the sacraments. The description of the Army as spiritualistic, without broader evaluation, allowed for some misunderstandings by the commission. The members simply took hold of this label without further reflection and connected it to the idea of the invisible church. A discussion or dialogue that had connected this to some of the Army's roots instead never took place. Such a discussion could have concerned the Army's belief in the baptism of the Holy Spirit as the essential baptism, or perhaps the pneumatological roots of some of the Army's teaching, or the influence of these roots on the founders of the Army. Concerning the pneumatological roots, R. David Rightmire[1] in his research analyzed the Quaker influence amongst others. He considered that to be more implicit that explicit. He was pursuing "the possible connection between Booth's theological mindset and the non-sacramental theology of the Spiritualist tradition." There was some influence, but the spiritualistic label that Block-Hoell gave the Army could hardly stand alone in light of how strong a practice the Army employed in developing the outward and visible signs of grace. A contemporary of William Booth noted how ironic it was that the Army, which placed such an emphasis on drama/symbol and action, abandoned the sacraments:

> "The whole character and nature of the Army, all its methods of action, would lead one to expect that it would be strongly sacramental. To anyone who understands the nature of the movement, it must come as a surprise that the leaders do not lay stress on sacraments. They lean much upon externals and ritualism; they believe tremendously in their place and positions, one would expect them to go on to sacraments. . . . How is it then possible that they should fail to grasp the idea of the sacraments, and not readily see that God, wishing to convey himself to us, graciously condescends to treat us as men with bodies as well as spirits, and gives us earthly material sacraments whereby to convey heavenly grace? In absolute and manifest contradiction to their whole character and nature they abandon the sacrament altogether."[2]

The astonishment of William Booth's contemporary was relevant as the Army's chosen methods and expressions were very far from the Quakers' silent meetings and spiritual revelations. The non-observance of the sacraments was what the Army and the Quakers had in common, not very much else. The emphasis on symbols and drama has remained part of Army life, as it was not only in the beginning that this was the case. What happened in the early days and beyond was that the Army expressed the need for symbols and ceremonies by creating its own forms and means of grace, not that all outward signs were removed. Some of these expressions were mentioned in the appendix of the 1923 Doctrine Book such as the ceremonies of Dedication (of infants) and the Soldier's Enrollment, as well as the mercy seat and the uniform. The Army has never called these things symbols of grace, but whatever the symbols and ceremonies were called,

---

1. Rightmire, *Sacraments and The Salvation Army*, 107–17.
2. Heathcote, *My Salvation Army Experience*, 69.

these seemingly filled the void there might have been without them, as the Army never really propagated a spiritualistic religion, at least not in praxis.

Rightmire gave this description:

> "The early Army sought to bring together the cognitive and affective dimensions of religious life in dramatic ways. In addition to the preached Word, which was central to Army worship, Booth employed various symbols and expressions in eliciting spiritual results. The chief symbol of early Army worship was the mercy seat, which served the psychological, spiritual, and unconscious focus of the worship experience. In responding to the invitation to come forward to the mercy seat, the penitent was encouraged to seek not only instantaneous conversion, but also the indwelling of the divine presence. Hence the mercy seat was more than a place where communion with God was experienced."[3]

Even though this quotation refers to the early Army, the mercy seat has kept up its central position through the years. Michael Neiiendam[4] focused on the mercy seat, or penitent form as it has been called in translation to the Nordic languages. He viewed it as a confessional and the Army administering the sacrament of confession. This was one view seen from the outside, but a view that hardly would be supported by the Army itself, even though confessions take place at a mercy seat. It would rather be the seeking of the "indwelling of the divine presence," that would be considered even more central than confession. Today the mercy seat in many places would be considered a place "to feed upon Christ"—a place to experience his real presence and therefore close to the place of the Eucharist. The role of the mercy seat can be interpreted differently, but irrespective of the interpretation it was still central in Army worship in 1976, when this discussion took place as well as it is today, at least in Scandinavia. Concerning the use of the mercy seat the body is in focus: the person will rise from his/her seat in the congregation or on the platform and walk towards the mercy seat and thereby make the whole act very visible. Very often another Salvationist will kneel beside the person in order to listen, counsel, or just offer a prayer for the seeker. It is a spiritual communion, but it is also a concrete act in a concrete place where the body is engaged by moving and kneeling as well as experiencing fellowship by another person and the congregation supporting by songs and prayer. Another example could be the Soldier's Enrollment as a bodily experience. The soldier will dress in uniform for the first time, and by this action change from a private person to a person in somebody's

3. Rightmire, *Sacraments and The Salvation Army*, 65.
4. Neiiendam, *Frikirker og sekter* Vol.3, 188.

service. He/she will stand under the flag (symbolizing the triune God), publicly confirm promises given, and kneel under the flag for prayer and confirmation of this new status as a soldier of Christ. As with the use of the mercy seat this is a concrete, visible act symbolizing the spiritual experience of salvation. In Salvationist theology personal experience, listening to God and responding to him, has played a central role from the beginning, not ruling out Scriptures and doctrine.

The departure from the general practice of the Church concerning the sacraments was originally to a certain degree based on a pneumatological understanding, but the actual practices that took their place were by no means spiritualistic. They were very concrete—meals with strangers presided over by Christ, the enrollment ceremony for soldiers as a sort of baptism into the body of Christ and the stress on the sacramental life of each Salvationists, a life with a very practical, down to earth outcome. In a way diaconia has found its central place as constitutive of being a church in The Salvation Army, perhaps even to be likened to the place of the sacraments for the majority of churches where they are constitutive for being a church. The foot washing in the Gospel of John (13:1–17) as the symbol of diaconia, not as a concrete act of washing feet, has been a central commandment to Salvationists, where the breaking of bread and the sharing of the cup of the synoptic gospels was the irrefutable commandment for the majority of Christians from the early age of the church.

Frelsesarmeen had pneumatological influences in its foundations, but in my interpretation it poses difficulties to identify the Army as an expression of spiritualistic Christianity alone.

The invisible/visible church

The reports from the two commissions claimed that Frelsesarmeen had a spiritualistic ecclesiology, as it only referred to the invisible church. The visible church could take very different forms, it was only temporal.[5] The report sought to prove that the founders of the Army had not developed any teaching concerning the visible church—only the invisible church mattered. To further support this claim, the report used a quotation from Bramwell Booth. This quotation happened to come from a chapter in Bramwell Booth's memoirs concerning the visible church. Bramwell Booth wrote about the purpose of Christ to gather his followers in a "visible society—The Society spoken of in the Bible as the Church or Congregation." Bramwell Booth

---

5. *FA-Utvalgets rapport,* 3 (Frelsesarmeen'e Commission's Report).

stressed that no specific church order was advocated by the New Testament. The original quotation of Bramwell Booth was:

> "Of this, The Great Church of the Living God, we claim, and have ever claimed, that we of The Salvation Army are an integral part and element—a living fruit-bearing branch in the True Vine."[6]

The report of the commissions "quoted" Bramwell Booth's original saying in this way taking single words or sentences from his arguments concerning the visible church:

> "There is one church . . . and being one, yet it is to be for all peoples and all classes. . . . The Salvation Army has always claimed that we are an organic part of the great church of the living God—a living fruit-bearing branch in the true vine."[7]

The sentence of the one church being for all peoples and classes was taken from a longer paragraph where Bramwell Booth explained the visible Church of Christ being one, and yet included very different people. The report used it to support the idea of an invisible church. The idea of the invisible church was never a part of Bramwell Booth's exposition, nor of Salvationist thinking. On the contrary, the universal church was considered a visible reality, including very different peoples and forms.

With their background of the Lutheran State Church, the idea of an invisible church within the visible was known to the writers of the report. This was generally understood as meaning the visible church embracing everybody, as in the parable of the wheat and the weeds that "grow together" (Matthew 13:24–30), while the invisible church was considered the wheat that would be revealed as the true church in the end. The notion of the invisible church within the visible went back to Augustine's ecclesiology. Those who were baptized and received the sacraments were members of the church, but not all were united to God by true faith and love. There was an inner core of saved that was invisible, because only God knew their inner dimension of faith. They would be the future church of the predestined. The background was the rapid growth of the church during the fourth century after it had been legitimized in the empire. This could include conversions of convenience. The reformers of the sixteenth century also referred to Augustine's interpretation of the invisible church within the visible, but they gave other interpretations as well, as for instance the wish to include others than those defined by their reforms as true Christians or the true church.

---

6. Booth, *Echoes and Memories*, 79.
7. *FA-Kirkeutvalget Rapport*, 19 (Frelsesarmeen's Church Commission).

The true church existed when the gospel was preached purely and the sacraments administered truly. The visible church was the empirical church, while the invisible church could refer to Christians gathered in one authentic faith around gospel and sacraments. The invisible church could also refer to Christians united in one faith as distinct from the Roman institutional structures. In contrast, Roman ecclesiology did not separate an invisible church from the empirical Roman church.[8]

Harald Hegstad, who is a Lutheran theologian, argues that, "the belief in the church cannot be understood as a distinction between the visible and invisible church." Hegstad's thesis is, "that there is only one church, namely the church as visible and one that can be experienced in the world."[9] He refers to Matthew 18:20: "Where two or three are gathered in my name, I am there among them" as the kernel of the New Testament understanding of the church, as it was understood first and foremost as a real and visible fellowship of believers. The confession of faith in the church, according to the historic creeds, concerns the visible church that can be experienced. This claim concerning the church presupposes an eschatological perspective. Salvation Army ecclesiology would be much closer to the ecclesiology developed in *The Real Church* than in the thoughts of the invisible church. Any idea of predestination was opposed in Salvation Army doctrine six: "We believe that the Lord Jesus Christ has by his suffering and death, made an atonement for the whole world so that whosoever will, may be saved" and any uncertainty of being saved was refuted by doctrine eight: "We believe that we are justified by grace through faith in our Lord Jesus Christ and that he that believeth hath the witness in himself." The church in Salvation Army ecclesiology was the visible empirical church, not an invisible unknown group within the visible church. The claim from the reports of the two commissions that the Army only related to the invisible church was mainly based on a misunderstanding of Bramwell Booth's arguments concerning the visible church. The other reason for this claim was the influence from the Lutheran perception of the invisible church within the visible, as it was generally understood. With a functional ecclesiology, such as the Army's, any idea of an invisible church would be foreign. The universal church is not considered an invisible church, but the sum of churches of all kinds around the world. It can be concluded that The Salvation Army does not operate with any idea of an invisible church in its teaching. It considers the church to be a visible actor in the world.

8. Haight, *Christian Community in History* Vol. III, 185–88.
9. Hegstad, *The Real Church*, 2.

The Army's engagement in WCC from its beginning was to relate to these visible churches around the world and therefore also to give a response to the BEM manuscript as part of this fellowship.

Important aspects of ecclesiology coming out of The Salvation Army's response to BEM

The Salvation Army's response to *BEM* was marked by the fact that the Army, non-observant of the sacraments, was relating to a document that concerned baptism and Eucharist as well as ministry. The Army believed in the visible church and considered the universal church as visible churches from around the world, and made it clear in its response to *BEM* that it supported a fellowship of churches on basis of the constitution of WCC:

> "A fellowship of churches which confess the Lord Jesus Christ as God and Savior according to the Scriptures and therefore seek to fulfil together their common calling to the glory of the One God, Father, Son and Holy Spirit."[10]

The Army disagreed with the notion that unity between the churches had to be manifested by a basic agreement on baptism, Eucharist, and ministry, or a visible unity in one Eucharistic fellowship as expressed in the document. The Army believed in oneness in Christ revealed in a shared faith and confession, not in visible unity as Eucharistic fellowship. It also underlined that this oneness was given from the beginning and opposed the idea that Christians started divided, searching to achieve unity.

> "The unity of the church should and can most effectively be made visible in Christian witness and service, in common life in Christ ... to make any act of worship, however sacred and meaningful, the basis of unity, created the risk of losing the emphasis on life together in Christ."[11]

In this clarification, central issues of the Army's ecclesiology could be seen: Christian witness (martyria), Christian service (diaconia) and the life together in Christ (koinonia). It made clear the implications of its focus on Christian witness and Christian service with this plea:

> "The Salvation Army urges that 'mission' remains paramount in all ecumenical discussions and that the spiritual and social

---

10. WCC, *Baptism, Eucharist and Ministry*, vii.
11. The General, *A Response from The Salvation Army*, 4.

implications of the gospel in relation to 'human community' be fully realized."[12]

Mission was paramount for Salvationists. It was stated in its name—The Salvation Army—and the implications of the gospel should be understood as concrete and visible while the life together in Christ is understood as "a spiritual unity as is manifest in the oneness of the Father, Son and Holy Spirit."[13] The document stressed its understanding of unity further by this statement:

> "The unifying force in the Christian church has always been and is today fidelity to the cardinal doctrines concerning Christ and salvation—the atonement, repentance, justification by faith, adoption into God's family by regeneration, the infilling of the Spirit—strong biblical doctrines not dependent on any sacramental rite."[14]

Unity was manifested in Christian faith, witness, and service. These belonged to life together in Christ or to the koinonia. Any further understanding of koinonia was not explicitly stated. That came twenty years later:

> "Koinonia . . . means a fellowship which occurs when you are part of something or have a share in something. This something is the love of God, the grace of Jesus Christ and the fellowship of the Holy Spirit. This fellowship is reflected in Paul's use of the expression being '*in Christ*' or '*in the Holy Spirit*.'"[15]

The document did not make use of the words martyria, diaconia, and koinonia, but I see these three pillars of Salvationists ecclesiology all related to mission coming out of this document. As *BEM* was concerned about Baptism, Eucharist, and Ministry, a large part of the response was to underline the freedom of the Holy Spirit to manifest his presence outside time-honored ways and boundaries. It made clear that the Army's founders had sought the guidance of the Holy Spirit in their interpretation of New Testament on the sacraments:

> "Gradually but positively there emerged that conviction which Salvationists cherish to this day, that the Holy Spirit was confirming this new expression of Christian faith and practice as a part of the Body of Christ, his Church, with a distinctive witness

12. Ibid., 5.
13. Ibid.
14. Ibid.
15. The International Doctrine council, *Salvation Story Study Guide*, 46.

and purpose, which included the non-observance of the traditional sacraments on theological as well as practical grounds."[16]

The Salvation Army saw itself as part of the Body of Christ as it was responding to the voice of Christ in its own voice and culture, while it took hold of "the freedom to be different, and yet in that difference to be part of the freedom which Christ has brought us."[17] In the concluding paragraphs of the introduction, the Army again underlined the belief that its being was confirmed by the Holy Spirit even as a movement with a particular commission and vocation. It then outlined the essentials of the faith it had been called to focus on: The need for regeneration, the call to sanctification, and the grace of ministry and service open to all believers. It stated on the basis of this clarification that the response was in the nature of an apologia and a witness to the experience "granted by the Holy Spirit to many Salvationists of succeeding generations and different nationalities."[18]

When it concerned the chapter on baptism, the response stressed that "the church of the New Testament was entered by a personal profession of faith" and the Army believed likewise, but still it mentioned the dedication ceremony of infants taking place within congregational worship as a commitment by the parents and the local congregation to bring up the child in the Christian faith. The encouragement of family worship and Bible study was implicit in the promises given here. The soldier's enrollment was highlighted and described as follows:

> " . . . marks acceptance as a member of the visible church—for the believer, a public confession of Christ as Lord and Savior; for the church, a sign that the believer is received and welcomed into Christian fellowship. The Salvationist so received would attest to the same sense of incorporation into the family of God and the life and service of Jesus Christ, with the beginnings of the inner work of the Holy Spirit, as does his baptized believer brother."[19]

The Dedication Ceremony was likened to the blessing, Jesus gave the children he called to himself, and the Soldier's Enrollment was compared to baptism, incorporation into the body of Christ.

Concerning the Eucharist, the response referred to every meal as "sacramental to those who partake with remembrance of him who provides

16. The General, *Baptism, Eucharist and Ministry*, 2.
17. Ibid., 2.
18. Ibid., 6.
19. Ibid., 12–13.

for both material and spiritual needs" and to the sacramental life as it was expressed in Albert Orsborn's song *My Life must be Christ's Broken Bread* as well as the experience of Christ's real presence where two or three are gathered together in his name.

> "My life must be Christ's broken bread, / my love his outpoured wine, / a cup o'erfilled, a table spread/ beneath his name and sign, / that other souls, refreshed and fed, /may share his life through mine."[20]

The sacramental life was explained further:

> "For the man of faith there is no need for part of life to be essentially sacred while the every-day is secular. For the Salvationist the 'anamnesis' of the sacrifice of Jesus on the cross is of central importance in his personal faith, his worship, his preaching and his daily living."[21]

The response welcomed the link from the Eucharist to the social implication of the gospel as responsible care and practical service, an area that was seen by Salvationists as a natural interpretation of the gospel. At the end of the response to the Eucharist chapter it was stated that one of the outcomes of the study of *BEM* would be a re-emphasis on the significance of the doctrine of holiness, as the Army saw a connection of its understanding of the Eucharist to the proclamation of sanctification that was lived out in a holy life, a sacramental life.

When it came to the ministry chapter, The Salvation Army agreed that the basis was the calling of the whole of God's people. Out of this calling some were called to full-life dedication as officers. It took up the importance of the equal ministry of men and women, and disagreed with a three-fold ministry as three levels of bishops, presbyters, and deacons. In the Army it was seen as operating in all levels of ministry, as "all officers are expected to exercise caring oversight and to undertake the humblest service with their people."[22] It warned that historic continuity alone did not guarantee apostolicity, but being sent by God in the power of the Spirit according to the scriptures. It saw the apostolic faith being preserved by faithfulness to the word of God and an openness to the Holy Spirit on each successive genera-

---

20. The General, *The Songbook of The Salvation Army*, 1986 no. 512. First published in *The War Cry*, May 3, 1947. Albert Orsborn was General from 1946–54. The song became the Army's sacramental hymn and has been translated to several languages including all the Nordic.

21. The General, *A Response from The Salvation Army*, 18.

22. Ibid., 24.

tion of Christians. At the end of the chapter it claimed the right of officers to be accepted as part of an ordained ministry as they had been called and their call proven by the Army, they had been trained and they had been accepted by the ceremonies of covenant-making, dedication, and ordination, commissioning and appointing of Salvation Army officers.[23]

From the response to *BEM* it can be concluded that The Salvation Army believed, as a foundation for its ecclesiology, that it "had been raised up by God and was sustained and directed by him,"[24] that the Holy Spirit confirmed this new expression of a Christian community, and that in Christ there was freedom to be different responding in its own voice and culture to the voice of Christ. The notae ecclesiae coming forth were martyria, diaconia, and koinonia as relating to the overall purpose of mission. It considered the church as the people of God based on the calling of the whole people of God. The priesthood of all believers was the foundation for the ordained ministry, a ministry for both men and women. It had its own ceremonies of incorporation into the body of Christ which it considered equal to baptism. It had doctrines in accordance with the classical creeds. It interpreted the Eucharist as all meals being sacramental, remembering Christ and as a sacramental life linked to the social implication of the gospel. This response was translated into Norwegian. As an outcome of the *BEM* process and in order to expand further on the issues appearing in the response, a Salvationist ecclesiology was published in 1987.

Community in Mission and its ecclesiology

The Salvation Army invited Major Phil Needham[25] to write a book as a supplement to The Salvation Army's official response to the Lima Document. The foreword by General Eva Burrows gave the following explanation "This book, therefore is not a theological statement emanating from the deliberations of an official group, but is something more vital—a positive statement from a dedicated Salvationist working from a biblical and experiential perspective." By this she was stating that this was not an official Salvation Army ecclesiology, but still published by IHQ with copyright belonging to the General. It expanded the issues already dealt with, but had a much stronger and clearer focus on mission and on the community as well. It made

23. See appendix III.
24. Articles of War, an opening statement see appendix II.
25. Needham, *Community in Mission*. He was a member of the International Doctrine Council, has been in international leadership as TC and Commissioner. He was also member of the Spiritual Life Commission.

use of the military metaphor all through the book. Each of the six chapters started with a statement on different aspects of being church. These statements deepened the understanding of what it meant to be a Salvation Army church. The three aspects of martyria, koinonia, and diaconia are present in the statements. The statement in chapter three however stands out:

> "The Church is a band of pilgrims who are called to separate themselves from the oppressive patterns of the present world order and to keep moving toward the possibilities which the new Kingdom in Christ offers. (The pilgrim people)."

It is different because of the image of separation. This was addressed in the first paragraph of the chapter as a contradiction at first sight to the affirmation of God's presence in common life. The first section affirmed that the world was the place where the church was called to witness and carry out its mission. It underlined that the Church could not exist in isolation from the world, for a church out of touch with the world was denying the call of God to go into the world. It was the tension between *being in* the world and not *being of* the world that was the aim of the chapter. Stating the separation was to signal opposition against oppressive patterns, and implicitly to take social action. The military metaphor was addressed, as one that captured both the mobility of the pilgrim Church and its focus on the world. In this way it gave a broad inspiration to diaconia. Chapter four developed the military metaphor further: "the characterization of the Church as an army derives from the reason for which it exists in the world."[26] The Church existed for the sake of its mission in the world, because of its missionary nature and calling. The calling was explained as evangelism and social action. The chapter developed the purpose, implications, structures, and celebration. Concerning structure, the principle of adaptation from William Booth was highlighted and explained with concrete suggestions.

The book reflected both on theory and practice as its aim was inspiration for Salvationists to identify themselves with these images. In the epilogue Needham expressed the aim of his book, that Salvationists would be stimulated to rethink, formulate, and reformulate their understanding of the Church, as well as the Army's place in the Church and in its mission in the world. Another equally important aim was to encourage Salvationists to be confident in their understanding of the Army as a church among churches. The conclusion of the book was the following quotation of Bramwell Booth:

> "We believe that our Lord Jesus Christ has called us into his Church of the redeemed, that our call has not been by man or

---

26. Needham, *Community in Mission*, 52.

the will of man, but by the Holy Spirit of God; that our salvation is from him, not by ceremonies or sacraments or ordinances of this period or that, but by the pardoning life-giving work of our divine Savior. We believe also that our system for extending the knowledge and power of his gospel, and of nurturing and governing the believing people gathered in our ranks, is as truly and fully in harmony with the spirit set forth and the principles laid down by Jesus Christ and his apostles as those which have been adopted by our brethren of other times and other folds."[27]

It seemed important to refer to one of the founders in order to underline that what was being argued was in accordance with what was taught by the early Army. This gave credibility, perhaps even authority to what had been stated for Salvationists. It should also serve as an encouragement for Salvationists to be confident in who they were. It was clearly a message to Salvationists, not so much for people of other churches. *Community in Mission* was not translated into any of the Scandinavian languages, so only those who were comfortable with English would be influenced by the book.

Another eleven years passed by before the issue of ecclesiology was addressed again. This time it came out as an official statement in the doctrine book, *Salvation Story*, a book that would be translated around the world into different languages and which had to be used in teaching of cadets and recruits. Doctrine books therefore had great influence.

Salvation Story and its ecclesiology

Salvation Story influenced Frelsesarmeen in the years just before registration. It had a chapter, "People of God," concerning Salvation Army ecclesiology. It was the first time in the history of Salvation Army doctrine books such a chapter was included. It was vital to express a belief in the Church in a tradition and theology, that otherwise could be individualistic and concentrate on the personal experience of faith and sanctification. The Salvation Army had no doctrine on the Church, but all doctrines started with "We believe," implying that the doctrines belonged to a community of faith. The well-known quotation from General Bramwell Booth headed the chapter:

> "Of This Great Church of the living God, we claim and have ever claimed, that we of the Salvation Army are an integral part and element—a living fruit-bearing branch in the True Vine."[28]

27. Booth, *Echoes and Memories*, 79.
28. Ibid., 79.

This quotation focused on the Army's belonging to the Church Universal, rather than expressing its belief in the church. The image used was the True Vine describing the Church as a living organism and the Army as part of this living organism with potential for growth and changes, and able to bear fruit.

The images used in the chapter are the body of Christ as well as the people of God. The significance of the Army's name for the community of believers—"the corps"—corpus Christi is important in this image of the Church. The concrete and visible is in focus as is underlined by the following:

> "We mean that the Church is Christ's visible presence in the world, given life by the indwelling of the Holy Spirit and called to grow in conformity to Christ."[29]

There is no room for any invisible church in this understanding of the church as Christ's visible presence in the world. The sentence just prior to this one explains what the Army means by the church as the body of Christ: "That all believers are incorporated in spiritual union with Christ, their head," and it adds, "with one another as fellow members working in harmony." There is a spiritual union with Christ, but the Church is his visible presence. It states that, "membership in the body of Christ is not optional for believers: it is a reality given to all who know Christ, the head of the Church". A belief similar to this was the basis for the Army's resistance against the assumption in WCC that Christians started divided and had to work toward unity. Later it states, "The unity of the Church depends upon incorporation into Christ, not necessarily organic union." The image of the people of God is to see the Church as a people called to faith and obedience to Christ similar to the people of Israel, who were identified as God's people and called to be examples of faith and obedience. The Church was seen as a continuing community:

> "As an integral part of its mission to continue the ministry of Christ, the Church passes on the gospel from one generation to another. While subject to the authority of Scripture the Christian community, led by the Spirit, provides a consensus of interpretation that ensures the preservation of the gospel message. The Church is one, though diverse in its expressions."

The Army's ecclesiology expressed in this chapter was in line with the Nicene signs of the church—the church as unam, sanctam, catholicam, and apostolicam. The church was one, led by the Spirit, with a consensus of interpretation and a preservation of the gospel message. It preserved a

---

29. The Doctrine Council, *Salvation Story*, 100–15.

tradition "that originated with the first Christians and their response to the risen Lord."

In *Salvation Story* the Trinitarian aspect was underlined more strongly than previously. It could be seen in chapter two, "The God who is never alone."[30] An outcome of this was a clear focus on the Holy Spirit as the agent for different aspects of the church as for example visualized by the headlines in chapter ten: the church is created by the Holy Spirit for fellowship, the church is created by the Holy Spirit for healing, The church is created by the Holy Spirit for nurture, the church is created by the Holy Spirit to equip for ministry and mission, The Holy Spirit empowers the whole church for witness, The Holy Spirit empowers the church for mission. These headings all belong to the two sections called the gathered community and the scattered community. The church gathers in order to be sent out. In The Salvation Army's perception of the church these two belong together, they are dependent upon each other as well as upon the agency of the Holy Spirit. The functional aspect of Salvation Army ecclesiology is clear. The gathering is fellowship, healing, nurture, and empowerment, or being equipped for the purpose of mission and ministry to the world. This aspect of mission and ministry is clear in the summary. The summaries at the end of each chapter were originally rewritten doctrines as the International Doctrine Council was asked by Eva Burrows to rewrite the eleven doctrines. However, they were never published as such, but came as summaries in *Salvation Story*. It stated this belief:

> "We believe in the Church, the body of Christ, justified and sanctified by grace, called to continue the mission and ministry of Christ."

All three notae ecclesiae of martyria, koinonia, and diaconia relating to the overall focus on mission, which is already seen in the Army's response to *BEM* as well as in *Community in Mission* also appear in this short statement. Koinonia is present in the description of the church as the body of Christ, and martyria, as well as diaconia, in the call of the church to continue the mission and ministry of Christ. Both salvation and sanctification are highlighted in the description of the body of Christ.

In the chapter the sacramental community stands between the gathered community and the scattered community, but here it is connected to the appendix on the sacraments, because both the section as well as the appendix show how the terminology had changed over the years in explaining the issue, and how new aspects had been added to explain the Army's view

---

30. Ibid., 14–22.

upon the sacraments. Sacramental living had always been an important aspect of the understanding of sanctification, but the focus had been on the individual, not so much on the community. Army teaching had highlighted the personal experience of the presence of God, and how the sacramental life was lived in the world in the power of the Holy Spirit. In this section the spotlight is on the sacramental community gathered around the source of sacramental living—Jesus Christ the one original Sacrament-and feeding upon him:

> "Jesus Christ is the center of the church which lives to be a sign of God's grace in the world. As the sacramental community, the Church feeds upon him who is the one and only, true and original Sacrament. Christ is the source of grace from whom all other sacraments derive and to whom they bear witness. He is what is signified in the sign of the sacraments.
>
> As the body of Christ the Church is his visible presence in the world. It is God's sign (sacrament) of the life together to which Christ calls the world, the visible expression of atoning grace. Rooted in the risen life of Christ, the one and only, true, and original Sacrament, the Church daily discovers, celebrates—and is transformed by—his grace. It gathers around Jesus Christ, lives by faith in him and is blessed to be his sacramental community."

The sacramental community appears as the visible presence of the body of Christ. For Salvationist ecclesiology once again it is the visible rather than the invisible community that is in focus. By combining the sacramental life, which used to have a more individualistic notion, with the sacramental community it embraced fellowship as well as mission and the personal life of holiness. By using the significant meaning of Christ as the original sacrament, it took hold of sacramental language and an image it could connect to, and from which it could explain Salvation Army practice. In contrast to Catherine Booth's reluctance to convey any importance to visible signs, it underlined the value of celebrations and stated:

> "Celebrations are needed in the life of any community, and celebrations of new life in Christ are needed in the life of the Church. . . . Celebrations and rituals can be vehicles through which the Holy Spirit brings renewal and hope to the fellowship of believers."

On the basis of such a change, it could be questioned whether the non-observant status would be altered. This did come up as an issue, but was not the eventual outcome, rather this focus on the importance of celebrations and rituals became foundational for another development of Salvationist understanding of its own practice as an expression of sacraments. The apologetic tone had left the doctrine book. It just stated the experience of a hundred years of living as a faith community, an experience expressed in this way:

> "We are a sacramental community because our life, our work, and our celebrations center on Christ, the one true Sacrament. Our life together is sacramental because we live by faith in him and our everyday lives keep stumbling onto unexpected grace, his undeserved gift, again and again."

The appendix showed that the Army took hold of the word sacrament and made it part of Salvationist experience, interpreting it in a way that it covered the Army's non-sacramental practice:

> "A sacrament is an event in which the truths of our faith move into something that is quite beyond theological formulation and our attempts at comprehension. It brings the Incarnation to our doorstep, invites us to swing open the door of our intellectual caution and calls us to allow God's incomprehensible grace to enter—and transform—our ordinary lives. Sacraments deal with the extraordinary in the ordinary—extraordinary things like God's saving sacrifice, his inclusive fellowship, his call to discipleship, his forgiving family—ordinary things like a meal shared with those we care about, or a meal for strangers, water for washing, a flag to stand under, a joining of hands."[31]

This interpretation of what a sacrament meant, connected with Salvationist practice and confirmed Salvationists that their experiences were valid, not something strange or second-rate in comparison to the experience of Christians from other traditions. It took the Salvationist practice even further by claiming actually to observe the sacraments:

> "We observe the sacraments, not by limiting them to two or three or seven, but by inviting Christ to suppers, love feasts, birth celebrations, parties, dedications, sick beds, weddings, anniversaries, commissioning, ordinations, retirements—and a host of other significant events—and, where he is truly received, watching him give a grace beyond our understanding. We can see, smell, hear, and taste it. We joyfully affirm that in

---

31. This interpretation not only covered the Army's non-sacramental practice, it was claimed by Salvationists gathered at the first Salvation Army Theology-and Ethics Symposium in Winnipeg in 2001 that it could also allow for a re-introduction of the sacraments.

our presence is the one, true, original Sacrament. And we know that what we have experienced is reality."

This claim of observing the sacraments by interpreting them as part of Salvationist practice and experience was new in comparison to the Army's traditional apologetic dealing with the issue. It connected to the interpretation of the sacrament in the previous paragraphs, but took the interpretation a step further by claiming that the Salvationist understanding was "an observance" of the sacraments. In other doctrine books the appendix used to have long explanations of the reasons for the Army's non-observance. In the appendix in *Salvation Story* there was just one sentence giving the facts that the Salvation Army had chosen not to observe sacraments as prescribed rituals and then the text added:

> "However, we do identify with the historic Church through its confession of one faith, one Lord, one baptism of the Holy Spirit, one salvation, and one Church universal. We confess one sacramental meal, not administered ritually, but presided over by Christ himself at any table he is received and honored."

As mentioned the apologetic tone had disappeared and a confidence rooted in Salvationists' experience was visible in this chapter. The stress on experience as a credible basis for decisions in matters of faith had been central from the Army's beginnings and was evident here. At the same time as the Army highlighted and confirmed its own experience it identified with the Church universal and claimed to be part of it.

Frelsesarmeen translated *Salvation Story* in loyalty to the text apart from the little paragraph starting, "We observe the sacraments. . . . " This paragraph was left out. At the same time that *Salvation Story* was published, the Spiritual Life Commission's report[32] also came out and was translated into Norwegian. *Krigsropet* had two articles with reference and extracts from the report.[33] A dialogue concerning the sacraments took place in the Spiritual Life commission as Salvation Army worship was a central point.

International dialogue concerning the sacraments

The headings of baptism and Holy Communion from the report of the Spiritual Life Commission was crucial, as the whole question of the sacraments, including the Army's non-observance, was up for discussion, as well

---

32. International Spiritual Life Commission, *Move Forward in Freedom*.
33. *Krigsropet* nr. 48, 6–7 and 49, 16–17 1998.

as reintroducing the sacraments into Army worship. This did not happen. Instead the focus was on interpreting the sacraments in such a way that Army tradition reflected the meaning of the sacraments.

An example from the Spiritual Life Commission could be the Soldier's Enrollment that was placed under the heading "A statement on Baptism". It stressed how the Soldier's Enrollment fulfilled the membership of Christ's Church on earth, because all who are in Christ are baptized into the one body by the Holy Spirit. There were ten points to explain the relationship between the soldier's enrollment and baptism, especially point 4-9 had this focus:

> "4) They also express publicly their desire to fulfil membership of Christ's Church on earth as soldiers of The Salvation Army. 5) The Salvation Army rejoices in the truth that all who are in Christ are baptized into the one body by the Holy Spirit (1 Corinthians 12–13). 6) It believes, in accordance with Scripture, that 'there is one body and one Spirit . . . one Lord, one faith, one baptism; one God and Father of all, who is over all and through all and in all' (Ephesians 4:5–6). 7) The swearing-in of a soldier of The Salvation Army beneath the Trinitarian sign of the Army's flag acknowledges this truth. 8) It is a public response and witness to a life-changing encounter with Christ which has already taken place, as is the water baptism practiced by some other Christians. 9) The Salvation Army acknowledges that there are many worthy ways of publicly witnessing to having been baptized into Christ's body by the Holy Spirit and expressing a desire to be his disciple."[34]

The non-observance of the sacraments needed no longer to be an issue of division from other churches as the meaning of baptism was adhered to in the soldier's enrollment, at least in Salvationists' view. There was a similarity to the claim in *Salvation Story*: "We observe the sacraments. . . . "

There were also ten points' statements on Holy Communion. Here points 5–7 are of special interest:

> "5) Christ is the one true Sacrament, and sacramental living—Christ living in us and through us—is at the heart of Christian holiness and discipleship. 6) Throughout its history The Salvation Army has kept Christ's atoning sacrifice at the center of its corporate worship.7) The Salvation Army rejoices in its freedom to celebrate Christ's real presence at all meals and in all meetings, and in its opportunity to explore in life together the significance

---

34. Spiritual Life Commission, *Move Forward in Freedom*, 7.

of the simple meals shared by Jesus and his friends and by the first Christians. 8) Salvationists are encouraged to use the love feast and develop creative means of hollowing meals in home and corps with remembrance of the Lord's sacrificial love."[35]

This continued the theme of clothing Army practice and worship in sacramental language. What was new here in comparison to earlier statements was point eight about the love feast, as well as encouragement to creativity in order to highlight the meaning of ordinary meals. The love feast has been used in the Army from its beginning, reflecting its Wesleyan roots, but it was practically unknown in Scandinavia. To underline the central message of Christ's atoning sacrifice in Army worship had always been present, but the visual response to the message had been related to the mercy seat, not in the significance of simple meals in this setting. The message wasn't new, but to stress it here was. Even though an effort was made in *Move Forward in Freedom*, as well as in *Salvation Story*, to take hold of sacramental language and to point to Salvation Army practice as sacramental expressions, the discussion in The Salvation Army internationally concerning the sacraments was not silenced.

A further discussion concerning the reintroduction of the sacraments into Army worship took place at The Salvation Army Theology and Ethics Symposium in 2001, and as an outcome the International Doctrine Council was asked to work on this issue. The Symposium was held at Booth University College in Winnipeg, Canada, and gathered Army theologians and ethicists from different parts of the world. The theme was the Trinity. It was planned and arranged by the International Doctrine Council. During the symposium the question of the non-observance of the sacraments appeared during discussions. The focus was on Holy Communion, rather than on baptism. The Chief of Staff, John Larsson, promised to follow up on the question of reintroducing the sacraments. The following year he was elected General. The Doctrine Council was asked to work on the question of what Larsson called "a third way":

> "However, as I said I would, I have been looking into the question of whether it would be possible to affirm our non-sacramental position more clearly than ever before, and yet find a way of permitting the greater use of 'symbols'—like water and bread— in ways that would not carry the baggage of twenty centuries of theological debate and controversy. This would be a kind of

---

35. Ibid., 7.

'third way'—somewhere in between observing the sacraments and not observing them."[36]

This article was written three years after the Doctrine Council had been asked to work on this issue. The task of making something in between given to the Doctrine Council was not easy, but even so the council debated the whole issue, worked on it and gave its input. The manuscript was considered confidential and placed in the General's files. John Larsson decided to leave matters as they were and not to circulate or publish the paper from the council.[37] Larsson explained this in his article:

> "I have consulted closely with the Doctrine Council on this matter. But after much thought and reflection I have to share with you that I have come to the conclusion that there really is no realistic third way. To use these symbols ceremonially in ways that most observers would interpret as being sacramental, whilst maintaining that we do not practice the sacraments, would require an impossible degree of sophistication from our people. So I have concluded that it has not been possible to find a realistic middle ground."[38]

The pressure for a reintroduction of the sacraments came most strongly from South America and Canada, but also from countries in the developing world, even though it was not an issue in all countries the Army worked in. Officers worldwide who read *The Officer* would be aware from his article that a discussion had taken place, but as nothing of the material was published there was no further discussion. There had not previously been pressure from the Nordic countries concerning a reintroduction of the sacraments, most probably because Salvationists who wanted to celebrate especially Holy Communion would do so in the Folk Churches in their countries, as a number had double membership anyhow. This situation would cover Norway, Sweden, Finland, Iceland, and Denmark. However, the question concerning an observance of the sacraments within Frelsesarmeen came in

---

36. John Larsson: "Being true to ourselves."

37. The interaction with the Doctrine Council and the papers from this, John Larsson described as "close consultation" in the article. In a letter to him of 15 November 2011 I wrote concerning the papers and a possible use of them. In his answer he stated: "One of the key functions of the Doctrine Council is to advise the General on matters he or she seeks advice—and papers responding to such requests for advice remain confidential unless the General decides to circulate them for comment." Letter of response from John Larsson 20 November 2011.

38. *The Officer*, November/December 2004.

Norway in connection with registration as an independent faith community as will be unfolded in the following section.

Ecclesiological tensions?

The Salvation Army's non-observant position concerning the sacraments has not been openly opposed through Frelsesarmeen's history in Norway, which cannot be a surprise in view of the translations of the doctrine books up to 1975, when the translation included the Army's non-sacramental views for the first time. The silence during all these years concerning the Army's position would not call for reflection on matters not generally known. Because of the 1975 translation the situation in 1996 was different. The Army's position was generally known, and at the time registration as an independent faith community was seemingly close to becoming a reality. Therefore, the non-observance of the sacraments was questioned.

The results from the questionnaire from Frelsesarmeen's Commission in 1978 did not reveal any strong beliefs concerning the sacraments or a wish for an observance within the Army, rather a practice that accommodated them to the general religious culture of the country. Twenty years later in 1996 the question of the sacraments came up. Seemingly a change in attitudes had happened from 1978 to 1996. The change could rest on the publication of the 1975 translation of the Doctrine Book. A period of twenty years would most probably have given most Salvationists some insight to the Army's position. There were no questions in the brochure concerning the sacraments, but in spite of that a number of corps simply took it up. 24 corps out of the 45 raised the question. The two main issues were: 1) It was difficult to see how Frelsesarmeen's non-observance could still be the case, when it registered as an independent faith community. Apparently sacraments belonged to the being of a church. 2) The Salvation Army's position of non-observance had to be taught more clearly.

In these two statements there are ecclesiological tensions. The group that wanted clear teaching would most probably identify Frelsesarmeen as an independent faith community as it presently was. Its characteristics had to be highlighted. The other groups most probably had been influenced by Lutheran ecclesiology on the true nature of the church—the gospel preached purely and the sacraments administered truly. There were comments on the importance of the sacraments, but also indifference to the actual observance of them. What they had in common was that sacraments had to be present in order to be a church. As there were no specific comments from all the 24 corps identifying why the sacraments had to be discussed, it was not possible to identify the percentage of these positions, only that attitudes were present from belief in the importance of the sacraments in order to be a proper church to the Army's position of non-observance that needed to be taught more clearly. There was a tension within Frelsesarmeen having these two positions. The first position of having the sacraments in order to be a church need not exclude Salvationist faith, nor an attitude to the sacraments as symbols. It could be similar to the teaching of the 1881 Doctrine Book (translated in 1901) for some, while others saw the sacraments as important means of grace indispensable for Christian life. Registration as an independent faith community would demand an administration of the sacraments for both of these attitudes to live up to the demands of being a church. From the examples above it can be concluded that there were tensions concerning ecclesiology, but how deep they were or how widespread is not possible to interpret from the material available.

All this happened before the publication of *Salvation Story* and the report from the Spiritual Life Commission, so the new approach to the sacraments where the Army interpreted its own celebrations in light of them was not known. As Salvationist faith has been dominant in Norway among Salvationists throughout its history, this new approach of taking hold of the concept of sacraments as part of Salvationist practice might have had an impact, had it been ready at this stage. The Norwegian translation of the response to *BEM* was known, *Krigsropet* had focused on it rather prominently. This meant that the readers of the paper, both Salvationists and the public, were informed about the document and the main points of its content. Knud Welander mentioned *BEM* as something of significance which he scrutinized. When the actual registration took place in 2005 there was still an expectation by some officers that the introduction of the sacraments was a natural outcome.[39] The determination of the leadership to avoid any conflicts resulted in the choice of placing all that described Frelsesarmeen's essence under the organization instead of under the congregation in the registration. Frelsesarmeen had always called itself an organization and it seemingly had to stay that way. This decision was needed not only be to keep tradition, but also to avoid a conflict over the meaning of being an independent faith community. Such a conflict might have occurred, if Lutheran ecclesiology was so dominant that it was difficult to see Frelsesarmeen as an independent faith community without adhering to the Lutheran ecclesiology. Such an

39. This is based on a mail of 15 March 2014 from the CS of the time, Miriam Frederiksen as a response to my question if such an expectation had been present at the time of registration. As an example she mentioned that a corps officer had ordered a chalice to the corps, because she knew registration was on its way and expected sacraments to be observed in the faith community.

adherence was present among at least some Salvationists. An adherence to Lutheran ecclesiology could be a reason why the majority of Salvationists did not register within the first months. Other Salvationists might wish to keep membership of the Norwegian Church of cultural reasons or to leave things as they had always been as in the case of Lisbeth Welander. There was tension, then, within Frelsesarmeen concerning ecclesiology to do with the observance of the sacraments, and the question of whether this was constitutive for being a church/faith community, or whether the Army's position of non-observance could be accepted as belonging to a proper church. The possible implicit tension between Frelsesarmeen and The Salvation Army also concerned these matters. The translation of the first doctrine book was most probably a way for Frelsesarmeen to accommodate itself within Norwegian society accepting the sacraments as an observance, but without any specific value. Because of the silence on the matter from 1930 it is difficult to know, if at some stage prior to the 1975 Doctrine Book disagreement, something had developed with the Army's non-observant position. The teaching from the Norwegian Church concerning the sacraments would be known, as Salvationists generally had followed confirmation classes. There was not much to balance Lutheran teaching apart from the influence of TCs of different nationality, Norwegian cadets being trained in London, Norwegian officers serving in other countries, and the circulation of Salvation Army papers and books published by the International Army. For years it seemed to have been an issue not debated.

The pragmatism which William Booth expressed through his attitudes and decisions marked The Salvation Army from its early beginnings as well as further on in its history, as it spread around the world. It was seen in its determination to find practical solutions to problems arising, as for instance how to accommodate itself into different countries and cultures for the sake of its mission of communicating the gospel and establishing its work. The Army expected some degree of accommodation into the local culture from the pioneers, and the consequences of this enculturation were generally accepted by the international leadership. Frelsesarmeen took the accommodation a step further than the other Scandinavian countries, and most probably further than IHQ imagined, because Frelsesarmeen also tried to accommodate the doctrines through its translations into a Norwegian setting, in order to make room for the dual membership among soldiers and officers. The accommodation also went further in Norway than in the other Scandinavian countries concerning conditions for soldiership.[40] The Orders

---

40. *O&R for Pastoral Care Councils*, section 4.11.d., 3 (The name changed from Senior Census board to Pastoral Care Councils in 2002).

and Regulations (O&Rs) that are strikingly different concerned the O&R for Senior Census Boards in the section of reasons for non-acceptance as a soldier. Since 1925 it has stated: "A person may not be accepted as a soldier ... who is a member of another religious body?" In Norway this had been translated: "A person may not be accepted as a soldier ... who is a member of a non-Christian denomination." 1981 a modification was added in the paragraph: "National law or so may modify this in some countries." Even after 1981 Norway continued its translation.

The wish to introduce sacraments became vocal in 1996 in these responses concerning registration as an independent faith community. It would be outside the scope of the accepted cultural difference officially to introduce the sacraments within Salvation Army worship. A change of this kind would have to come from the General. Because of Frelsesarmeen's enculturation the tensions between Frelsesarmeen and the international Army concerning the sacraments might never have been acknowledged or admitted. It might have been implicit in some of the choices of translation, but never explicit or vocal.

Conclusion

From the different published papers and books I conclude that The Salvation Army understands the church as a visible, empirical reality, that has no concept concerning the invisible church. It was difficult to identify the Army as an expression of spiritualistic Christianity alone, as was done in the reports from Frelsesarmeen's Commission 1975–78 and Frelsesarmeen's Church Commission 1993–96, even though there were pneumatological influences. As a foundation for its ecclesiology, the Army believed that it "had been raised up by God and was sustained and directed by him,"[41] that the Holy Spirit confirmed this new expression of a Christian community, and that there was freedom in Christ to be different, responding in its own voice and culture to the voice of Christ. The notae ecclesiae were martyria, diaconia, and koinonia as they related to the overall focus on mission. It considered the church as the People of God based on the calling of the whole people of God. The priesthood of all believers was the foundation for the ordained ministry, a ministry for both men and women. It had its own ceremonies of incorporation into the body of Christ, which it considered equal to baptism. It had doctrines in accordance with the classical creeds. It interpreted the Eucharist as all meals being sacramental remembering Christ, and as a sacramental life linked to the social implication of the gos-

---

41. Articles of War, an opening statement see appendix II.

pel. From a comparison of what is constitutive for The Salvation Army for being a church with the Lutheran it is clear that two different traditions are at stake. The Lutheran tradition focus on orthodoxy compared to a Salvationist tradition where orthopraxy is as important. The visible concrete expressions of martyria, koinonia, and diaconia are vital. In Salvationist tradition the preaching of the word also has to be based on the Bible and to be true to Christian doctrines, but as important is the expectation that the interpretation of these comes to life through personal experience and testimony. There is focus on freedom in the Spirit, and the fellowship is vital for discipleship and for mission. Diaconia is based on the sacramental life, that is challenged by the foot washing, to be a servant of all.

It seems as if the *BEM* process was an eye opener for the Army and inspired it to work on its own ecclesiology. By answering to *BEM* it both expressed its disagreement with some main statements, and while doing this it expressed more clearly its own belief. It also tried to interpret its own practice in view of *BEM*, and in this way to relate to the practice of other churches. The process of committee work, and the openness of inviting an international response to the outcome of this paved the way for both an ownership of the response document given, as well as an interest in the issue of ecclesiology and Salvation Army theology. The process of *BEM* became an inspiration for the work of the International Doctrine Council concerning the new doctrine book, where it became paramount to include a chapter on Salvationist's ecclesiology. The Spiritual Life Commission worked parallel with the doctrine council and two of the members were in both commissions. The Army's non-observance of the sacraments was debated. In both publications a new way of interpreting the Army's practice as sacramental expressions was encouraged. The newfound interest in Army theology became visible by calling for an International Theology and Ethics Symposium in 2001.[42] This was made possible by the fact that a number of Salvationist theologians and ethicists were around in different countries. Scholarly research concerning the Salvation Army had been published from early 80s. One outcome of the symposium was to look into a possible third way concerning observance of the sacraments. The report from the Doctrine Council was never published, but the international Army was made aware that considerations had been given to this option by an article in *The Officer* by General John Larsson.

In Norway the influence from the published documents was probably most evident among those who advocated registration as a faith community

---

42. This symposium was followed up by another one in 2006 in Johannesburg, South Africa with the theme of Ecclesiology. The most recent one was arranged in 2010 in London with the theme of Holiness.

as could be seen with Knud Welander. They might have found affirmation of their views and a deeper insight into Salvation Army belief. However, tensions surfaced in connection with the prospect of the registration becoming a reality. They concerned ecclesiology, and it was clear that a number of Salvationists were influenced by Lutheran ecclesiology and therefore could not imagine Frelsesarmeen as a registered faith community without observing the sacraments. Others wanted the Army's position to be taught more clearly. The actual registration ascribed what belonged to the essence of the Army as a faith community to the organization in the constitution, while the congregation was only described as a legal entity. The notae ecclesiae for being a true church or a true Salvation Army have been evident in Frelsesarmeen's corps in Norway, but it seems as if it had not been part of any Norwegian discussion. This concerned the sacraments alone. An adherence to martyria, koinonia, and diaconia, as relating to mission, can be seen in the different corps programs, and would be considered to belong to the essence by any of Frelsesarmeen's corps. The popular quotation of John Gowans from 2000 meant recognition of the mission of the Army and of each soldier also in Norway: "To save souls, grow saints and serve suffering humanity." Translation of this into the Scandinavian languages was more difficult (not the meaning but the flow). This quotation picked up the notae ecclesiae as they were understood around the Salvation Army world, as well as in Norway. The influence of Lutheran ecclesiology on some Salvationists could be detected. This raised the question whether they also saw their membership of the Norwegian Church as church membership in the true sense of being incorporated into the body of Christ, or whether they experienced that incorporation within Frelsesarmeen living out their Christian vocation in mission, fellowship, and service.

Chapter 11

Conclusion

AT THE HEART OF this book has been The Salvation Army's enculturation into Norwegian society, especially the relationship between Salvationists and the Norwegian State Church. Even though there has been freedom of religion in Norway since 1845, when "the Law concerning Christian Dissenters and others who were not members of the State Church" was passed by the government, the State Church kept the vast majority of the population as its members. Only a few percentages registered as dissenters, and Frelsesarmeen did not belong to these. The early officers within Frelsesarmeen resigned their membership of the State Church, and as a consequence were not members of any registered church or religion, but between 1900 and 1910 a number of them regained their membership of the State Church. From then on the large majority of officers and soldiers had dual membership, the State Church and Frelsesarmeen. I have connected the change with the time of the dissolution of the union with Sweden and the formation of an independent Norway in 1905. Salvationists wished to be counted as proper Norwegian citizens, who identified with Norway in all areas of life, including the State Church, even if the membership was a nominal one. One of the questions throughout the study has been to ask whether Salvationists considered the State Church as a civil religion, because of their nominal membership and strong adherence to this as a state institution. The attitude of Salvationists of implicitly considering the church as an expression of civil religion might have developed over a number of years, but it was not until the main period of this study 1975–2005 that their attitude to the church gave reason for such an interpretation. The prospect of a separation between state and church made the question of registration as an independent faith community urgent, as it seemed inconceivable for at least Frelsesarmeen's leadership, and a number of Salvationists, to be members of a Lutheran free church.

The overall concern for Frelsesarmeen during its history in Norway was to pursue its mission of "saving souls, growing saints and serve suffering humanity." Movement growth was necessary for this to be achieved and so was enculturation into Norwegian society. Even though the Army was ultimately international in its governance, Frelsesarmeen focused on being considered a Norwegian movement and Salvationists as true Norwegian citizens. For individual Salvationists, as well as for Frelsesarmeen, there was unwillingness to be counted as dissenters, perhaps even a fear of such a situation as it might hamper the overall mission. The focus was on the goal of the mission, making the compromises necessary for the sake of the principle of accommodation. The situation worked and Frelsesarmeen extended its work and also initiated different social outreach all over Norway. One of the reasons why the doors were opened to the Army was, I believe, that it did not dissent from the State Church. The example from Karl Larsson's diary about Norway in the 1930s gave a glimpse of the situation. As Salvationists were not asked to defect from the State Church and by this from tradition and culture, soldiers were made all over the country even in the smallest places. Soldiership might not have been so widespread had the Army required new soldiers to resign their membership of the church. Furseth mentioned the difference between the Methodists, where the members were asked to resign their membership, and the labor movement that did not demand the same, even though members were encouraged to do so. Methodism suffered because of this as it became an obstacle to movement growth. The majority of the members of the labor movement chose to keep their membership of the church.[1] The Army was close to both of these movements. It had its roots within Methodism, while it drew its members and culture from the working class and developed its methods parallel with the labor movement. The choice of Salvationists concerning keeping membership in the church was similar to that of the members of the labor movement and not that of the Methodists.

In order to avoid conflicts with the State Church at the beginning of the century, because many Salvationists kept their membership of the church, a translation of the very first doctrine book from 1881, speaking of the Army's early observance of the sacraments, was published in 1901. This version was chosen in spite of later doctrine books having removed this section in view of the decision in 1883 for the Army to be non-observant. The tradition of dual membership seemed to have been so firmly established,

---

1. Furseth, *A Comparative Study of Social and Religious Movements in Norway 1780s–1905*, 384–85.

that when the 1923 doctrine book was translated in 1930, the appendix explaining the Army's non-observance was excluded. There was seemingly no wish to change the status quo. By excluding the appendix concerning the Army's non-observant position, Frelsesarmeen could continue its work without having to face conflicts concerning attitudes to the sacraments. Thus it encouraged an identity of a religious organization rather than an independent faith community. With such a situation lasting until 1975 there was no impetus for starting a process of registration. The Army's traditional pragmatism won the day. I interpret the doctrine books of 1901 and 1930 as reflecting matters of faith and practice as they had developed, therefore the books were used to support the present situation, rather than being instrumental in new traditions. When the full doctrine book was published in 1975 it did not in itself start a new situation, it rather signaled that things were changing, and that there was a wish for Salvationists to be well informed concerning the Army's position. I do not see this as Frelsesarmeen departing from its traditional pragmatism, rather that bonds to the Norwegian Church had weakened generally in society and therefore also among Salvationists. Concerning Salvationists' affiliation to the Norwegian Church they seemingly acted similarly to ordinary Norwegians.

When, in 1964, Commissioner Westergaard took up the question of the Army's non-observant position in the public through the press it was not welcomed by Salvationists. A number of officers and soldiers were unaware of the Army's position and did not know what to answer when local people asked them. But during his time of leadership signs of change were on their way. He considered dual membership as a problem and wanted to strengthen Salvationist identity. There was also a conference for leading officers concerning the issue of officers being able to perform marriages and funerals, resulting in a letter being sent to the Department for Church and Education in order to obtain this. These were the first signs of a new awareness of being an independent denomination rather than being a mission movement. The work and reports from commissions within the Norwegian Church, with an agenda of evaluating the needs and possibilities of reform for empowering the church for its missions, influenced Frelsesarmeen to evaluate if the time had come to look into such matters for the Army. It became urgent for Frelsesarmeen in 1975, when the report from the State/Church Commission recommended a separation between state and church, to start its own commission. Commissioner Solhaug was convinced that Frelsesarmeen had to register as a faith community if state and church separated, and that such a situation would be a Kairos moment for taking this step. He could not imagine Salvationists being members of a Lutheran free church. In my interpretation he considered the Norwegian Church an expression of civil religion. As long as it was a state church it would be natural for Salvationists to have a nominal membership, but the moment the two separated, the Lutheran church identity would be dominant. It would be difficult for Salvationists to stay as members.

Frelsesarmeen's Commission 1975–78 worked on measures to strengthen Salvationist identity as well as making a survey concerning registration as a faith community among Salvationists. There was a majority of no votes, but yes and no were close. During the three years that Frelsesarmeen's Commission worked, the urgency diminished because the results of the hearing on the State/Church Commission did not support the majority recommendation of a separation between state/church. The final recommendation from the Commission was to leave matters as they were, legally, but to work towards strengthening Salvationist identity by giving greater attention to Frelsesarmeen's teaching, and to keep alert to changes in the Norwegian Church as a separation between state and church would demand that registration be considered. The interim years between the two commissions were centered round strengthening Salvationist identity and meeting the challenges from society that influenced internal matters within Frelsesarmeen, from a process of giving voice to ordinary soldiers in decisions and planning, to changes in worship life through new musical styles, as well as teaching being renewed. It became an overall updating of the Army's work to meet the present age.

The changes in Salvationists identity became visible during the 1992 congress where a group of officers suggested registering a faith community on their own initiative, expressing impatience with the present situation. For that group the state/church relation seemingly did not play a role. They thought registration was timely and independent of a separation between state and church. They wanted a legal confirmation of what, for them, was a reality, that Frelsesarmeen was a faith community of its own. It initiated the start of Frelsesarmeen's Church Commission. The result of the survey from the commission revealed that just over half of the corps wanted to keep the situation as it was, but with an openness to make room for the wishes of the minority. The fact that the question concerning the sacraments came up from nearly half the corps that had answered, signaled that there were unresolved matters of theology and ecclesiology. Frelsesarmeen's Church Commission recommended a registration as independent faith community within the overall registration as an organization in 1996, though the actual registration took place in 2005.

During these years legal matters, as well as a constitution, were looked into. The opponents against registration were vocal and forceful, because they considered the timing to be wrong as the state and church had not separated, and they feared that Frelsesarmeen would be split up into A and B members by a registration, where only some would be in the registered faith community. By leaving matters for some years, the leadership ensured that tensions calmed down, especially by communicating that things would stay as usual, and that no changes needed to happen, only for those who wanted to have a legal church registration within Frelsesarmeen. Registration was only a legal matter that need not influence the Army as such. The Army's pragmatism won the day again. It achieved a registration that could work within the present situation and which also fitted into the new image the Army had presented to the public and to itself through its new communication strategies.

In my interpretation the main reason for Frelsesarmeen's registration as a faith community in 2005 was that a consensus on the dual membership of the Norwegian Church and Frelsesarmeen no longer existed. But the reason that the constitution was made as a two-fold registration, organization, and congregation, giving the organization the notae ecclesiae and the congregation just being a purely legal matter, was firstly to calm those who opposed the situation and give the impression that nothing had changed. The Army was still an organization and could be a faith community as such. The influence from the ecclesiology in *Salvation Story* and *Move Forward in Freedom* described the church identity of the Army and interpreted well known practices of the Army in sacramental language. Nothing new needed to be added in order for Salvationists to recognize their church membership within the Army. However, I also see something new being introduced into Frelsesarmeen by making a registration of a value free congregation. By such a registration Frelsesarmeen introduced and offered people a low commitment model of membership or even a nominal membership. It corresponded to the image it communicated to the public of open doors to everybody to join and of a low threshold. This was illustrated in the ceremonies of dedication, marriage and juniors in the new book of ceremonies. The traditional Frelsesarmee faith community was present within the registration of the organization. Here the demanding soldiership was the main membership, though it also included the less demanding adherency. Membership here was a totally different matter than in the congregation. It was based on a declaration of faith and a commitment to a simple life style for instance being tee total, and with promises of investing oneself in the Army's mission including giving financial support. Registration in the congregation was something extra for the soldiers and others to choose in order to have a legal membership also.

A question concerning a change of emphasis in theology, or shift in theology, became relevant in this situation. The impact of the 1975 doctrine book, with the appendix concerning the Army's non-observance, became clear, even though it apparently had not reached out to all corps to the same degree. The comments concerning the sacraments covered three different attitudes, that further teaching concerning the Army's non-observance position was necessary, that a faith community without sacraments was unthinkable because sacraments belonged to the being of a church, and the importance of the sacraments for Christian life. These were questions raised, but there were no statistics to show how strong each position was. It showed that the question of the sacraments was unresolved. For seventy-five years the non-observant position of the Army had more or less been left to silence, so what was originally an accommodation (the 1901 and 1930 doctrine books) into Norwegian culture and custom developed into a tension in ecclesiology between Frelsesarmeen and The Salvation Army, internationally and within Frelsesarmeen. For those Salvationists who had scrutinized the response to *BEM* in order to strengthen their own position, the notae ecclesiae of martyria, koinonia, and diaconia as relating to mission the Army considered as essential and constitutional for being a church were sufficient, but for others, the importance of the sacraments for being a church was evident. The three important signs of a church would be supported by all Salvationists, but the question remained as to whether they were enough to be a true church. However, it also made clear a tension between those who agreed with the Army's positions concerning ecclesiology and those who amalgamated what was essential for Army ecclesiology and what was essential to Lutheran ecclesiology.

In the study, sociological factors have been related to Frelsesarmeen's mission as the aim for Frelsesarmeen has always been to serve the present age. Through this process it has become clear that changes in society have been reflected in Frelsesarmeen's development during these years. It has reacted to changes by accommodating itself to changing needs, but also to more fundamental changes in society. The desire to be intelligible to the surrounding culture was so strong that it has developed a listening and open approach to what was happening in society, a sort of musicality or sensitive ear. It retained some strong distinctives, while it also allowed enculturation to happen. The most visible example of this in recent time was the new communication strategy that influenced the Army internally as much as the general public. It was a response to new communication technology, but it became much more because it "washed the foundation" of the movement in the process of communication. The image of an open fellowship with a low threshold and high ceiling became an ideal within Frelsesarmeen, and not only an image for the public. The results of it could be seen in corps activities, such as baby song and similar events. This wish to live up to the image was reflected in the registration of a congregation, that opened up for nominal membership and ceremonies that would be more inclusive than traditional Army ceremonies had been. The use of the internet throughout the Army world gave a different and stronger influence on Frelsesarmeen from the international Salvation Army. It could bind all territories together and even in remote places make a great difference. The fact that IHQ made use of this possibility from the early beginning of the World Wide Web gave an impetus to use it straight away. It gave impulses from many different perspectives of Army life.

A summary of findings

The study reveals that theological ideas have an impact on religious history, here illustrated by Frelsesarmeen's history and the influence from Lutheranism upon Frelsesarmeen. The doctrine books, as they were translated, influenced the development for a century. In their reception in Norway some of them have been misrepresented and as such they had long term influence on the ecclesiology and identity of Frelsesarmeen as a faith community. The reception had to go via translation into Norwegian and therefore issues internal to Norway decided how the doctrines were communicated and received. Because of this the reception of the doctrines has been as significant as the doctrines themselves. This also illustrates that the process of reception within Frelsesarmeen has been influenced by the dominance of the State Church, because the principle of adaptation was so central for the Army. The policy of translation could also be seen as a pragmatic solution. Throughout this study Frelsesarmeen has come across as a pragmatic organization. In my interpretation it has been possible to choose pragmatic solutions in its accommodation into Norwegian society as well as in the actual registration, because the overall goal of mission has been clear and unchallenged. This also included the way it expressed its mission through martyria, koinonia, and diaconia. Not only has the overall goal of mission not been challenged, but also the important principle of adaptation, which the Army took hold from its very beginning has been unchallenged.

Recent research within Norwegian Church history has focused on the situation of the Norwegian Church in relation to the state as well as to society. I have made use of this research as a background for my research on Frelsesarmeen, because of the links Salvationists have had to the Norwegian Church during Frelsesarmeen's history in Norway. Some of the questions and processes from within the church have been reflected within Frelsesarmeen. Parallel with the commissions within the Norwegian Church and the State.

Church commissions Frelsesarmeen has had its own commissions such as Frelsesarmeen's Commission 1975–78 and Frelsesarmeen's Church Commission 1993–96. These not only looked into the question of registration, but also evaluated its identity, mission, and relevance for society, in later years for a postmodern society. Here, registration provided the possibility of low commitment membership, as well as a relationship to the State Church as a small minority religious organization. Into this recent focus within Church history the research on Frelsesarmeen could contribute to give a broader picture of the Norwegian religious situation, because it shows how a minority religious group has accommodated itself both doctrinally as well as practically to the situation of a dominant state church. By abandoning the possibility of being dissenters it cooperated with the State Church and adapted as far as it was necessary for the sake of its overall goal of mission. It benefitted from this situation in movement growth, in acceptance by the general public as well as the State Church and public authorities. This situation was expressed by economic support for its work and open doors for its mission.

Within studies in the sociology of religion, Salvationists have not appeared in statistics because they were not a registered religious group as such. Because of this the study could contribute by showing that a minority religious group has similar relationships and attitudes to the Norwegian Church as other nominal members of the church, but at the same time also has a lot in common with the lay organizations within the church. This can be seen in the question of civil religion and to what extent the Norwegian Church can be experienced as an expression of civil religion in Norway.

Concerning ecclesiology, the study reveals that the ecclesiology of the Norwegian Church has had an impact on a smaller denomination like Frelsesarmeen in defining what constitutes a church. The non-observance of the sacraments had been interpreted as a natural outcome of being an organization that had not registered as dissenters or as an independent faith community. This was possible because of the official silence concerning the reasons for the non-observance for such a long time. The influence from the Norwegian Church mainly concerned the sacraments as notae ecclesiae, an influence that revealed itself both during the work of Frelsesarmeen's Church Commission and at the time of registration, even though the available sources did not specify how widespread the influence was. Such an influence could give reason for identifying some Salvationists as Lutheran Salvationists. Another influence from the Norwegian Church was the distinction between the visible and invisible church. Frelsesarmeen's two commissions accepted this description without evaluating what it really meant, and if there was any support of this in Salvationist ecclesiology. The study reveals that there is no support for such a distinction within Salvation Army theology. Salvationist ecclesiology in this matter is much closer to Harald Hegstad's *Ecclesiology of the Visible* than to a distinction between a visible and an invisible church. The study also reveals what constitutes a Salvation Army church in Salvationist understanding—that the notae ecclesiae are martyria, koinonia and diaconia as they relate to mission as the overall sign. This could contribute to further dialogue concerning the fundamental signs of a church seen from a minority denomination.

This study has aimed at giving new input into an unexplored field of Norwegian church history by giving insight into a well-known brand in the mind of the Norwegian public (including public administration on all levels), but less known within academia as no research has been available previously concerning Frelsesarmeen in Norway. The aim has also been to set the situation of The Salvation Army in a country dominated by a Lutheran State Church such as Norway into international research concerning Lutheran churches /state churches as well as concerning The Salvation Army. The Salvation Army/Frelsesarmeen has its reputation mainly because of its social work, but I have concentrated on what I consider the sources of the ability to innovate itself over a period of 125 years. By making use of the process towards registration as an independent faith community I have dealt with central matters of its faith as well as its ecclesiology which I consider crucial for its identity as a faith community. The Salvation Army's ability to accommodate itself within different cultures has mainly been due to its pragmatism that has been dominant in most areas. This pragmatism has been at work within Frelsesarmeen in Norway from its beginning to the present day.

Appendix I

Doctrines of The Salvation Army

We believe that the Scriptures of the Old and New Testaments were given by inspiration of God, and that they only constitute the Divine rule of Christian faith and practice.

We believe that there is only one God, who is infinitely perfect, the Creator, Preserver, and Governor of all things, and who is the only proper object of religious worship.

We believe that there are three persons in the Godhead—the Father, the Son and the Holy Ghost, undivided in essence and co-equal in power and glory.

We believe that in the person of Jesus Christ the Divine and human natures are united, so that He is truly and properly God and truly and properly man.

We believe that our first parents were created in a state of innocency, but by their disobedience they lost their purity and happiness, and that in consequence of their fall all men have become sinners, totally depraved, and as such are justly exposed to the wrath of God.

We believe that the Lord Jesus Christ has by His suffering and death made an atonement for the whole world so that whosoever will may be saved.

We believe that repentance towards God, faith in our Lord Jesus Christ, and regeneration by the Holy Spirit, are necessary to salvation.

We believe that we are justified by grace through faith in our Lord Jesus Christ and that he that believeth hath the witness in himself.

We believe that continuance in a state of salvation depends upon continued obedient faith in Christ.

We believe that it is the privilege of all believers to be wholly sanctified, and that their whole spirit and soul and body may be preserved blameless unto the coming of our Lord Jesus Christ.

We believe in the immortality of the soul; in the resurrection of the body; in the general judgment at the end of the world; in the eternal happiness of the righteous; and in the endless punishment of the wicked.

Appendix II

Soldier's Covenant

Having accepted Jesus Christ as my Saviour and Lord, and desiring to fulfil my membership of His Church on earth as a soldier of The Salvation Army, I now by God's grace enter into a sacred covenant.

I believe and will live by the truths of the word of God expressed in The Salvation Army's eleven articles of faith:

> We believe that the Scriptures of the Old and New Testaments were given by inspiration of God; and that they only constitute the Divine rule of Christian faith and practice.

> We believe that there is only one God, who is infinitely perfect, the Creator, Preserver, and Governor of all things, and who is the only proper object of religious worship.

> We believe that there are three persons in the Godhead-the Father, the Son and the Holy Ghost-undivided in essence and co-equal in power and glory.

> We believe that in the person of Jesus Christ the Divine and human natures are united, so that He is truly and properly God and truly and properly man.

> We believe that our first parents were created in a state of innocency, but by their disobedience they lost their purity and happiness; and that in consequence of their fall all men have become sinners, totally depraved, and as such are justly exposed to the wrath of God.

> We believe that the Lord Jesus Christ has, by His suffering and death, made an atonement for the whole world so that whosoever will may be saved.

We believe that repentance towards God, faith in our Lord Jesus Christ and regeneration by the Holy Spirit are necessary to salvation.

We believe that we are justified by grace, through faith in our Lord Jesus Christ; and that he that believeth hath the witness in himself.

We believe that continuance in a state of salvation depends upon continued obedient faith in Christ.

We believe that it is the privilege of all believers to be wholly sanctified, and that their whole spirit and soul and body may be preserved blameless unto the coming of our Lord Jesus Christ.

We believe in the immortality of the soul; in the resurrection of the body; in the general judgment at the end of the world; in the eternal happiness of the righteous; and in the endless punishment of the wicked

I will be responsive to the Holy Spirit's work and obedient to His leading in my life, growing in grace through worship, prayer, service and the reading of the Bible. I will make the values of the Kingdom of God and not the values of the world the standard for my life.

I will uphold Christian integrity in every area of my life, allowing nothing in thought, word or deed that is unworthy, unclean, untrue, profane, dishonest or immoral.

I will maintain Christian ideals in all my relationships with others; my family and neighbours, my colleagues and fellow salvationists, those to whom and for whom I am responsible, and the wider community.

I will uphold the sanctity of marriage and of family life. I will be a faithful steward of my time and gifts, my money and possessions, my body, my mind and my spirit, knowing that I am accountable to God.

I will abstain from alcoholic drink, tobacco, the non-medical use of addictive drugs, gambling, pornography, the occult and all else that could enslave the body or spirit.

I will be faithful to the purposes for which God raised up The Salvation Army, sharing the good news of Jesus Christ, endeavouring to win others to Him, and in His name caring for the needy and the disadvantaged.

I will be actively involved, as I am able, in the life, work, worship and witness of the corps, giving as large a proportion of my income as possible to support its ministries and the worldwide work of the Army.

I will be true to the principles and practices of The Salvation Army, loyal to its leaders, and I will show the spirit of salvationism whether in times of popularity or persecution.

I now call upon all present to witness that I enter into this covenant and sign these articles of war of my own free will, convinced that the love of Christ, who died and now lives to save me, requires from me this devotion of my life to His service for the salvation of the whole world; and therefore do here declare my full determination, by God's help, to be a true soldier of The Salvation Army.

Appendix III

Officer's Covenant

My Covenant
Called by God
To proclaim the Gospel of our Lord and Saviour Jesus Christ
as an officer of the Salvation Army
I bind myself to Him in this solemn covenant
to love and serve him supremely all my days,
to live to win souls and make their salvation
the first purpose of my life,
to care for the poor, feed the hungry, clothe the naked,
love the unlovable, and befriend those who have no friends,
to maintain the doctrines and principles of The Salvation Army, and,
by God's grace to prove myself a worthy officer.

Signed _____

Witnessed by _____

Appendix IV

Commissioning and Ordination

Ceremony for the Commissioning and Ordination of persons about to become officers of the Salvation Army

Declaration of Faith by the Cadets

The cadets about to be commissioned and ordained say in unison:

> In the name of God, the Father, God the Son, and God the Holy Spirit, and in the presence of the officers, soldiers and friends of The Salvation Army here assembled, we declare that:

There then follow the words of the Eleven Doctrines (Articles of Faith): The officiating officer will say:

> Do you promise faithfully to maintain and proclaim these truths?

The cadets will reply:

> We do!

The officiating officer will say:

> Do you regard it as your duty to bear this witness everywhere, to strive to lead all persons to their only Savior, and for his sake to care for the poor, feed the hungry, clothe the naked, love the unlovable, and befriend those who have no friends?

The cadets will reply:

> We do!

The officiating officer will say:

> Do you promise by holy living, boundless charity and adherence to the principles and discipline of the Army to show yourselves at all times to be faithful officers of The Salvation Army?

The cadets will reply:

> We do!

The officiating officer will say:

> In the name of God, I accept the declarations and promises you have made this day. We will now proceed to your commissioning and ordination.

The Commissioning and Ordination

Recognizing that God has called you, has equipped you and gifted you for sacred service, I now ordain you as a minister of the gospel of our Lord and Savior Jesus Christ, and commission you as an officer of The Salvation Army with the rank of lieutenant.

Prayer of Dedication

Bibliography

Agøy, Nils Ivar. *Kirken og arbeiderbevegelsen*. Bergen: Fagbokforlaget, 2011.
Anon. *Gjennem 40 år*. Oslo: Frelsesarmeen, 1927.
———. *Under Blods-og Ildsfanen*. Kristiania: Frelsesarmeen, 1900.
———. *Vort Korstog*. Kristiania: Frelsesarmeen, 1914.
Arweck, Elisabeth and Martin D. Stinger, eds. *Theorizing Faith* The Insider/Outsider Problem in the Study of Ritual. Birmingham: The University of Birmingham Press, 2002.
Astley, Jeff. *Ordinary Theology* Looking, Listening and Learning in theology. Aldershot: Ashgate, 2002.
Balling, J.L. and Lindhardt, P.G. *Den nordiske kirkes historie*. København: Nyt nordisk, 1979.
Barnes, Cyril J. ed. *The Founder speaks again* A Selection of the Writings of William Booth. London: Salvationists LTD, 1960.
Bebbington, D.W. *Evangelicalism in Modern Britain* A History from the 1780s to the 1980s. London: Routledge, 1989.
Begbie, Harold. *Life of William Booth* Founder of the Salvation Army. Vol.I & II London: Macmillan and Co., 1920.
Bellah, Robert N. *The Broken Covenant* American Civil Religion in Time of Trial. Chicago: The University of Chicago Press, 1992.
———. "Civil Religion in America". *Dædalus* Fall 2005, 40-55 (*Dædalus* Winter 1967).
Berger, Peter L. ed. *The Desecularization of the World* Resurgent Religion and World Politics. Grand Rapids: William B. Eerdmans, 2005.
———. *Modernity, pluralism and the crisis of meaning. The orientation of modern man*. Gütersloh: Batesmann Foundation, 1995.
———. *The sacred Canopy: Elements of a Social Theory of Religion*. Garden City: Doubleday, 1967.
Booth, Bramwell. *Echoes and Memories*. London: Hodder&Stoughton, (1925) 1977.
Booth, Catherine. *Aggressive Christianity*. London: The Salvation Army, 1880.
———. *Female Ministry: Women's Right to Preach the Gospel*. London: Salvation Army, (1870) 1975.
———. *Popular Christianity*. London: The Salvation Army, 1887.
———. *Practical Religion*. London: The Salvation Army, 1891 (4th edition).

———. *The Salvation Army in relation to the Church and State*. London: The Salvation Army, 1889.
———. *Utredninger om lærespørsmål*. A summary by Gauntlett, S. Cavosso. Oslo: Salvata, 1953.
Booth, William. *Addresses to Staff Officers*. London: The Salvation Army, 1907.
———. *All the World* January 1889. London: The Salvation Army.
———. *The Christian Mission Magazine* 1870-78. London: The Salvation Army.
———. *Doctrines and Disciplines of the Salvation Army*. London: The Salvation Army, 1881.
Different editions published 1892, 1900, 1904, 1907, 1911, 1913, and 1917.
———. *The Founder's Messages to Soldiers* during years 1907-08. London: Salvationists, 1921.
———. *How to reach the Masses with the Gospel?* London: Morgan, Chase & Scott, 1872.
———. *In Darkest England, and the Way Out*. London: Carlyle, 1890.
———. *International congress Addresses*. London: The Salvation Army, 1904.
———. *Letters to Salvationists on Religion for Everyday*. London: The Salvation Army, 1902.
———. *The Salvation Army Directory*, No II. London: The Salvation Army Books, 1900.
———. *The Salvationist* January 1879. London: The Salvation Army.
———. *The War Cry* 27 December 1879, 17 January 1883, 10 November 1884, 23 December 1893, 14 April 1894. London: The Salvation Army.
Booth Tucker, Frederick St. George de Latour. *The Short Life of Catherine Booth* (Abridged Edition). London: IHQ, 1893.
Breistein, Ingunn Folkestad. *Har staten bedre borgere? Dissenternes kamp for religiøs frihet 1891-1969*. Trondheim: Tapir, 2003.
Brohed, Ingmar ed. *Church and People in Britain and Scandinavia*. Lund: Lund University Press, 1996.
Brown, Arnold. *The Gate and The Light*. Toronto: Bookwright, 1984.
Brown, Fred. *Secular Evangelism*. London: SCM, 1970.
Callahan, Daniel ed. *The Secular City Debate*. New York: The Macmillan company, 1966.
Carpenter, Samuel. *A man of Peace in a World of War*. Montville: Privately published, 1993.
Casanova, José. *Public Religions in the Modern World*. Chicago: The University of Chicago Press, 1994.
———. "Religion, the New Millennium, and Globalization". *Sociology of Religion* Vol. 62 No. 4, 415-441.Oxford University Press, 2001.
Clark, William ed. *Dearest Lily. . . . A selection of the Brengle correspondence*. London: IHQ, 1985.
Collier, Richard. *The General Next to God*. London: Collins, 1965.
Cook, William. *A Catechism embracing the most important doctrines of Christianity*. London, 1851.
Coutts, Frederick. *The Better Fight: The History of the Salvation Army* Vol. VI. London: Hodder and Stoughton, 1973.
———. *Bread for my Neighbour*. London: Hodder and Stoughton, 1978.
———. *The Call to Holiness*. London: SA, 1975.
———. *In Good Company*. London: SA, 1980.

BIBLIOGRAPHY

———. *No Continuing City*. London: SA, 1976.
———. *No Discharge in this War*. London: Hodder and Stoughton, 1981.
———. *The Splendor of Holiness*. London: SA, 1983.
———. *The Weapons of Goodwill: The History of the Salvation Army* Vol. VII. London: Hodder and Stoughton, 1986.
Coutts, John. *The Salvationists*. London: Mowbrays, 1977.
Cox, Harvey. *The Secular City*. New York: Macmillan, 1965.
Davies, J.G. *A New Dictionary of Liturgy & Worship*. London: SCM, 1986.
Dulles, Avery, S.J. *Models of the Church*. New York: Doubleday, Random House, (1975) 2002.
Eason, Andrew Mark. *Women in God's Army: Gender and Equality in the early Salvation Army*. Waterloo, Ont.: Wilfred Laurier University Press, 2003.
Ellis, Gilbert. "Omsorg for hele mennesket" in *Suppe, såpe, frelse siden 1888* edited by Anna Rebekka Solevåg, 97–99. Oslo: Verbum, 2013
Elstad, Hallgeir. "Hundre års debat om stat og kyrkje i Noreg". *Syn og Segn*, 2010.
———. *Nyere norsk kristendomshistorie*. Oslo: Universitetsforlaget, 2005.
———. "Næsten Alting er ualmindeligt og ubeskrivelig excentrisk'. Kyrkjeleg motstand mot Frelsesarmeen dei første åra i Noreg". *Norsk Teologisk Tidsskrift* no.3 2008, 243–261.
Ervine, St John. *God's Soldier, General William Booth*. Vol. I&II. London: Heinemann, 1934.
Field, Benjamin. *The Student's Handbook of Christian Theology*. New York: The Methodist Book Concern, 1868.
Finney, Charles G., *Revivals of Religion*. New York: Leavitt, Lord & Co., 1835.
Fotland, Roar. "Når livet påvirker teologien". Unpublished paper, 2008.
Fougner, Even. "Church and State." In *The Church and Civil Religion in the Nordic Countries of Europe*, edited by Harmati, Bela. Geneva: LWF Studies, 1984
Furre, Berge. *Norsk historie 1914–2000*. Oslo: Det norske samlaget, 2013.
Furseth, Inger. "Civil Religion in Low Key: The Case of Norway". *Acta Sociologica* 1994 no. 37, 39–54.
———. *A Comparative Study of Social and Religious Movements in Norway 1780s–1905*. New York: Edwin Mellen, 2002.
Furseth, Inger and Pål Repstad. *Inføring i religionssociologi*. Oslo: Universitetsforlaget, 2003.
Gadamer, Hans-Georg. *Sandhed og Metode*. Aarhus: Academica, 2007.
Gariepy, Henry. *The History of the Salvation Army* Vol. VIII. Atlanta, Ga: SA, 2000.
The General. *Chosen to be a soldier* Orders and Regulation for Soldiers. London: IHQ, 1977.
———. *Dåp, Nattverd og Embete* Limadokumentet. Frelsesarmeens svar. Oslo: Frelsesarmeens Hovedkvarter, 1986.
———. *Frelsesarmeens læresætninger*. Kristiania: Frelsesarmeens Hovedkvarter, 1907.
———. *Frelsesarmeens læresætninger*. Kristiania: Frelsesarmeens Hovedkvarter, 1913.
———. *Frelsesarmeens troslære*. Oslo: Frelsesarmeens Hovedkvarter, 1975.
———. *Frelsesarmeens seremonier*. Oslo: Frelsesarmeens Hovedkvarter, 1981.
———. *Handbook of Doctrine*. London: International Headquarters, 1923.
———. *Handbook of Doctrine*. London: International Headquarters, 1940.
———. *Handbook of Doctrine*. London: International Headquarters, 1968.
———. *Håndbok i Troslære*. Oslo: Frelsesarmeens Hovedkvarter, 1930.

———. *Håndbok i Troslære*. Oslo: Frelsesarmeens Hovedkvarter, 1946.
———. *Move Forward in Freedom*. The Spiritual Life Commission. London: IHQ, 1998
———. *The Officer*. London: IHQ, 1970-2005.
———. *The Officer's Review*. London: IHQ, 1944.
———. *One Faith, One Church*: The Salvation Army's Response to Baptism, Eucharist and
Ministry. London: IHQ, 1990.
———. *Orders and Regulations for Territorial Commanders and Chief Secretaries*. London: IHQ, 1995.
———. *Orders and Regulations for Pastoral Care Councils*. London: IHQ, 2004
———. *The Sacraments—The Salvationist's Viewpoint*. London: IHQ, 1960.
———. *The Salvation Army Ceremonies*. London: IHQ, 1989, 2004
———. *The Salvation Army Year Book*. London: IHQ, 1976-2013.
———. *Seremonier i Frelsesarmeen*. Oslo: Frelsesarmeens Hovedkvarter, 2005.
———. *The Songbook of The Salvation Army*. London: IHQ, 1986
Gowans, John. *There's a boy here*. London: IHQ, 2002.
Green, Roger J. *Catherine Booth*. Grand Rapids: Baker, 1996.
———. *The Life and Ministry of William Booth*. Nashville: Abingdon, 2005.
———. *War on Two Fronts, the Redemptive Theology of William Booth*. Atlanta: The Salvation Army, 1989.
Grane, Leif. *Confessio Augustana*. København: G.E.C. Gad, 1981.
———. *Den danske Folkekirkes Bekendelsesskrifter*. København: Det danske Bibelselskab, 1981.
Gustafsson, Göran and Thorleif Pettersson, eds. *Folkkyrkor och religiös pluralism Den nordiske religiöse modellen*. Stockholm: Verbum, 2000.
Haight, Roger S.J. *Christian Community in History* Historical Ecclesiology Vol. I–III. New York: Continuum International, 2004, 2005, 2008.
Harmati, Bela ed. *The Church and Civil Religion in the Nordic Countries of Europe*. Geneva: LWF Studies, 1984.
Hattersley, Roy. *Blood and Fire*. William and Catherine Booth and Their Salvation Army, London: Little, Brown & Co., 1999.
Hegstad, Harald. *The Real Church* An Ecclesiology of the Visible. Cambridge: James Clarke & Co, 2013.
Heathcote, Wyndam. *My Salvation Army Experience*. London: Marshall Brothers, 1891.
The High Council. *Speeches of Nominees 1981, 1986*. Unpublished papers London: IHQ.
Hill, Harold. *Leadership in the Salvation Army* A Case Study in Clericalisation. Milton Keynes: Paternoster, 2006.
Horridge, Glen K. *The Salvation Army: Origins and Early Days 1865-1900*. Goldaming: Ammonite, 1993.
The International Doctrine Council. *Minutes* 6-8March, 26-28 June, 16-18 October 1995, 22-24 September 1997. London: IHQ.
———. *Ordet om frelse* Frelsesarmeens håndbok i troslære. Oslo: Frelsesarmeen, 1999.
———. *Salvation Story*. London: IHQ, 1998.
———. *Salvation Story Study Guide*. London: IHQ, 1999.
———. *Servants together*. London: IHQ, 2002.
———. *Unpublished Papers International Theology and Ethics Symposium* 2001 and 2006. London: IHQ.

Iversen, Hans Ravn, ed. *Rites of Ordination and Commitment in the Churches of the Nordic countries*. København: Museum Tuscalanum, 2006.
———. ed.*Vinduer til Guds rige*. København: Anis, 1995.
Jensen, Bent Dahl, ed. *Suppe, sæbe, frelse i 125 år*, Frelsens Hær i Danmark 1887–2012. København: Frelsens Hærs Hovedkvarter, 2012.
Kjeldstadli, Knut. *Fortida er ikke hva den en gang var* en innføring i historiefaget. Oslo: Universitetsforlaget, 1999.
Kjäll, Torsten:" Frälsningsarmeen som trossamfunn i Sverige". *Frälsningsofficeren* 1962 (The article is only available in copy).
———. "Frälsningsarmeen och Svenska Kyrkan". *Frälsningsofficeren* No. 1 1970.
Kew, Clifford. *Closer Communion: The Sacraments in Scripture and Tradition*. London: IHQ, 1980.
Kitchen, Theodore, ed. *The Salvation Army Year Book* 1913. London: The Salvation Army
Kitching, Wilfred. *Soldier of Salvation*. London: IHQ, 1963.
Küng, Hans. *The Church*. New York: Image Books, 1976.
———. *Credo*. The Apostles' Creed explained for today. London: SCM, 1993.
Könönen, Elsa. *En Arme på marsch* Frälsningsarmén i Finland. Helsingfors: Söderström&Co, 1964.
Larsson, Karl: "Sakramentspørgsmålet". *Frelsesofficeren* No. 11 November 1931, No.1 January 1932, No.2 February 1932, No. 4 April 1932, No. 5 May 1932, No. 6 June 1932.
———. *Under ordrer* Vol. III. Stockholm: Frälsningsarméns Högkvarter, 1951.
Larsson, John. "Being true to ourselves", *The Officer* November/December 2001.
———. *1929 A crisis that shaped the Salvation Army's Future*. London: IHQ, 2009.
———. *Saying Yes til Life*. London: Salvation Books, 2007.
Leaders Conference. *Minutes* 1975–2004. Oslo: THQ.
Link, Hans-Georg. *Apostolic Faith Today* Faith and Order Paper No.124. Geneva: WCC, 1985.
Lundby, Knut ed. *Religion across media: From Early Antiquity to Late Modernity*. New York: Peter Lang, 2013.
Lundin, Johan A. *Predikande kvinnor och gråtande män* Frälsningsarmeen i Sverige 1882–1921. Malmö: Kira, 2013.
Lunn, Henry S. "The Salvation Army and the Sacraments" *Review of the Churches* Vol. 7 No. 2 April 1895.
Lydholm, Gudrun. *Ceremonies and Symbols in Worship*. Unpublished paper from the Salvation Army International Theology and Ethics Symposium, Johannesburg, 9–13 August 2006.
———. "Den hundred år gamle bog af William Booth-In Darkest England and the Way out genlæst i dag". *Nordisk Missionstidsskrift*, Mission 4, November 1990, 2–5.
———. "Is Wesleyan Theology Only British and American? Reflections on Salvationist theology within a non-Wesleyan context". *Word&Deed* May 2004 Vol.6 No.2.
———. "Kristustjeneste for Verden. Om Frelsens Hærs storbymission i Danmark". *Kirkefondets skriftsserie*. Temahæfte 11. 1992, 31–36.
———. "Memoirs from The Salvation Army's 'Outpost War' in Norway" *Word&Deed* November 2016 Vol. XIX No. 1, 33–50.
———. " Rites for Commissioning/Ordination to Ministry in the Salvation Army in the Nordic countries related to the Theological development in the Salvation

Army internationally" in *Rites of Ordination and Commitment in the churches of the Nordic countries* edited by Hans Ravn Iversen, 391–415. København: Museum Tusculum, 2006.

———. "Salvation Army Doctrines". Bilateral Theological Dialogues between the World Methodist Council and the Salvation Army. *Word&Deed* November 2005 Vol.8 No. 1.

———. ed. . . . *teaching them.* Festschrift in honor of General(R) Eva Burrows. Oslo: Frelsesarmeens Hovedkvarter, 2009.

Lønning, Per. *Derfor . . .* Oslo: Gyldendal, 1975.

Løvlie, Birger. *Kirke, Stat og folk i efterkrigstid.* Doctoral Dissertation. Lund: Lund University, 1995.

McBrien, Richard P. *Katolsk Tro gennem to Årtusinder.* København: Niels Steensens Forlag, 1987.

McLeod, Hugh. *Religion and the People of Western Europe 1789–1970.* Oxford: Oxford University Press, 1981.

Merrit, John G. *The A to Z of The Salvation Army.* Plymouth: Scarecrow, 2009.

Metcalf, William. *The Salvationist and the Sacraments.* London: IHQ, 1965.

Molland, Einar. *Konfesjonskunnskap.* Oslo: Land og Kirke, 1960.

Moyles, Robert Gordon. *A Bibliography of Salvation Army Literature in English 1865–1987.* New York: Edwin Mellen, 1988.

———. *The Salvation Army and the Public.* Edmonton: AGM, 2000.

Murdoch, Norman H. *The Origins of the Salvation Army.* Knoxville: University of Tennessee Press, 1994.

Needham, Philip. *Community in Mission: A Salvationist Ecclesiology.* London: IHQ, 1987.

———. *Mission in Community: A Salvationist Perspective.* Unpublished Doctoral Ministry Dissertation. Emory University, 1981.

Neiiendam, Michael. *Frikirker og sekter.* København: G.E.C. Gads, 1939

Nicol, Alex M. *General Booth and the Salvation Army.* London: Herbert and Daniel, 1911

Nielsen, May-Brith Ohman, et al., eds. *Norvegr Norges historie* Vol. I–IV. Oslo: Aschehoug & Co., 2011.

Norborg, Sven. *Seksti selsomme år.* Oslo: J.W. Cappelens, 1962.

Norun, Charles. *Med Kjærlighetens Våpen.* Oslo: Salvata, 1987.

———. *Med en stjerne i hjertet* Biografiske blade. Oslo: Ansgar, 1991.

———. *Med Omsorg for hele mennesket.* Oslo: Frelsesarmeens Socialtjeneste, 1991.

Oftestad, Bernt T. *Den norske statsreligion.* Kristianssand: Højskoleforlaget, 1995.

———. "Fra "forgård" til "helligdom". Folkekirken i Ole Hallesbys og Ludvig Hopes vekkelsesteologi." *Folkekirken-status og strategier.* Presteforeningens Studiebibliotek nr. 29, 1988.

Oftestad, Bernt T. et al. *Norsk kirkehistorie.* Oslo: Universitetsforlaget, 1993.

Pallant, Dean. *Keeping Faith in Faith-Based Organizations* A Practical Theology of Salvation Army Health Ministry. Eugene, Oregon: Wipf&Stock, 2012.

Pannenberg, Wolfhart. *Den apostolske Trosbekendelse.* København: Anis, (1972) 1991.

Parsons, Gerald. *Perspectives on Civil Religion.* Aldershot: Ashgate, 2002.

Percy, Martyn. *The Ecclesial Canopy* Faith, Hope and Charity. Farnham: Ashgate, 2012.

———. *Shaping the Church* The Promise of Implicit theology. Farnham: Ashgate, 2010.

Petri, Laura. *Cathrine Booth och Salvationismen*, Akademisk Avhandling. Lund: Berlingska, 1925.
———. *Hanna Cordelia Ouchterlony*. Lund: Berlingska, 1924.
Railton, George Scott. *General Booth*. London: Hodder & Stoughton, 1912.
———. *Heathen England* London: S.W. Patridge, 1878.
———. *Twenty-One Years Salvation Army*. London: The Salvation Army, 1886.
Read, John. *Catherine Booth* Laying the Theological Foundation of a Radical Movement. Eugene, Oregon: Pickwick, 2013.
Repstad; Pål. "Civil Religion in Modern Society". *Kirchliche Zeitgeschichte* 1995 Heft 1.
———. *Mellom nærhet og distanse* Kvalitative metoder i samfunnsfag. Oslo: Universitetsforlaget, 2007.
———. *Religiøst liv i det moderne Norge* Et sociologisk kart. Kristianssand: Høyskoleforlaget, 2000.
Rhemick, John. *A New People of God: A Study in Salvationism*. Des Plaines: The Salvation Army, 1993.
Rightmire, R. David. *Sacraments and The Salvation Army: Pneumatological Foundations* Metuchen, NJ: Scarecrow, 1990.
———. *Sanctified sanity* The Life and Teaching of Samuel Logan Brengle. Alexandria: Crest, 2003.
Rousseau, Jean-Jacques. *The Social Contract and Discourses*. London: Dent (1762), 1973.
Sandall, Robert. *The History of The Salvation Army* Vol. I–III. London: Nelson 1947, 1950, 1955.
Sandvik, Bjørn, ed. *Folkekirkens status og strategier*. Præsteforeningens Studiebibliotek nr. 29 1988.
Schreiter, Robert. *The New Catholicity* Theology between the global and the local. New York: Orbis, 1997.
Schillebeeckx, Edward. *The Church with a Human Face*. London: SCM, 1985.
Schjørring, Jens Holger ed. *Nordiske folkekirker i opbrud* National identitet og international nyorientering efter 1945. Aarhus: Aarhus Universitetsforlag, 2001.
Schmidt, Ulla ed. *Endring og Tilhørighet* Statskirkespørgsmålet i perspektiv. Trondheim: Tapir, 2006.
Shakespeare, Karen. *Knowing, being and doing: The spiritual development of Salvation Army officers*. Unpublished PrD thesis. Anglia Ruskin University, 2011.
Skartveit, Emil. *Frelsesofficer nr. 6* Historien om Kristine Saksill—mor og pioner. Oslo: Frelsesarmeen, 2010.
———. *Jeg er ingen blomst* En rejse gjennom kommandør Haakon Dahlstrøms liv. Oslo: Lunde, 2008.
Solevåg, Anna Rebekka. *Likestilling i Frelsesarmeen?* En kvalitativ undersøgelse av kvinnelige offiserers arbeidssituation. Hovedopgave i kristendomskunnskap. Oslo Universitet, 2000.
———. ed. *Suppe, såpe, frelse siden* 1888. Oslo: Verbum, 2013.
Street, Robert. *Called to be God's People*. London: IHQ, 1999.
Størksen, Jan Aasemann. "Vaske grunnmuren." In *Suppe, såpe, frelse siden* 1888, edited by Solevåg, Anna Rebecca, 105–107. Oslo: Verbum, 2013.
Sundback, Susan. "Folk Church Religion—A kind of Civil Religion." In *The Church and Civil Religion in the Nordic Countries of Europe*, edited by Hamati, Bela. Geneva: LWF Studies, 1984

———. "Medlemskapet i de lutherske kyrkorna i Norden." In *Folkkyrkor oche religiös pluralism* Den nordiske reliöse modellen, edited by Gustafson, Göran and Thorleif Petterson. Stockholm: Verbum, 2000.
Tandberg, Henry Albert. *Femti års korstog for Gud og Norge*. Oslo: Frelsesarmeens Forlag, 1937.
Tandberg, Henry Albert, and Per Raubakken. *Hæren Gud gav Våpen, Frelsesarmeen i Norge, 75 år*. Oslo: Salvata, 1965.
Taylor, Charles. *A secular Age*. Harvard: The Belknap Press of Harvard University Press, 2007.
Taylor, David W. *Like a Mighty Army*. Eugene, Oregon: Pickwick, 2014.
Territorial Commander. *Annual Report* 1969, 1977, 1986, 1987 Oslo: THK.
———. *Executive Council Minutes* 2000–05 Oslo: THK.
———. *Farewell Report* 1966, 1972 Oslo: THK.
———. *FA-Kontakten* 1976–89 Oslo: THK.
———. *FA-Utvalget* 1975–78 *Minutes*. Oslo: THK.
———. *FA-Utvalget* 1975–78 *Rapport*. Oslo: THK.
———. *FA-Kirkeutvalget* 1993–96 *Minutes*. Oslo: THK.
———. *FA-Kirkeutvalget* 1993–96 *Rapport*. Oslo: THK.
———. *Frelsesoffiseren* 1975–2005 Oslo: THK.
———. *Krigsropet* 1970–2005 Oslo: THK .
———. *Krigsråbet* 1990, 1996 København: THK.
———. *Årsmelding* 2005 *for trossamfunnet Frelsesarmeen*. Oslo: THK.
Thompson, Paul. *The Voice of the Past* Oral History. Oxford: Oxford University, 1982.
Thorkildsen, Dag. "Nasjonalitet, identitet og moral" Norges Forskningsråd *Kult* nr. 33 1995.
———. "Stat og kirke i historisk og nordisk perspektiv". *Norsk Teologisk Tidsskrift* Årg. 103, nr. 2–3, 113–124.
Thorsen, Donald A.D. *The Wesleyan Quadrilateral*. Grand Rapids: Zondervan, 1990.
Troeltsch, Ernst: *The Social Teaching of the Christian churches*. Louisville: John Knox, (1912) 1992.
Tønnessen, Aud V. *"Et trygt og godt hjem for alle"? Kirkelederes kritikk av velferdsstaten etter 1945*. Trondheim: Tapir, 2000.
Vertovec, Steven. *Transnationalism*. London: Routledge, 2009.
Ville, Johannes. *Lys og mørke*. København: Gyldendal, 1950.
———. *Korstog i Køge*. København: Frelsens Hærs Forlag, 1951.
Wahlström, Jarl. *En Vallfartssång*. Vasa: Församlingsförbundets Förlags Ab, 1989.
Wahlström, Tor. *Frälsningsarmeen i Finland som Trossamfund*. Avhandling for Teologie Licentiatexamn. Åbo Akademi, 1975.
Walker, Pamela J. *Pulling the Devil's Kingdom down*. Berkeley: University of California Press, 2001.
Ward, Pete ed. *Perspectives on Ecclesiology and Ethnography*. Cambridge: William B. Eerdmans, 2012.
Watson, Bernard. *A Hundred Years' War: The Salvation Army 1865–1965*. London: Hodder and Stoughton, 1964.
Weber, Max: *Sociology of Religion*. Boston: Beacon, (1922) 1963.
Wickberg, Erik. *Inkallad*. Stockholm: Harriers, 1978.
Wiggins, Arch. *The History of The Salvation Army* Vol. IV–V. London: Nelson, 1964, 1968.

Wilson, Bryan. *Religious Sects* A sociological study. London: Weidenfeld and Nicolson, 1970.
Winston, Diane H. *Red Hot and Righteous* The Urban Religion of the Salvation Army. Cambridge, Mass: Harvard University press, 1999.
Wiseman, Clarence. *A Burning in My Bones.* Toronto: McGraw-Hill Ryerson, 1979.
Woodhead, Linda and Paul Heelas, eds. *Religion in Modern Times* An Interpretive Anthology. Oxford: Blackwell, 2000.
World Council of Churches. *Baptism, Eucharist and Ministry* Faith and Order Paper no. 111. Geneva: WCC, 1982.
Volf, Miroslav. *After Our Likeness* The Church in the Image of the Trinity. Grand Rapids: Eerdmans, 1998.
Aagaard, Anne Marie. *Identifikation af kirken.* København: Anis, 1991.
Åhlberg, Ragnar: "Frälsningsarmeen som trossamfunn i Sverige." *Frälsningsofficeren* 1963 (The article is only available in copy).

Index

Adaptation
    The principle of, ix–x, xii, 19, 196, 218, 240
Akerø, Hans Anker, 72n4
Anamnesis, 216
Apostolic
    Faith, 114–15, 216
Augustine, Saint, 211

BEM, xiv, 96, 109, 165–67, 213–14, 216–17, 221, 229, 232, 239
Bebbington, D.W., 13n4, 16–17, 25, 35
Bellah, Robert N., 193–94, 197
Berg, Odd, 132, 136–38, 145
Block-Hoell, Niels, 9, 11, 73–74, 77, 207–8
Booth, Bramwell, 3, 16n14, 20, 29–30n2, 210–12, 218–19
Booth, Catherine, ix, xi, 8, 13–15, 19, 22–23, 25, 27, 34, 38, 47, 120
Booth, William, xi, 3, 8, 12–26, 28–29, 33, 36–37n20, 39n27, 47, 73, 85, 91, 120, 141, 148, 151, 178n34, 208, 218, 230
Burrows, Eva, 126, 165–66, 217, 221
Bjartveit, John, xv, 107n24, 116n50, 127
Breien, Carl, 37, 44, 107–108n25
Breistein, Ingunn Folkestad, 35n16, 42–43

Casanova, José, 203
Church
    Visible, 11, 91, 150, 210–15, 220, 241–42
    Invisible, 11, 76n9, 91–92, 150, 210–12, 220, 222, 231, 241–42
Communication Strategy, 10, 172, 188, 239
Constitution
    The Christian Council of Norway, 118
    The Christian Mission 1870, 20
    The Deed of 7 August 1878, 16
    The Deed Poll 26 July 1904, 16n13
    The Norwegian of 17 May 1814, 2, 64, 66–67, 164, 204
    The Norwegian of 21 May 2012, 165
    Frelsesarmeen's, 156–57, 172–73, 177, 179, 188, 190, 205, 233, 237–38
    WCC, 213
County Governor, 152, 171, 173

Dahlstrøm, Haakon, 70, 116n49, 117–18, 132, 135–36, 138, 145, 174, 199–200, 205
Democratization, 9, 73, 95, 98, 103, 106, 165
Deprivatization, 203–4
Digitalization 9, 127

Doctrine Books
  The Doctrines and Disciplines of
    The Salvation Army 1881, 14,
    39
  Norwegian translation of 1901,
    8, 39, 43, 45, 48–49, 113, 137,
    229, 235–36, 239
  of 1930, 8, 45, 48–49, 137, 144,
    170, 230, 236, 239
  of 1975, 45, 49, 74, 144, 169–70,
    228, 230, 238
  of 1999, 169–71, 174, 224

Ecumenism, 9, 110, 115–16, 118
Enculturation, 5, 230–31, 234–35
Enstad, Nils-Petter, 119, 153–54, 179
Evangelical religion
  Activism, 13, 16, 25, 35
  Conversionism, 13, 16–17, 35
  Biblicism, 16, 35, 112–13
  Crucicentrism, 13, 16–17, 35

Female Ministry, 14, 29
Finney, Charles, 18
Fougner, Even, 196–99
Frelsesarmeen's
  Folk High School—Jeløy, 53, 73,
    80, 109, 151–52
  Outpost work, 52–54, 79–82, 105,
    149–50
  Salvage vessel, 38
Fundamentalism, 74, 204–5
Furseth, Inger, 11, 30–31, 42, 196–97,
  199, 205, 235

Gowans, John, 109, 233
Green, Roger J., 14n7, 20n24, 27n43–44
Gulliksen, Thorleif, 158

Hallesby, O., 2
Halvorsen, P. Th., 36
Hannevik, Edward, 153–55
Hansen, Astrid, 182n39, 188n48
Harmati, Béla, 194
Hegstad, Harald, 212, 242
Hope, Ludvig, 45
Horridge, Glenn K., 15, 30

Iconoclast, 135
Individualism, 97
Information technology, 10, 162, 189
Internet, 9, 127–28n8, 162, 240
Iversen, Helge, 65

Johnson, Gisle, 33

Kairos, 68, 136, 160, 236
Kennedy, John F., 193
Kolde, Theodor, 33–34

Larsson, John, 109, 173, 226–27, 232
Larsson, Karl, 47, 235
Larsson, Sture, 53, 59, 61
Legislation
  Dissenter Law of 1845, 1, 34n15,
    234
  Dissenter Law of 1891, 34n15, 61
  Non-Conformist Act of 1969, 1,
    3–4, 35n17, 60–63, 69, 80, 116,
    131n11, 140, 147n42, 155–56,
    176, 204
Linder, Robert, 194, 197–98
Ljungholm, Kathy, 127
Ljungholm, Sven-Erik, 127
Love Feast, 78, 169, 223, 226
Lunn, Henry S., 74
Lønning, Per, 65, 67, 69, 71

Madsen, Einar, 113, 116
Methodist, xi, 13–14, 15, 35, 39n27,
  117, 235
  Wesleyan, 13, 15, 107, 226
Military metaphor, 8, 13, 16, 29, 120,
  175, 218
Multiculturalism, 198
Music, 9, 32, 95, 98–99, 103, 103–9,
  123
  Brass bands, 107–9
  Strings Bands, 107–108n25, 109
  Musicals, 108–9
  Electronic, 108
Mæland, Erling, 132, 137–38, 143,
  145, 170

INDEX

Needham, Philip, 96, 115n46, 121, 165n7, 169n16, 217
Neiiendam, Michael, 209
Notae ecclesiae, 8, 10, 25, 27, 84, 117, 189, 217, 221, 231, 233, 238–39, 241–42
   Unam, sanctam, catholicam and apostolicam, 174, 220

Olav, Saint, 46
Onarheim, Knut Johan, 156–58, 161
Order
   Jesuit, 33, 85
   Religious, 85, 89, 92, 122, 130
Orsborn, Albert (Staff Captain), 36–37
Orsborn, Albert (General), 216
Orthodoxy, 90, 204–5, 232
Orthopraxis, 30
Ouchterlony, Hanna Cordelia, 29–30n2, 36–38

Parehk, Bhikhu, 201
Parsons, Gerald, 11, 194, 199–200, 205
Petard, Richard, 194
Percy, Martyn, 200–03, 205
Pluralism, 7, 9, 11, 35, 53, 87, 193, 198, 200, 202–6
Polarization, 156
Pragmatism, 5, 8, 14, 17–19, 29, 35, 178, 196, 230, 236, 238, 242
Priesthood of all believers, 217, 231
Privatization, 202–3

Rasmussen, Roger, 118–19, 179
Regeneration, 13, 21–23, 214–15, 243, 246
Repstad, Pål, 197
Rightmire, David R., 13n6, 17–18, 20, 208–9
Rousseau, Jean-Jacques, 11, 192–93
Russia, 9, 16, 35n17, 47, 126–27
Røros, 179, 182–84, 188n48, 190

Sacerdotalism, 3
Sacramental images, 21
Sacramentalism, 3
The Salvation Army's
   Governance, 7, 235

Hierarchy, 132, 153
High Council, 16, 110, 166
International Doctrine Council, 134, 146, 165–69n16, 174n29, 217n25, 221, 226–27, 232
International Spiritual Life Commission, 10, 157n55, 169, 217n25, 224–25, 229, 232
International Theology and Ethics Symposium, 223n31, 226, 232
Orders and Regulations, 20, 33, 78, 85, 121n65, 122, 129, 140, 173, 176
Slum sisters, 51
Training college, 47, 106, 108n26, 170, 180–81
Sanctification, 13, 23, 33–34, 38, 114, 215–16, 219, 221–22
Sacramental living, 23, 216, 222, 225
Save souls, grow saints, serve suffering humanity, 27, 233, 235
Schjelderup, Kristian, 2
Secularization, 9, 54–55, 58, 68, 104, 203–4
Silfverberg, Anne-Lise, 108
Silfverberg, Erik, 108
Slettholm, Bernhard, 72, 91–92, 129
Smemo, Johannes, 56
Smith, Peter, 155–56, 158, 173, 177
Social democratic, 50, 98, 163
   Welfare State, 50, 52, 96, 162, 197, 201
Solhaug, Karsten Anker, 11, 61–71, 92, 116, 132–39, 150, 156, 174, 182, 191, 199–200, 236
Soviet Union, 9, 110n36, 126
Sowton, Charles, 36–37n20
Spiritualistic Christianity, 11, 74–75, 207, 210, 231
Støylen, Kaare, 62, 88, 92
Sundback, Susan, 195, 197
Symbols of The Salvation Army
   Flag, 17, 210, 223, 225
   Mercy Seat, 33, 55, 137, 208–210, 226
   Uniform, 101, 182, 208–9

Tandberg, Henry T., 42, 107–8
Taylor, Charles, 54, 203
TC 's
   Annual report, 37n21, 55–61, 97n5
   Farewell Brief, 57–58, 61
Trinitarian, 221, 225
Trinity, 226

Walker, Pamela J., 12n3, 14n7, 15, 20n24, 23, 30
Wahlström, Jarl, 9, 110n36, 111n39
Wahlström, Tor, 9, 33, 84, 87, 110, 119
Washington, George, 193n5
Weber, Max, 84
Welander, Knud David, 179, 182, 184, 190, 229, 233
Welander, Lisbeth, 179–82, 184, 190, 230
Westergaard, Kaare, 55–58, 61, 236

Wille, Vilhelm, 37
Wilson, Bryan, 84
Wilson, Richard W., 38
Wiseman, Clarence, 89
WCC, 75, 96, 111, 116, 213, 220
Women's Liberation, 9, 54
Working class, 8, 12–13, 18, 29–32, 44, 48, 107, 235
   Labor Movement, 31–33, 44n36, 235

Youth culture, 9, 53, 58, 68, 95, 98, 107–8, 123

Ødegaard, Arne, 132, 136, 138
Ødegaard, Berit, 177
Ødegaard, Donald, 175, 177–78
Ødegaard, Tor Martin, 92, 100, 153–54
Østby, Klaus, 107–8n25

www.ingramcontent.com/pod-product-compliance
Lightning Source LLC
Chambersburg PA
CBHW071244230426
43668CB00011B/1576